Domestic Abuse Disclosure Schemes

Jamie Grace

Domestic Abuse Disclosure Schemes

Problems with Policy, Regulation and Legality

palgrave
macmillan

Jamie Grace
Department of Law and Criminology
Sheffield Hallam University
Sheffield, UK

ISBN 978-3-030-89038-4 ISBN 978-3-030-89039-1 (eBook)
https://doi.org/10.1007/978-3-030-89039-1

This Palgrave Macmillan imprint is published by the registered company Springer Nature Switzerland AG.
The registered company address is: Gewerbestrasse 11, 6330 Cham, Switzerland

To Sara and Bennett, and the criminal justice professionals who handled more than 30,000 applications under 'Clare's Law' in England and Wales in the year to March 31, 2021—and for the victims of domestic abuse those applications represent.

Foreword

In 2011, when Clare's Law was initially piloted in England and Wales, domestic violence service providers and researchers were curious to know one thing: would it work? With annual rates of approximately two women a week being killed by a current or former partner, any political commitment to reducing domestic abuse was welcomed. Fast forward a decade later and Clare's Law, or the Domestic Violence Disclosure Scheme, is not only embedded across England and Wales but has been used as a template for similar schemes in the UK and New Zealand, as well as parts of Canada and Australia. It regularly features in the British media, from local news stories (particularly around International Women's Day) to major storylines in popular television programmes. Members of the public have capitalised on social media platforms to create online networks where they can provide insight, guidance and emotional support to people curious about, or accessing, Clare's Law.

As public engagement with the Scheme grew, so too did the demand for a comprehensive, evidence-based understanding of how the policy was operating and whether it was achieving its intended aim of preventing domestic abuse. A wealth of feminist research has indicated important characteristics of domestic abuse: victims often minimising their experiences, blaming themselves, excusing the perpetrator and telling no-one about their situation (particularly the police). Therefore, initial caution and scepticism focused on the policy's approach—responsibilising the *victim* to recognise their partner's behaviour as problematic, to contact the police, to request information, to wait to see if any would materialise and then to decide whether to continue or end the relationship. This all seemed at odds with everything that was known about domestic abuse; therefore, one question remained pertinent throughout: is Clare's Law working?

In this book, Jamie Grace provides an incredibly timely, detailed and accessible public policy analysis which helps to answer that question. Not only is this the first book to offer a forensic examination of Clare's Law but it is also currently the only text to offer a comparative analysis of the various domestic abuse disclosure schemes emerging internationally. Reflecting on the importance of adopting a socio-legal approach in this exploration, Grace employs freedom–of-information requests, case law, policy documentation, domestic homicide reviews and Hansard transcripts to investigate the role of Clare's Law in preventing domestic abuse. His findings demonstrate the importance of interrogating how criminal justice institutions conduct evaluations or measure 'successes', particularly as the police hold data indicating that many disclosure recipients are later victims of domestic abuse, sometimes by the original subject of the Clare's Law application. Therefore, it appears as though the degree to which Clare's Law is *preventing* abuse is as questionable now as it was at the time of its inception.

In an excellent synthesis of data, theory and insight, the book outlines a clear argument for a review into current operating procedure given that little substantive analysis of the policy exists beyond a procedural overview of application and disclosure rates. This is a judicious suggestion as, in England and Wales, the recently enacted Domestic Abuse Act 2021 places Clare's Law on a statutory footing, meaning that the police will have to pay due regard to the updated policy guidance. Helpfully, Grace goes beyond a retrospective analysis by providing practical recommendations designed to inform this guidance. While many will find this book informative, those with the power to improve the nature and impact of this Scheme should comprise its main target audience, particularly in countries where it is being adopted or adapted for implementation.

Clare Wood's tragic experience has resulted in a legacy of the scale of which even her late father—whose campaign in her memory prompted the Scheme—may not have anticipated. This book offers a fitting contribution to this legacy, while highlighting the importance of critically scrutinising political efforts aimed at ending violence against women.

University of Kent, Canterbury, UK

July 2021 Marian Duggan

Preface

When I started writing about criminal records disclosures as a public protection issue, in 2012–13, I thought of myself as a black-letter law academic, and primarily a teacher of law, not a writer. Two things have happened to me in writing the body of research that became my PhD thesis, and then this book. Firstly, I broadened my teaching approach and research interests to accommodate the social sciences perspectives I needed to adopt to understand my subject more thoroughly. Secondly, and more importantly, I came to reflect a great deal more on the way that domestic abuse has occurred in my own family in the past, and why it was important to give the rights of victims of domestic violence the main focus of analysis in my work on Domestic Abuse Disclosure Schemes (DADS).

I struggle to understand what it must be like to be informed by the police of the dangers a partner poses to you, and perhaps your children, and then be unable to know for certain if you could leave them, and whether doing so would make you, or your children, safer, or whether it would in fact put you (and them) at risk. Some disclosure recipients will know their partner is abusive, all too clearly, or in some way or to some degree—others will have no inkling before the police make contact. Others still will have suspected as much, and will have applied for a disclosure themselves, or will have been coaxed into doing so by a third party. What unites these people, in this range of situations, thousands of them every year in England and Wales, is surely their fearful questioning. What to do with the information? Can I keep myself safe now? Are my children safe from this person?

This book is an attempt at a combined analysis of the law, policy and regulation relating to the operation of different DADS, in a number of common law jurisdictions. DADS typically deploy a 'right to ask' strand and a 'right to know' strand. These strands represent the ability to ask the police for information on the domestic violence offending history of a current or former partner, and the ability of a police to proactively consider the sharing of such information, respectively. Notably, under the common law that operates in each jurisdiction of the UK as a whole, such disclosures can be made where a 'pressing need' to do so exists, while other legal considerations under data protection law and human rights law also apply.

This interdisciplinary research argues that DADS have risen to a disproportionate prominence in the landscape of public protection, and in policy on the prevention of domestic violence. Problematically, no thorough government study has ever been undertaken to rigorously explore whether the disclosure of information concerning the criminal history of one person, to that person's intimate partner, will ultimately increase the likelihood of keeping the recipient safe. The main criticism in this book, however, is not levelled at the core aims of DADS, per se, but at the manner in which they have proliferated in the common law world (in what can be described as a 'policy spiral' (Walker, 2018)) without proper critical evaluation to date by policymakers, the police or any other government agency in the UK or elsewhere. This book argues that DADS must be evaluated, where they have entered or might enter a public protection landscape, in terms of the exposure to victimisation that faces the recipients of disclosures. This book also makes recommendations for reforming DADS policy in the UK.

I am very much professionally indebted to Sara Grace, Marion Oswald, Marian Duggan, Kat Hadjimatheou, Mark Taylor, Richard Kirkham, Adam White, Kevin Bampton, Dave Walsh, Joel Klaff, Tony O'Neill and the late Chris Poole. Each of these brilliant academics has helped me in my research and teaching career to date in one or more fundamental ways. Along with these mentors and coaches, I am blessed to have talented friends in the higher education sector who continue to inspire me with their own successes—thank you. Great thanks also to my students at Sheffield Hallam University, and particularly on the module 'Human Rights and Crime' in the spring of 2021, for asking lots of questions during my online lectures concerning criminal records, public protection, offender registers and domestic abuse disclosure scheme policies. I would also like to thank my colleagues in Law and Criminology at Sheffield Hallam University, past and present, as well as former colleagues at the University of Derby and, for a brief period during my Visiting Fellowship there in 2020, at the Institute of Advanced Legal Studies at the University of London. I was especially grateful to be able to present a research webinar on domestic abuse disclosure schemes in the summer of 2020 as part of my Visiting Fellowship, and I am thankful to the audience that dialled in and gave me a lot of advice on my ideas. Particular thanks as well to Sara Grace, Marian Duggan and Clive Walker for agreeing to look at a draft of the manuscript—it was very kind of you. Any errors in the book remain my own. A great 'thank you' to Marian Duggan for contributing a Foreword, and finally, my particular thanks of course must go to Josie Taylor at Palgrave Macmillan for helping with the commissioning of this book.

Sheffield, UK Jamie Grace

About the Book

This book is based on the doctoral thesis of the author for a PhD awarded by the University of Sheffield in March 2021:

Grace, Jamie (2020) *Domestic Abuse Disclosure Schemes: Regulatory Responsibility and Coherent Legality, or a Vulnerability 'Policy Spiral'?* PhD thesis, University of Sheffield.

Contents

About the Author

Jamie Grace is Senior Lecturer in Law in the Department of Law and Criminology at Sheffield Hallam University, UK, holding this post from January 2014. He was course leader of both the MA and LLM in Applied Human Rights courses in the Department for four years and the LLB Law for one year. He is an active researcher in the Helena Kennedy Centre for International Justice, and a fellow of the Sheffield Institute for Policy Studies, both part of Sheffield Hallam University. He has been appointed as Vice-Chair to the Data Analytics Ethics Committee established by the West Midlands Police and Crime Commissioner. Grace also serves on the West Midlands Police general force ethics committee.Grace held a visiting fellowship at the Institute of Advanced Legal Studies (IALS), University of London, in the summer of 2020, as part of the Centre for Information Law and Policy at the IALS. Grace was previously Senior Lecturer in Law in the School of Law & Criminology at the University of Derby (with various roles from June 2007 until January 2014). He was a programme leader for full-time LLB awards at the University of Derby from August 2012 to January 2014. Grace will hold a visiting scholarship at the University of Birmingham Law School in the first six months of 2022.

Abbreviations

ACPO	Association of Chief Police Officers
DADS	Domestic Abuse Disclosure Schemes
DMF	Decision-Making Forum
DSDAS	Disclosure Scheme for Domestic Abuse (Scotland)
DVADS	Domestic Violence and Abuse Disclosure Scheme
DVDS	Domestic Violence Disclosure Scheme
ECHR	European Convention on Human Rights (1950)
FOI	Freedom of Information
FVIDS	Family Violence Information Disclosure Scheme
HMIC	Her Majesty's Inspectorate of Constabulary
HMICFRS	Her Majesty's Inspectorate of Constabulary, Fire and Rescue Services
HMIP	Her Majesty's Inspectorate of Probation
HRA	Human Rights Act 1998
IDVA	Independent Domestic Violence Adviser
LGBTQ	Lesbian, Gay, Bisexual, Transsexual and Queer
MAPPA	Multi-Agency Public Protection Arrangements
MARAC	Multi-Agency Risk Assessment Conference
MoJ	Ministry of Justice
MPS	Metropolitan Police Service
NPCC	National Police Chiefs' Council
NSW	New South Wales
PNC	Police National Computer

PND	Police National Database
QLRC	Queensland Law Reform Commission
UKSC	United Kingdom Supreme Court
UNCRC	United Nations Convention on the Rights of Children (1989)
ViSOR	Violent and Sex Offender Register

List of Tables

1 Introduction

1.1 The Original Domestic Abuse Disclosure Scheme

Domestic Abuse Disclosure Schemes (DADS) are the police practice of sharing information to warn potential victims of domestic violence about the dangerousness of their partners based on the abusive past behaviour of those partners. The concept of such a policy is now widely known as 'Clare's Law', named for Clare Wood who was murdered in Salford, England in 2009 (Duggan, 2018a). However, as Marian Duggan (2019) has noted in her reflections on the Domestic Violence Disclosure Scheme (DVDS) in England and Wales, the effectiveness of the Scheme is assumed: recipients of this information are supposed to end relationships, or take steps to safeguard themselves somehow; yet no systematic record of the end result of this process is kept by police forces in England and Wales. As a result, Duggan (2019) argued, the effect of the DVDS, the first such 'Clare's Law', is unknown. Amongst other findings, my research for this book tries to estimate the prevalence with which recipients of disclosures of such information are in any event still abused by their current or former partners.

J. Grace, *Domestic Abuse Disclosure Schemes*,
https://doi.org/10.1007/978-3-030-89039-1_1

This book examines a number of policies around the globe, in common law jurisdictions, where such Domestic Abuse Disclosure Schemes (DADS) have been adopted. This book uses policy analysis, regulatory theory and legal analyses to do this. Although this book does not use a solely human rights-based approach, it should be noted from the outset that the use of DADS can be seen as a human rights issue situated within policing practice, and in essence the policing practice of preventing violence against women. At the United Nations level, the prevention of violence against women is the responsibility of the Committee on the Convention on Elimination of All Forms of Discrimination Against Women (CEDAW). The 2017 CEDAW Committee General Recommendation No. 35, on gender-based violence against women, stipulates that state parties should "[a]dopt and implement effective measures to protect and assist women complainants of and witnesses to gender-based violence before, during and after legal proceedings, including by … [p]roviding appropriate and accessible protective mechanisms to prevent further or potential violence" (CEDAW, 2017a: 10). DADS *may* be such measures—but this book examines whether it can be said that DADS are indeed such appropriate or protective mechanisms.

At the time of writing, the UK now features five different DADS: in England and Wales, Scotland, Northern Ireland, Jersey and the Isle of Man; as do parts of Australia (New South Wales, South Australia and Tasmania), Canada (Alberta, Saskatchewan and Newfoundland and Labrador) and New Zealand. The UK (in 1986), Australia (1983), New Zealand (1985) and Canada (1981) have now all signed or ratified CEDAW. The UK government explicitly mentioned the DVDS, the original 'Clare's Law', in its eighth periodic report, to the CEDAW Committee, in relation to the UK strategy for preventing violence against women and girls (CEDAW, 2017b: 45). So it is important for policy-makers to establish whether, and if so, how DADS can be shown to be appropriate, accessible and effective as protective measures in dealing with potential violence against women outside of established reporting, investigation and prosecution processes. Certain human rights standards will apply in specific regional and jurisdictional contexts; for example, Article 3 of the European Convention on Human Rights and Freedoms (ECHR) (1950) has been determined by the European Court of Human

Rights (ECtHR) to place a positive obligation on member-state governments to deploy "law-enforcement machinery for the prevention, suppression and punishment of breaches" of the criminal law protecting victims of harm by private parties (like abusive partners) (*Valiulienė v. Lithuania* (2013)—33234/07 at 75). Additionally, the ECtHR states, "a State may be held responsible [if] in the view of the [ECtHR], [it can] be shown that the domestic legal system … failed to provide practical and effective protection of the rights guaranteed by Article 3", that is to say, freedom from domestic violence as a form of inhuman and degrading treatment (*Valiulienė v. Lithuania* (2013)—33234/07 at 75).

The effect of 'lockdowns' during the 2020–21 coronavirus pandemic in England saw a 60% surge in calls to a national abuse reporting hotline (Grierson, 2021), and the impact of the pandemic presumably led to a greater number of members of the public considering applications under the 'Right to Ask'. The National Police Chiefs' Council (NPCC) certainly encouraged members of the public to come forward to their respective police forces during 'lockdown' in order to report domestic abuse (NPCC, 2021). The coronavirus pandemic has led to some early evidence from Police Scotland that, as pressures in households under lockdown increased, so too did the relative number of requests from members of the public in relation to the Disclosure Scheme for Domestic Abuse in Scotland (DSDAS), with an 18% rise in early 2020 on a comparable period in early 2019 (Picken, 2020). Cleveland Constabulary figures, for example, even show a 44.8% increase in DVDS applications for 2020 versus 2019 (Dawson, 2021). In Wiltshire, applications to the DVDS increased significantly between the year to end of March 2019 and the year to the end of March 2021—from 348 in the year to March 2019, to 457 in the year to March 2020 and to then 558 in the year to March 2021 (McLaughlin, 2021). This last bit of information, about an increase between the year to March 2020 and the year to March 2021, merely continues the trend of annually increasing numbers of applications and disclosures for England and Wales between 2016 and 2020. This has seen the number of applications under the DVDS in England and Wales increase from 8490 in the year to March 2017 to 20,147 in the year to March 2020; and an increase from 3410 disclosures for the year to March 2017 to 8715 disclosures for the year to March 2020 (see Table 1.1,

Table 1.1 The operation of the DVDS in England and Wales with partner/former partner domestic homicides

Year to	RtA apps.	RtA discs.	RtA disclosure rate (%)	RtK apps.	RtK discs.	RtK disclosure rate (%)	Total apps.	Total disclosures	Overall disclosure rate (%)	P/FP domestic homicides (ONS) (female victims 16+)	P/FP domestic homicides (ONS) (male victims 16+)
March 2017	3045	972	31.9	5445	2438	44.8	8490	3410	40.2	79	13
March 2018	4655	2055	44.1	6313	3594	56.9	10,968	5649	51.5	66	9
March 2019	6496	2575	39.6	7252	4008	55.3	13,748	6583	47.9	87	15
March 2020	11,556	4236	36.7	8591	4479	52.1	20,147	8715	43.3	61	9

Source: ONS.gov.uk (2021a, 2021b)
RtA = Right to Ask; RtK = Right to Know; P/FP = Partner/former partner

below). This trend of more and more applications and disclosures year on year is at odds with the picture we have of the way that police forces in England and Wales operating the DVDS struggle to bring a prosecution to bear on an abuser. In the year to March 2020, nearly 75% of reported cases in England and Wales were dropped by forces in England and Wales before prosecution—54.8% because a victim, it was claimed by police forces, no longer supported prosecution, and 20% because there were perceived evidential difficulties even when a victim did support prosecution (HMICFRS, 2021: 6).

Her Majesty's Inspectorate of Constabulary, Fire and rescue Services (HMICFRS) have recently observed that the coronavirus pandemic "did not prevent this important tool [the DVDS] from being used to prevent future offending" (HMICFRS, 2021: 5). During the coronavirus pandemic, a number of police forces in England and Wales were using online technology to communicate non-disclosure decisions under Clare's Law, or were accepting scanned copies of ID documentation sent remotely in order to process DVDS applications (Walklate et al., 2021: 8). At the end of the first year of the pandemic, in early 2021, English forces were also considering how to best respond to the public pressure and scrutiny arising from the media focus on the abduction and murder of Sarah Everard in London in March. The Everard murder provoked pressure on the police and government across the UK to be seen to be doing more to prevent violence against women. Norfolk Constabulary mentioned more proactive use of the DVDS as part of their response to this urgent pressure (Norfolk Constabulary, 2021). Some of the policies that HM Government briefed the media about, however, such as the use of plain-clothes officers to police the night-time economy, were derided as 'kneejerk' and 'performative' by the End Violence Against Women coalition (Topping, 2021). On the other hand, at least one reform announced in this period had been long-awaited: the police in England and Wales will soon be required to record hate incidents on the basis of perception of misogyny (Devlin, 2021).

But while government policy in England and Wales, like that in other common law jurisdictions today, is under scrutiny for the manner in which it does, or does not, protect women and girls from male violence, this book is primarily concerned with distinct issues (and key problems) with 'Clare's Law', in terms of the legal, policy and regulatory features in relation to what can be collectively termed Domestic Abuse Disclosure Schemes (DADS). This book also addresses similar DADS from outside of England and Wales, namely in Scotland, Northern Ireland, New Zealand, parts of Australia and parts of Canada. This comparative approach helps this book investigate the problematic 'policy spiral' (Walker, 2018) that we can observe in the growth of DADS globally.

Since its inception as a Home Office policy, the Domestic Violence Disclosure Scheme has been predicated in part on a so-called Right to Ask. This is the ability to ask the police whether a new partner has a previous history of perpetrating domestic violence (BBC News, 2012). There is also the option in public policy for the police to consider making a disclosure of such a history, without any prior request from the recipient—the so-called Right to Know (HM Government, 2012). However, this book argues that DADS might be poor public policy because of the current lack of evidence of the effectiveness of DADS, as they purport to protect vulnerable people at risk of abuse from their partners. Indeed, this book compiles enough evidence to suggest that DADS are poor public policy based on the limited knowledge we have about their operational effectiveness, in the context of what we know about the difficulties of preventing domestic violence. Furthermore, and regardless of the overall effectiveness of DADS, this book argues there is a considerable public policy issue concerning the nature of DADS as ongoing initiatives which are typically not well-monitored by those public bodies, like the Home Office, who are responsible, as regulators, for their operation.

The DVDS in England and Wales operates on the basis of the disclosure of criminal histories of domestic abusers to their partners, as potential victims. First introduced and piloted by the Conservative-Liberal Democrat coalition government in four police force areas in 2012–13, the Scheme has been operated in every police force across England and Wales since 8 March 2014 (Home Office, 2016a). At the time of writing the DVDS in England and Wales has been re-founded, in terms of a duty on police forces to 'have regard' to making disclosures under the DVDS, in accordance with a statutory code of practice, as it is framed in the new Domestic Abuse Act 2021. The continuing premise of the Scheme is that if a person were to be informed about the violent past of their intimate partner, they would take steps to prevent themselves from being the next victim in a series of victims abused by that partner. Conceptually speaking, in order to be effective the Scheme, if operating in isolation, relies on the recipient of a disclosure then making appropriate self-preserving and rational decisions about ending, or presumably somehow otherwise managing, their personal relationship with an offender. On a practical basis, the Scheme relies on the disclosure of information to individuals from police records. From the perspective of the subject of any possible disclosure, this public protection measure requires an interference with their private and family life.

The DVDS is more of a novel intervention, on a theoretical and policy basis, than one might initially consider. As Helena Kennedy (2018: 87) has acknowledged, since domestic violence is often by its very nature a human rights abuse conducted in a private setting; it "has not been easy shifting the culture to acknowledge that human rights is not only about obscenities which take place in Kosovo or Sudan, Somalia or Iraq, but also about the abuse of people closer to home". But the adoption of a DADS sees public policy in a given jurisdiction take a new position on personal relationships, in terms of policies designed to prevent domestic abuse as a human rights issue 'closer to home', in a literal sense.

So the DVDS and other DADS are fairly novel intrusions by the state into personal relationships, in public policy terms, and are intrusions that are motivated by public protection purposes. Policy formulation in the arena of public protection has typically, however, been complex. As Bill Hebenton and Terry Thomas would no doubt agree, today, and as they wrote in 1993, the concept of 'public protection' and who is deemed to be "'at risk' forms part of the discourse for an ever widening set of targets" (Hebenton & Thomas, 1993: 10). Hebenton and Thomas highlighted in their work on criminal records policy in the early 1990s that the "piecemeal developments of criminal record disclosure, bureaucratic demands and technological developments … makes the meaning of 'protection' by no means [self-explanatory]" (Hebenton & Thomas, 1993: 10). Firm targets for the effective use of the DVDS in England and Wales, however, have never been set—as this would require measuring the actual impact of disclosures under the Scheme, potentially, and this has never been done in a thorough manner. As a result, policy pressure in relation to UK

DADS has simply taken the form of demands and hints from criminal justice inspectorates to make more disclosures and raise more awareness of DADS amongst officers and public protection professionals (as discussed later in this book).

The policymaking process that initially unfolded in the creation of the DVDS roughly accorded with the broad outlines of a policy formulation process in the relevant academic literature. As Frank Fischer (2013: 4) has outlined, in giving an overview of an archetypal process of public policy formulation:

> Decision-makers first identify empirically the existence of a problem, then formulate the goals and objectives that would lead to an optimal solution. After determining the relevant consequences and probabilities of alternative means to the solution, they assign a numerical value to each cost and benefit associated with the consequences. Combining the information about consequences, probabilities, and costs and benefits, they select the most effective and efficient alternative.

Certainly, the relevant Home Office policy impact assessment underpinning the DVDS tried to be clear about the possible benefits of the introduction of the new measure (Home Office, 2013a: 1):

> Domestic violence and abuse has the highest rate of repeat victimisation of any crime with around two-thirds (63%) of all incidents of domestic violence experienced by repeat victims … preventing domestic violence will bring significant benefits in terms of public protection and reducing health and criminal justice costs.

A major aim of the DVDS is to assist the police and other public protection agencies in preserving life. The relevant Home Office policy impact assessment also noted that a "domestic violence and abuse incident which results in the death of the victim is often not a first attack, and serious injury and homicide may be prevented with early intervention such as a Domestic Violence Disclosure Scheme" (Home Office, 2013a: 6). Again, this book will show that there is as yet no thoroughly convincing evidence for the effectiveness, in the round, of such 'early intervention' via the DVDS, and explores why this may be a complex issue to address and measure.

1.2 Research Questions and Methods

This book seeks to address three key research questions: Firstly, to what extent do Domestic Abuse Disclosure Schemes evidence a lack of regulatory responsibility for preventing domestic violence? Secondly, to what extents do Domestic Abuse Disclosure Schemes adequately address issues of victim vulnerability, or contribute to them? And thirdly, to what extent do the Domestic Abuse Disclosure Schemes (i.e., the UK DADS in particular) pose issues of coherence in terms of their legality, and in relation to the context of disclosures?

This book therefore uses a method and approach of evaluating the evolving landscape of Domestic Abuse Disclosure Schemes by combining policy analysis with an application of regulatory theory conducted in the light of relevant legal standards. This combined approach allows for this book to draw on a wider body of sources and materials when assessing the place of the DADS in the public protection domain.

This book argues that the policy opportunity of a DVDS has been swept along in a 'policy spiral'. Clive Walker (2018: 726) has observed that:

> A 'policy spiral' describes a policy which lacks clear initial purpose or subsequent direction, progression, control and reflection. A policy spiral is therefore susceptible to unresolved contradictions or gaps, dramatic direction changes, and uncertain outcomes. As a result, policy spirals arise from inexact and contested meanings, objectives, and mechanisms.

The 'policy spiral' in relation to DADS in the UK and globally is taking place in a 'regulatory space' (Hancher & Moran, 1998) that is legalistic, in that it is governed by rule of law principles, but which is poorly equipped to stop that 'policy spiral', despite and perhaps because of the complex and interwoven 'multi-level governance' (Bache & Flinders, 2004) that exists in a politico-legal system like that of the UK. This DADS 'policy spiral' has largely been a result of the domination of the 'politics of public protection' (Nash, 2010) within the relevant policy sphere. It is argued in this book that without the sort of stronger regulation that would mandate policy evaluation, with regard to the effectiveness of DADS, this 'policy spiral' has led to a situation where, for some victims and potential victims of violence, the DADS in place in a jurisdiction may indirectly worsen their vulnerability as victims. Victim vulnerability is not the only issue that is under-explored by regulators in the 'regulatory space' of which those DADS are a part. The details of disclosure legalities are also something in which DADS regulators in the UK have so far shown little interest; particularly with regard to the wider legal standards that should feature in guidance for disclosure decision-makers in police forces.

The legal basis of the Scheme in UK jurisdictions rests, ultimately, upon the common law duty of the police to act to protect the public (Hale LJ in *Michael v The Chief Constable of South Wales Police* [2015] UKSC 2 at 195), and the power to disclose information to do so (as discussed in *A v B* [2010] EWHC 2361 (Admin)). According to an established line of case law that pre-dates the development of the DVDS in England and Wales as a piece of public policy from government, disclosures under the DVDS must be made on the basis of a 'pressing need' for those disclosures, and should only be made in a manner that is lawful and proportionate as well as necessary (*per* Bingham LJ in *R v Chief Constable for North Wales ex parte Thorpe* [1998] EWCA Civ 486). The case law concerned was already developed, at its core, prior to the development and piloting of the DVDS by the Home Office in 2012. In fact, two Home Office evaluations of the DVDS have highlighted that the legal tests for disclosures as articulated in the current Scheme guidance are difficult to interpret consistently, a likely partial explanation for the disclosure rates, measured by applications versus eventual disclosures, that vary considerably across force areas in England and Wales (Hadjimatheou & Grace, 2020; Grace, 2018; Home Office, 2016a). While much is hoped for, as yet little is known in detail of the true impact of schemes like the DVDS, in the sense of their effectiveness in making (potential) victims of domestic violence safer from harm (Fitz-Gibbon & Walklate, 2017).

Notably, the DVDS has come under academic criticism both in terms of its operation and its capacity to secure results, that is, its ability to actually safeguard potential victims from the risk of domestic violence (Fitz-Gibbon & Walklate, 2017; Hadjimatheou & Grace, 2020). This book extends and develops this criticism on the basis of new evidence, chiefly statistics either published by the Office for National Statistics or obtained by the author via freedom-of-information requests. Because the DVDS is a public protection measure and is aimed at helping to reduce levels of domestic violence in the UK, it weaves itself within the policy landscape, not just on offender rehabilitation but on the prevention of 'violence against women and girls' (VAWG) (as well as against men and boys). As such, the DVDS is affected by broader issues of social justice and accountability in the criminal justice system. The Scheme did not and could not, however, evolve spontaneously into its current form, as a matter of policy development, without regulatory oversight and design.

Given that many of the issues concerning DADS result from regulatory stances (or shortcomings), this book also addresses the scope, nature and operation of the Scheme from a regulatory theory perspective, and interrogates the policy input of various 'regulatory actors'. As such, this book addresses the core issue of the coherence of the Scheme given its competing policy tensions and the (sometimes) opposing bodies of legal doctrine—against a backdrop of policy critique, and according to a body of regulatory theory.

This book has used freedom-of-information (FOI) requests to produce some hitherto unavailable insight into the operation of DADS in the UK. (To pre-empt some details from Chap. 5, the research for this element of the book has shown that of a sample of 520 early recipients of disclosures under the Scheme, at least 45% (234) have been victimised by their partners following that disclosure, i.e., by the perpetrators of domestic violence that they were actually warned about, raising considerable questions about the purported effectiveness of the Scheme.) FOI requests have also been used to investigate how much self-evaluation police forces in the UK have entered into with regard to their operation of DADS (again, see Chap. 5).

Domestic Abuse Disclosure Schemes are *prima facie* a narrow topic of study, about which published research is quite sparse, but they are an important and growing area of public policy, and in fact DADS are a feature of a growing number of criminal justice systems (see Chap. 4). In terms of the regulatory concepts, policy areas and the bodies of doctrinal law that the development and operation of the Schemes concerned touch upon, when seen and taken together, it can be shown that DADS, in the common law jurisdictions that operate them to date, make for an important area of study.

1.3 The Nature of the Domestic Violence Disclosure Scheme

This section of the introduction chapter explains the nature of the policy guidance underpinning the Domestic Violence Disclosure Scheme (DVDS) in England and Wales—the original Domestic Abuse Disclosure Scheme-type policy in the common law world. This section also addresses the process for decision-making concerning a DVDS application, as outlined in the 2016 Home Office guidance that currently configures the common law power of the police to make reasonable, necessary and proportionate disclosures of information on a history of domestic abuse committed by a partner or former partner to an applicant or potential victim, according to, in essence, a 'pressing need' in terms of risk (Home Office, 2016b: 18). This section of the chapter also addresses the aims of the DVDS as set out in Home Office policy for England and Wales and highlights the extent of the multi-agency nature of the policy.

DVDS policy in England and Wales operates on the premise of an applicant ('A') approaching the police using their 'Right to Ask' about a partner or former partner ('B') who they feel may pose a risk of abusing them. Alternatively, the policy provides for A's 'Right to Know': the ability for other agencies and professionals to refer the potential need for a disclosure about B to the police. The current Home Office guidance on the DVDS includes a key statement about the nature, scope and purpose of the policy:

> The Domestic Violence Disclosure Scheme is focused on disclosure and risk management where B is identified as having a conviction, caution, reprimand, or final warning for violent or abusive offences; and/or information held about B's behaviour which reasonably leads the police and

> other safeguarding agencies to believe that B poses a risk of harm to A. (Home Office, 2016b: 6)

However, the Home Office did not create the DVDS in England and Wales entirely anew, given that the Scheme was based on pre-existing common law powers. This book argues that the national launch of the Scheme for England and Wales in March 2014 and the uncritical growth in its operation since then has allowed the Home Office and police forces to make the DVDS an increasingly prominent feature of policy around the prevention of domestic abuse. However, this intensification of the use of the Scheme has occurred despite gaps in the evidence as to the effectiveness of the Scheme (see Chap. 5).

The Home Office guidance on the DVDS makes it plain that under the 'Right to Ask' entry point for applications, where 'A' approaches the police, or a member of the public ('C') does so on their behalf, there is an integral stage to the process that involves an initial risk assessment. This takes place before a face-to-face meeting is used to verify an applicant's details and to feed into a more detailed risk assessment. There is a considerable emphasis in the later stages of the disclosure decision-making process on a multi-agency risk assessment conference approach, where there may be representation, dependent on local practices, of a range of agencies and organisations familiar with either 'A' or 'B', or both parties. However, the initial risk assessment stage, conducted by police officers using information at their disposal, renders the 'Right to Ask' strand of the DVDS a police-dominated public protection practice, as "it will be for the police member of staff to … make the decision on whether or not to progress the disclosure application following this [initial] risk assessment" (Home Office, 2016b: 10). However, one strength of the framing of the police as the chief operators of the Right to Ask strand, to be used by members of the public themselves ('A' applicants) or in making requests on behalf of their relatives or friends (as 'C' applicants), is that the police can be argued to have a primary victim safeguarding role and legal powers to match. As the 2016 Home Office guidance puts it, in relation to the outcome of an initial assessment using the contents of the Police National Computer (PNC), the Police National Database (PND), the ViSOR database (the Violent and Sex Offender register) and local police intelligence systems, "if it is identified there is an immediate/imminent risk of harm to A, then ACTION MUST BE TAKEN IMMEDIATELY to safeguard those at risk" (Home Office, 2016b: 10, emphasis in the original).

A full risk assessment will only take place with searches and checks on police databases and intelligence systems once a face-to-face meeting with an applicant ('A') has taken place to verify their identity, drawing on multi-agency information and insight from social services, probation services, any Multi-Agency Risk Assessment Conference (MARAC) in place in the locality, and local domestic abuse services (Home Office, 2016b: 14–15). Finally, whether the potential disclosure comes through the 'Right to Ask' route or the 'Right to Know' referral route, a multi-agency meeting is used to determine whether and how a disclosure should actually be made. This multi-agency forum will often be the local MARAC, but in any event the Home Office guidance stipulates that the agencies that must be represented at this decision-making stage are the police, the probation service and an Independent Domestic Violence Advocate (IDVA) (Home Office, 2016b: 18). However, the DVDS guidance puts primacy, in relation to disclosure decision-making, very much in police hands:

> The police should categorise either the disclosure application (under "right to ask") or the indirect information received (under "right to know") as either a "concern" or "no concern" before it is referred to the local multiagency forum for discussion and *final decision for disclosure by the police*. (Home Office, 2016b: 16) [Emphasis added.]

It is appropriate, in terms of the lawful use of legal powers, that the police can be held accountable for the final decision to disclose, since, as is discussed in detail in later chapters of this book, the common law position of the police power to disclose information is well-established, allowing for police discretion to make disclosures of information where necessary, reasonable and proportionate in relation to an identified 'pressing need' (following *R v Chief Constable of North Wales ex p Thorpe* [1999] Q.B. 396).

Home Office guidance suggests a disclosure can be made anywhere up to 35 working days following police receipt of a 'Right to Ask' request, and up to 25 working days from receipt of an inter-agency 'Right to Know' referral (Home Office, 2016b). Where a disclosure is made, the Home Office guidance prompts the local multi-agency forum or MARAC to consider referring the subject of the disclosure ('B') to either local Multi-Agency Public Protection Arrangements (MAPPA) or a local Integrated Offender Management (IOM) scheme, respectively (Home Office, 2016b: 22). MAPPA are statutory public protection approaches "where probation, police, prison and other agencies work together locally to manage offenders who pose a higher risk of harm to others" (HMIP and HMICFRS, 2020: 44). A joint inspection report on police and probation offender management practices explains that "[IOM] brings a cross-agency response to the crime and reoffending threats faced by local communities" (HMIP and HMICFRS, 2020: 44). MAPPA typically deal with higher risk offenders than IOM schemes, and so "IOM arrangements should add value to, but not duplicate, existing arrangements to tackle crime, reoffending and victimisation, including MAPPA" (HMIP and HMICFRS, 2020: 35). By prompting a consideration by the local MARAC or multi-agency forum as to the correct and necessary degree of offender management and monitoring for a disclosure subject, the Home Office guidance on the DVDS retains a multi-agency dimension in its public protection function, even if it stipulates police primacy in disclosure decision-making overall. However, the next section of this chapter begins to paint a picture of some of the problems apparent to date in the operation of the DVDS in England and Wales.

1.4 Building a Picture of the Original Disclosure Scheme in England and Wales

This section of the chapter gives a view of the statistical picture of the operation of the DVDS in England and Wales in the last few years, as the 'original' DADS. A later chapter of this book, Chap. 4, gives an overview of the operation of DADS in a number of other common law jurisdictions, namely, Scotland, Northern Ireland, New Zealand, parts of Australia and parts of Canada. This introduction chapter, however, establishes some basic principles and trends concerning 'Clare's Law', the proto-DADS, in the form of the Domestic Violence Disclosure Scheme in England and Wales.

The Domestic Violence Disclosure Scheme has been operational across all of England and Wales for more than seven years (and had been piloted in 4 of 43 police force areas since 2012). A Home Office impact assessment had noted that for the option of a dual approach of a national DVDS for England and Wales, operating both a Right to Ask and a Right to Know model, it was "estimated that this option will result in 4302 initial cases per year, of which 1237 will result in a disclosure" (Home Office, 2013b: 15). The Home Office report on the roll-out of the DVDS 'one year on' from national implementation in England and Wales in March 2014 suggested an initial figure of more than 5000 applications in a year of operation for the DVDS, since the period "between 8 March 2014 and 31 December 2014 [alone saw] a total of 4,724 applications … with 1,938 disclosures made" (Home Office, 2016a: 4). So the impact of the DVDS on policing was soon greater than was anticipated by the Home Office.

We can see that the initial estimates of the uptake of the DVDS were under-estimates. The estimate of more than 4000 applications per year to police forces in England and Wales, under both strands of the DVDS, was always very likely to grow if, for example, the twin pressures of a police inspectorate positively reinforcing a high rate of Right to Know disclosures by individual forces, and the media profiling of the Scheme as efficacious (twin factors considered in more detail later in the book), also continued to grow. Data from the Office of National Statistics on domestic abuse shows that across the four years ending March 2017, 2018, 2019 and 2020, the number of disclosures, using the legal 'pressing need' test as required by the policy known as 'Clare's Law', has entailed more than a doubling of the amount, from 3410 in a year to 8715 (ONS.gov.uk, 2021b). However, the greater embedding of the DVDS for policing in England and Wales has not had an effect on the number of domestic homicides in each of those three years, or not in a way that is measurable—with the number of killings by partners and former partners varying considerably year on year between 2017 and 2020 (see Table 1.1). There will be many factors that play a bigger role than the DVDS in terms of harm prevention, in terms of the work of the criminal justice system to prevent domestic violence, and not least with regard to the interoperation the criminal justice system must have with health, social care and local authorities. For that reason, it is interesting to see a *London Evening Standard* headline ('Domestic killings fall as women use Clare's Law to check partners') in February 2020 (France, 2020), which implied that an increasing number of disclosures by the Metropolitan Police led to a direct reduction in domestic homicides in London by nearly half, from 27 in 2018 to 15 in 2019—despite the national picture showing no such obvious relationship arising from the increase in disclosure (see Table 1.1, below).

With greater police prioritisation of the Scheme as a tool to combat domestic violence (and through the measuring and promotion of the use of the Scheme by HMIC, as it then was), the greater proportion of Right to Know (RtK) applications and disclosures compared to the those under the Right to Ask (RtA) strand shows that the DVDS has become an accepted part of public protection work by the police. The possibility that the Right to Know strand of the DVDS is increasingly embedded in police public protection work might be supported by the fact that the disclosure rate for RtK applications increased more than for RtA applications across 2016–19. Inter-agency 'backing' for applications in the Right to Know strand might perhaps be more likely to produce a result of a disclosure. However, given that typically nearly half of Right to Know referrals and applications to the police still do not result in a disclosure, we can only presume that for many (suspected) abusers the police do not hold information about any past perpetration of domestic abuse—or do not consider that there is a 'pressing need' for a disclosure if they do.

The key point to make is that there was quickly an intensification overall in the policing landscape in England and Wales as regards the DVDS. But extra resource pressures from targeting and 'upselling' of the Scheme by HMICFRS and the Home Office could perversely have a possible impact on the risks of not properly supporting the vulnerable victims of domestic violence. This could be very damaging, as Elizabeth Greene and Jodie O'Leary (2018: 76–77) have argued, since behaviour change by a potential victim, that is, discontinuing a potentially abusive and dangerous relationship, may be difficult in any event, following receipt of a disclosure; but would surely be harder without sufficient and adequate support services, and perhaps even with them (for some victims).

There are, though, considerable issues of scale and (in)consistency of use of the DVDS across different force areas. Assuming the Scheme, when disclosures are made, is actually working as intended and helping potential victims keep themselves safe, then the lower rate of disclosures as a proportion of the number of Right to Ask applications may suggest that victims independently seeking information to be disclosed about a partner, of their own initiative, may be increasingly likely to be left without any tangible benefit from the Scheme. With the comparative lack of any information to help them make decisions about their safety in an ongoing relationship, Right to Ask applicants may be at greater risk in the months following an approach to the police about their partner than someone considered by a multi-agency panel for a Right to Know disclosure. Indeed, in some of the only empirical (qualitative) research on the operation of the DVDS in England and Wales to date, Marian Duggan (2018b: 214–215) has found that "the DVDS is currently operating very differently according to the status of the person requesting information". Potential Right to Know disclosure recipients are far more likely to be supported by Independent Domestic Violence Advisers (IDVAs) from the outset compared to individuals approaching the police on their own using their Right to Ask.

The public protection landscape has been hit hard by austerity in public spending, which will no doubt contribute to and perhaps exacerbate the issue of a 'postcode lottery' in terms of not only how the DVDS is operated from police force to police force (see Table 1.2 below) but also how other policing strategies are used to make a contribution to the prevention of victimisation through domestic abuse (HMICFRS, 2020: 12). However, if the disclosure decision-making process is operating on a very different basis, potentially, from force to force, the large variation in ONS figures on disclosure rates might mean that there is a considerable variation in the application, amongst other factors, of the 'pressing need' test for disclosure. It must be noted that in November 2018, however, the BBC revealed, following a series of their own freedom-of-information

Table 1.2 High and low disclosure rates for the DVDS by police force area, ONS 2017–20

ONS data from year	Key forces for lowest disclosure rate(s)		Key forces for highest disclosure rates	
	Right to Ask	Right to Know	Right to Ask	Right to Know
Year to March 2017 (Average disclosure rate in E&W was 40.2%)	7% in Northumbria	3% in Kent	RtA 76% in Cumbria	RtK 98% in Cumbria
Year to March 2018 (Average disclosure rate in E&W was 51.5%)	9% in Kent 17% for Thames Valley Police (TVP)	10% for Thames Valley Police 12% for the Metropolitan Police	99.5% Hampshire 100% Wiltshire	100% Kent 99% Hampshire
Year to March 2019 (Average disclosure rate in E&W was 47.9%)	9% Kent 14% Essex	20% TVP	92% Hampshire	91% Cumbria 92% Cambridgeshire
Year to March 2020 (Average disclosure rate in E&W was 43.3%)	10% GMP 11% Essex	16% Essex	73% Cumbria	86% Dyfed-Powys 81% Norfolk

Source: ONS.gov.uk (2021b)

requests, that there are issues with forces not recording disclosure decision-making in a standardised way. BBC journalist Francesca Williams specifically cited Cumbria police, with their high disclosure rates as reported by the ONS, as a force acknowledging their own exclusion of so-called mischief-making applications, and applications for which there was nothing to disclose about a subject, from the data returned to the Home Office and the ONS about the DVDS (Williams, 2018). Figures for other forces may reflect that they do not take this approach.

The space in which the DVDS operates, involving police revelations of an abusive history, typically of a male perpetrator of violence, and made to a very possibly vulnerable woman, is one that is in principle appropriate as a method purporting to reduce the risk of the most serious harms or indeed, homicide. For one thing, as revealed by the Femicide Census project in February 2020, of the 149 women known to have been killed by men in the UK in 2018, over half (52%) of perpetrators of these killings were already known by the police to have a history of violence against women (Femicide Census, 2018: 35). However, Marian Duggan has consistently criticised the manner in which the DVDS in England and Wales, and as the proto-DADS, inappropriately 'responsibilises' victims of domestic violence because the Right to Ask strand appears to place the onus on the victim to contact the police about their fear of potential violence from a partner—while disclosures under both the Right to Ask strand and the Right to Know strand of the DVDS would appear, after all, to hand the hard task of cutting ties with a potentially violent partner directly to the victim (Duggan, 2018b). It is possible to argue that in a force area like Essex, with lower disclosure decision-making rates for both Right to Ask and the Right to Know strands (see Table 1.2, below), victims are being 'responsibilised' by their very awareness of the existence of 'Clare's Law', but left with little information to act upon, creating more stress for them. These disparities produce a 'postcode lottery' in the way that the DVDS is operated (Grace, 2018) and experienced, as is highlighted in Table 1.2.

This is at odds with the uniformly positive way that forces allow, or prefer, the DVDS to be presented to the public, that is, the use of the Scheme correlates with fewer intimate partner homicides, despite the fact that (as Table 1.1 shows) at the national level, there is no apparent statistical relationship between making more DVDS disclosures and any fall in domestic homicides over time. Additionally, we must remember that it is only natural that the way that an organisation applying a policy in difficult resource circumstances, and with difficult demands on its staff, such as police forces operating DADS, would see the fine detail of the usage of a certain approach fade into and out of a list of priorities over time. For the Metropolitan Police, for example, this is captured in the words of Acting Detective Chief Inspector Pam Chisholm, who was reported in a *London Evening Standard* article in February 2020 as saying there had been "a cultural change in the Met, so that all staff are talking about tackling and preventing domestic abuse" (France, 2020). But cultural change is not static, and is not uniform, across or within organisations.

So there are some real issues with the inconsistencies in the use of the police power to disclose information through the DVDS in England and Wales. *Inconsistent* use of police powers, even assuming that their use is always lawful should they be used, is itself inherently problematic. Inconsistent use of a police power smacks of arbitrariness, raising questions about the sufficiency of oversight and regulation. As Andrew Sanders (2008: 51) has written:

> In the context of police coercive powers, the question becomes whether there are clear rules of standards, whether compliance is monitored effectively, and whether there are adequate realignment mechanisms.

As we shall see later in this book, the attempts at the realignment of the operation of the DVDS in England and Wales have to date been piecemeal on the part of HMICFRS and the Home Office. Wide disparities in disclosure rates are not as much of a priority, as we shall see, as pushing the Scheme as a policy, despite evidence of a lack of clarity in the disclosure guidance itself, as discussed in later chapters, and the little effort made in monitoring police forces' compliance with that guidance from those same criminal justice regulators. So this quick growth in the use of the DVDS in England and Wales is problematic at least in part. And since the DVDS is at its core presented as a means of both empowering and 'responsibilising' (potential) victims of domestic violence (Duggan, 2018a), there is the serious issue that little oversight of the DVDS, and little certainty and accountability in its operation as evidenced by wide variations in disclosure rates between forces, suggests there is a risk that some forces are using the Scheme as a means of social discipline aimed at victims, not offenders. It can be argued that adding new police powers over time, without strong oversight and monitoring, creates regulatory difficulties. As Satnam Choongh (1997: 222) has observed, the police often seek to impose social discipline with the powers they are granted, "the exercise of which is difficult to review or control".

This book drew inspiration from Savage and Hyde's use of the Freedom of Information Act 2000 to generate fresh data to augment a regulatory, legal and policy analysis (Savage & Hyde, 2013). Westmarland et al. (2017) have also used a freedom-of-information-based approach to gather fresh statistical insight into the (worrying) trend of conducting the policing of reported domestic violence solely using only 'out of court disposals' in more than 5000 cases in 2014 alone. In order to provide context for this book, freedom-of-information requests were used to gather a picture in May 2018 as to how the first wave of recipients of disclosures under the DVDS were dealing with those disclosures. I used FOI requests to try to gain a sense of how many Clare's Law disclosure recipients were not necessarily safeguarded by the DVDS. This was an admittedly problematic attempt to gain a picture of the effectiveness of the first wave of disclosures using the measure of whether the recipients of disclosures were recorded in police systems as being victimised by the person the disclosure concerned (who would have been their intimate partner at the time of the disclosure). Costs rules for FOI mean that overly onerous requests will be rejected by public bodies. Police forces in England and Wales can only spend up to 18 hours in collating data in response to a request (i.e., for a request costed at £25ph up to a maximum of £450), so 20 disclosure recipients for each force to locate records upon seemed pragmatic.

It should be noted that this book did not initially require formal ethics approval for the research to be undertaken, since the mixed and incremental analysis of law, policy and regulation outlined above all draws upon primary legal and secondary (academic and or/policy) sources only, which are freely available. Any sources obtained using freedom-of-information requests are *de facto* in the public domain, and while an informal enquiry was made with the University of Sheffield School of Law ethics committee Chair, as I undertook my initial FOI research as a

PhD student, I was informed that as a result of the public domain feature of the research, my FOI requests did not require formal ethical scrutiny or approval. (However, in 2021, when completing my research for this book using another round of FOI requests, I did gain ethical approval for these from the Sheffield Hallam University Research Ethics Committee.)

My May 2018 freedom-of-information requests about the effectiveness of the DVDS asked:

1. Of the first 20 recipients of a disclosure under the DVDS in your force area, counting from the point when the DVDS went into national operation as a policing policy on 8 March 2014, how many of those 20 recipients have since reported, or have been reported, being the victims of some form of domestic abuse perpetrated by the person about whom they requested or were given information about under the DVDS?
2. Of the first 20 recipients of a disclosure under the DVDS in your force area, counting from the point when the DVDS went into national operation as a policing policy on 8 March 2014, how many of those 20 recipients have since reported, or have been reported, being the victims of some form of domestic abuse perpetrated by any person *other than* the person about whom they requested or were given information about under the DVDS?

The combined results of 26 responses to the FOI request, from a possible 43 responses from police forces in England and Wales, show that of 520 recipients of disclosures that would have been made in the first months of the national operation of the Scheme from March 2014, by around four years later, in May 2018, 45% (234 individuals) had been recorded as victimised by the person they were warned about by the police. The problematic nature of this figure is explored fully in Chap. 5, but suffice to say here the main concern with this figure of 45% as a rate of victimisation for 'early wave' recipients of DVDS disclosures is that police systems chronically under-record domestic abuse—through both under-reporting by victims and under-recording by police officers themselves (Dearden, 2020; Grierson, 2018). In other words, it is likely that the true rate of victimisation amongst 'early wave' disclosure recipients was even higher. If at least 45% of recipients are harmed by those they are warned against, however, we certainly need to ask questions of the rapid growth of DADS with little real evaluation.

I should further highlight that I have used a freedom-of-information approach to also research the extent to which police forces themselves have begun to reflect and address their own use of 'Clare's Law' as organisations. My 2018 and 2021 FOI requests about police force self-evaluation and monitoring of the use of the DADS in the UK informed the discussion in Chap. 5 on the extent of evidence of the efficacy of the use of those DADS, and the extent to which police forces in the UK have increasingly begun to self-regulate and monitor their use of DADS.

1.5 Conclusion

One common analytical framework for policy analysis is the model of the 'policy cycle' (Walker, 2018). This is inherently non-linear as a model, and maintains that policy will come about because policymakers, once an agenda is set in public discourse, will engage in policy *formulation*, *legitimation*, *implementation* and, finally, *evaluation* (Cairney, 2013). So a common approach to policy analysis is a longitudinal analysis, and in several parts or stages, with the last one being evaluative of the impact of the policy. However, this process is in no way standardised. As Paul Cairney has observed:

> There is no single theory applicable to public policy as a whole. The world is too complex to allow for parsimonious and universal explanations. Our choice is to produce a single theory that is so complicated it defeats the purpose of parsimonious explanation, or simpler theories that explain parts of the story in different ways. (Cairney, 2012: 282)

Because of the fragmented nature of the governance of DADS in operation worldwide (in five or more common law jurisdictions, for one thing), it would have been difficult to use a single analytical framework to articulate a critique of current DADS together. It can, however, be noted from the outset that this research adopts a method which sees regulation as a lens broader than either policy or law, and encompassing both, while in turn, "[t]he concept of policy is necessarily broader than legislation" as the Court of Appeal noted in *R (Plan B Earth and others) v Secretary of State for Transport* [2020] EWCA Civ 214 at 224. As such, the idea of 'policy analysis' is *partly* used in this research to examine the spread of DADS policy without much in the way, for most of the jurisdictions concerned, of an evaluative phase. This research will show that where evaluations or pilot assessments of DADS have been conducted in any given jurisdiction, they have been procedural in their focus, rather than with a substantive focus on determining how effective disclosures are in protecting victims; and so lacking sufficient rigour to steer the policy-making process on the DADS concerned away from greater entrenchment of the policy, if that were appropriate. As such, the chief policy analysis tool used in this research is not a 'policy cycle' but a 'policy spiral' (Walker, 2018: 726).

It should be noted that it is difficult to conclude that the spread of DADS accords with the nature of a full-blown 'policy disaster' (Dunleavy, 1995). Dunleavy (1995: 52) has written that 'policy disasters' are those policies "generally construed to mean significant and costly failures of commission or omission by government". This research overall finds that there is not yet sufficient evidence in the public domain to conclude as to whether the DADS policies in the UK and elsewhere are a 'policy disaster', but there is much to suggest that DADS are currently in a 'policy spiral' (Walker, 2018); a concept explored more fully across chapters that follow.

References

Bache, I., & Flinders, M. (2004). Multi-level governance and the study of the British state. *Public Policy and Administration, 19*(1), 31.

BBC News. (2012, March 5). Clare's Law' gives 'right to ask' on domestic violence. *BBC News*. Retrieved June 16, 2020, from https://www.bbc.co.uk/news/uk-17254163

Cairney, P. (2012). *Understanding public policy: Theories and issues*. Palgrave Macmillan.

Cairney, P. (2013). Policy concepts in 1000 words: The policy cycle and its stages. Retrieved June 16, 2020, from https://paulcairney.wordpress.com/2013/11/11/policy-concepts-in-1000-words-the-policy-cycle-and-its-stages/

CEDAW. (2017a). *General Recommendation No. 35*. Retrieved May 6, 2021, from https://tbinternet.ohchr.org/Treaties/CEDAW/Shared%20Documents/1_Global/CEDAW_C_GC_35_8267_E.pdf

CEDAW. (2017b). *United Kingdom's Eighth Periodic Report*. Retrieved May 6, 2021, from https://assets.publishing.service.gov.uk/government/uploads/system/uploads/attachment_data/file/698249/UN_convention_on_the_elimination_of_all_forms_of_discrimination_against_women_8th.pdf

Choongh, S. (1997). *Policing as social discipline*. Oxford University Press.

Dawson, K. (2021). Figures show how number of people using Clare's Law has increased. [online] *TeessideLive*. Retrieved March 30, 2021, from https://www.gazettelive.co.uk/news/teesside-news/clares-law-figures-show-number-19871311

Dearden, L. (2020, February 15). Police failing to record tens of thousands of crimes, inspection finds. *The Independent*. Retrieved June 16, 2020, from https://www.independent.co.uk/news/uk/crime/police-failing-record-thousands-crimes-uk-inspection-thames-valley-yorkshire-durham-hmicfrs-a8210831.html

Devlin, K. (2021). Police to record hate crimes motivated by misogyny. [online] *The Independent*. Retrieved March 30, 2021, from https://www.independent.co.uk/news/uk/politics/police-hate-crimes-misogyny-sarah-everard-b1818691.html

Duggan, M. (2018a). 'Idealising' domestic violence victims. In M. Duggan (Ed.), *Revisiting the ideal victim: Developments in critical victimology*. Policy Press.

Duggan, M. (2018b). Victim hierarchies in the domestic violence disclosure scheme. *International Review of Victimology, 24*(2), 199.

Duggan, M. (2019). Reflections on the Domestic Violence Disclosure Scheme (England and Wales). *Journal of Gender-Based Violence, 3*, 249–257.

Dunleavy, P. (1995). Policy disasters: Explaining the UK's record. *Public Policy and Administration, 10*(2), 52.

Femicide Census. (2018). *Annual Report on UK Femicides 2018*. https://femicidescensus.org/wp-content/uploads/2020/02/Femicide-Census-Report-on-2018-Femicides-.pdf

Fischer, F. (2013). *Reframing public policy: Discursive politics and deliberative practices*. Oxford University Press.

Fitz-Gibbon, K., & Walklate, S. (2017). The efficacy of Clare's Law in domestic violence law reform in England and Wales. *Criminology & Criminal Justice, 17*(3), 284.

France, A. (2020, February 21). Domestic killings fall as women use Clare's Law to check partners. *London Evening Standard*. Retrieved June 16, 2020, from https://www.standard.co.uk/news/crime/domestic-killings-fall-as-women-use-clare-s-law-to-check-partners-a4367966.html

Grace, J. (2018, March 8). Four years on: The postcode lottery of Clare's Law. SIPS blog. Retrieved April 14, 2018, from https://sheffieldinstituteforpolicystudies.com/2018/03/08/four-years-on-the-postcode-lottery-of-clares-law/

Greene, E., & O'Leary, J. (2018). Domestic violence disclosure schemes: Effective law reform or continued assertion of patriarchal power? *Bond Law Review, 30*(1), 55.

Grierson, J. (2018, March 7). Domestic abuse still under-reported in England, say Women's Aid. *The Guardian*. Retrieved June 16, 2020, from https://www.theguardian.com/society/2018/mar/07/domestic-abuse-still-under-reported-in-england-says-womens-aid

Grierson, J. (2021). Calls to domestic abuse helpline in England up by 60% over past year. [online] *The Guardian*. Retrieved March 30, 2021, from https://www.theguardian.com/society/2021/mar/23/domestic-abuse-covid-lockdown-women-refuge

Hadjimatheou, K., & Grace, J. (2020). 'No black and white answer about how far we can go': Police decision making under the domestic violence disclosure scheme. *Policing and Society*. https://doi.org/10.1080/10439463.2020.1795169

Hancher, L., & Moran, M. (1998). Organizing regulatory space. In R. Baldwin, C. Scott, & C. Hood (Eds.), *A reader on regulation*. Oxford University Press.

Hebenton, B., & Thomas, T. (1993). *Criminal records: State, citizen and the politics of protection*. Avebury.

HM Government. (2012, March 5). Police pilot right to find out about domestic violence. Retrieved June 16, 2020, from https://www.gov.uk/government/news/police-pilot-right-to-find-out-about-domestic-violence

HMICFRS. (2020). *PEEL spotlight report: Diverging under pressure*. Retrieved June 16, 2020, from https://www.justiceinspectorates.gov.uk/hmicfrs/wp-content/uploads/peel-spotlight-report-diverging-under-pressure-2018-19-overview.pdf

HMICFRS. (2021). *Review of policing domestic abuse during the pandemic—2021—HMICFRS*. [online]. Retrieved June 23, 2021, from https://www.justiceinspectorates.gov.uk/hmicfrs/publications/review-of-policing-domestic-abuse-during-pandemic/

Home Office. (2013a). *Domestic Violence Disclosure Scheme (DVDS) pilot assessment*. London: Home Office.

Home Office. (2013b). Domestic Violence Disclosure Scheme impact assessment. Retrieved June 16, 2020, from https://www.gov.uk/government/uploads/system/uploads/attachment_data/file/260899/DVDS_IA.pdf

Home Office. (2016a). *Domestic Violence Disclosure Scheme (DVDS): One year on—Home Office assessment of national roll-out*. Home Office.

Home Office. (2016b). *Domestic Violence Disclosure Scheme (DVDS) guidance*. Retrieved June 16, 2020, from https://www.gov.uk/government/uploads/system/uploads/attachment_data/file/575361/DVDS_guidance_FINAL_v3.pdf

Kennedy, H. (2018). *Eve was shamed: How British justice is failing women*. Penguin.

McLaughlin, M. (2021, April 15). Clare's Law requests in Wiltshire increasing year on year. *Gazette and Herald*. Retrieved June 6, 2021, from https://www.gazetteandherald.co.uk/news/19232970.clares-law-requests-wiltshire-increasing-year-year/

Nash, M. (2010). The politics of public protection. In M. Nash & A. Williams (Eds.), *Handbook of public protection*. Willan.

National Police Chiefs' Council (NPCC). (2021). *Domestic Abuse victims urged to keep seeking help during national lockdown*. [online]. Retrieved March 30, 2021, from https://news.npcc.police.uk/releases/domestic-abuse-victims-urged-to-keep-seeking-help-during-national-lockdown

Norfolk Constabulary. (2021). *Chief Constable responds to the kidnap and murder of Sarah Everard*. [online]. Retrieved March 30, 2021, from https://www.norfolk.police.uk/news/latest-news/chief-constable-responds-kidnap-and-murder-sarah-everard

Ons.gov.uk. (2021a). *Appendix tables: Homicide in England and Wales—Office for National Statistics*. [online]. Retrieved March 30, 2021, from https://www.ons.gov.uk/peoplepopulationandcommunity/crimeandjustice/datasets/appendixtableshomicideinenglandandwales/current

Ons.gov.uk. (2021b). *Domestic abuse and the criminal justice system—Appendix tables—Office for National Statistics*. [online]. Retrieved March 30, 2021, from https://www.ons.gov.uk/peoplepopulationandcommunity/crimeandjustice/datasets/domesticabuseandthecriminaljusticesystemappendixtables

Picken, A. (2020, April 29). Coronavirus: Rise in requests to reveal partners' abusive pasts. *BBC Scotland News*. Retrieved June 16, 2020, from https://www.bbc.co.uk/news/uk-scotland-52444555

Sanders, A. (2008). Can coercive powers be effectively controlled or regulated?: The case for anchored pluralism. In E. Cape & R. Young (Eds.), *Regulating policing: The Police and Criminal Evidence Act 1984—Past, present and future*. Hart.

Savage, A., & Hyde, R. (2013). Local authority handling of freedom of information requests: Lessons from a research project. *Web JCLI*, 19(2). (online)

Topping, A. (2021). Long-term funding and public campaign needed to end violence against women. [online]. *The Guardian*. Retrieved March 30, 2021, from https://www.theguardian.com/world/2021/mar/17/policies-to-end-violence-against-women-bizarre-say-experts

Walker, C. (2018). Counter-terrorism and counter-extremism: The UK policy spirals. Public Law. 725.

Walklate, S., Godfrey, B., & Richardson, J. (2021). Changes and continuities in police responses to domestic abuse in England and Wales during the Covid-19 'lockdown'. *Policing and Society*, 1–13. https://doi.org/10.1080/10439463.2021.1896514

Westmarland, N., Johnson, K., & McGlynn, C. (2017). Under the radar: The widespread use of 'out of court resolutions' in policing domestic violence and abuse in the United Kingdom. *The British Journal of Criminology, 58*(1), 1–16.

Williams, F. (2018, November 29). Clare's Law: The women who risk their lives by refusing information. *BBC News*. Retrieved June 19, 2020, from https://www.bbc.co.uk/news/uk-england-42920020

2

Victim Vulnerability, Risk Prediction and Victim Blaming

2.1 Introduction

This chapter is the start of a public policy analysis of the foundation and operation of Domestic Abuse Disclosure Schemes (DADS), in particular, to begin with, in England and Wales. The chapter therefore first sketches the scale of the problem of trying to prevent domestic violence in England and Wales, and will begin the process of building up a picture of the vulnerability of victims of domestic violence who might try to use DADS disclosures to keep themselves safe (and some problems with this). In this way, an assessment of the notion of DADS through the lens of 'victim vulnerability' will emerge. Policymakers adopting DADS have made some considerable assumptions about the ability of a potential victim of domestic abuse to protect themselves from harm following the disclosure of criminality information from the past of a domestic violence perpetrator. Indeed, the very existence, sparsely evaluated, of the DADS in the UK, and now Australia, Canada and New Zealand too, can be leveraged for considerable political capital by policymakers. Politicians, keen to look like they have left no avenue unexplored in seeking to combat domestic violence and keep victims safe, have been easily swayed by the

J. Grace, *Domestic Abuse Disclosure Schemes*,
https://doi.org/10.1007/978-3-030-89039-1_2

premise of DADS as opposed to evidence of their effectiveness. Conceptually, this should be unsurprising: in the words of Marian Duggan (2018b: 201), 'Clare's Law' in fact "links to existing debates about the symbolic mobilisation of victims for political gain".

Despite the overwhelming need to do more, in policy terms, to combat domestic violence in the UK and many common law jurisdictions, and as is highlighted below, there are enough reasoned objections against Domestic Abuse Disclosure Schemes available for consideration by policymakers that we should ask questions of the eagerness with which those policymakers have caused those Schemes to proliferate. This proliferation of DADS, in a 'policy spiral' (Walker, 2018), has developed across the UK and internationally without proper and critical evaluation as to their effectiveness. It is inherently laudable for policymakers to seek to combat domestic violence, but being blasé about the effects of an intervention, to the extent of it comprising a regulatory *failing*, is less so. This chapter begins the process of establishing the origins of the UK 'policy spiral' on DADS, with respect to the development of the policy position of the original Domestic Violence Disclosure Scheme in England and Wales.

2.2 The Problem of Domestic Violence in England and Wales

At this point we must remind ourselves briefly of the scale of the problem, that is, of the challenges facing any aim to prevent domestic violence as an aspect of public protection. First to note is that the task of preventing domestic violence in society is vital, but is exceedingly complex and far from straightforward. The best approach to criminalising abusive behaviour, conducted in private in relationships between two people, and using legal tools to shape the behaviour of one or both parties, is a difficult one to determine. The reasons that account for the prevalence of domestic violence in human society are numerous and wide-ranging: individual and psychological or neurological (Raine, 2014), as well as social and economic (Sharp-Jeffs, 2020). There are as many groups of causes for domestic violence and abuse as there are formulations and variations of the abuse itself—for example, while there may be economic causes of abuse, abuse itself can take economic forms (Sharp-Jeffs, 2020). Overall, as Merchant and Whiting (2018: 582) have noted, "violence is a complex interplay of context and behavior, where actions are affected by social, cultural, relational, and individual influences".

It is well-known that domestic violence is a widespread and socially harmful crime in England and Wales, with 1,316,800 domestic abuse-related incidents and crimes recorded by the police in the year ending March 2019 (ONS, 2019a). This number was an increase of 118,706 from the year ending March 2018 (ONS, 2019a). On top of police-recorded figures, the estimated prevalence of domestic violence in England and Wales is very extensive. Compared to the year ending March 2015, the first year of national operation of the DVDS in England and Wales, which resulted in approximately 2000 disclosures (Home Office, 2016a), the Crime Survey for England and Wales (CSEW) estimated that nationally there were 1.3 million female victims and 600,000 male victims of domestic abuse, or 8.2% of women and 4.0% of men (ONS, 2016). Domestic violence is also clearly gendered, therefore, in its manifestations in contemporary UK society. In November 2019, the ONS noted that in the year to March 2019, in relation to "75% of the domestic abuse-related crimes recorded by the police in the year ending March 2019, the victim was female" (ONS, 2019b). This is exacerbated in the uptake of the DVDS in England and Wales in terms of the relative numbers of men and women drawing on the Scheme. Issues of gender are plain in the take-up of the DVDS; statistics from the study undertaken by the Home Office of the pilot stage of the Scheme show that 98% of the applicants for potential disclosures under the Scheme were women (Home Office, 2013b). As a result, the term 'victims', at least in the sense of recipients of disclosures under DADS, should be taken in this book to be near-synonymous with 'women', and the notion of a 'subject' in relation to a disclosure under a DADS taken to be male, since the majority of victims of domestic violence in England and Wales in any given year will be women, and the vast majority of the worst perpetrators of domestic abuse will be men (ONS, 2019b).

With the police being happy enough to allow the media to refer to the Scheme as 'Clare's Law'—useful no doubt as a public information *aide memoire* and so on—the general PR approach to the promotion of the Scheme by the police has led it to be seen by many of the public as a tool for women only, when it is not (Grace, 2015). In one year in Lancashire, it has been reported (Lancashire Post, 2018), 7 men applied to the DVDS compared to 822 women, for example. This can be said to be problematic from a men's rights perspective; and it is likely to have been exacerbated by the labelling of the DVDS as 'Clare's Law' in the media and in police discourse. Of course, men are also victims of considerable domestic violence each year in England and Wales, up to and including homicide in terms of severity of harm. But the issue of gender in the perpetration of domestic violence remains one that is highly skewed. As for the single most important point concerning gender and domestic violence, the prevalence of men killing women each year in the UK through acts of domestic violence is shockingly high. In November 2019, the ONS noted that for three years between 2015 and 2018, "74% of victims of domestic homicide were female compared with 13% of victims of non-domestic homicide" (ONS, 2019b).

Another key issue in terms of sketching out the vulnerability of victims of domestic violence in England and Wales is the decreasing likelihood in recent years that their abusers will be brought to justice in criminal courts. While disclosures under the DVDS have climbed steadily year on year between 2017 and 2020, the number of Domestic Violence Protection Notices (DVPNs) issued by the police have not seem the same steady growth. And while the number of arrests for domestic abuse in that period in England and Wales have remained fairly constant each year, the numbers of domestic abuse-flagged prosecutions each year, and in particular the prosecution of domestic rapists, have dropped like a stone, by nearly two-fifths for domestic abuse prosecutions overall, and by nearly two-thirds for domestic rape prosecutions (see Table 2.1). Overall then, the majority of domestic abuse, and the far greater amount of fatal domestic violence, is enacted by men upon women, with the violence enacted by women on men of a qualitatively different and typically lesser order, as implied by the ONS findings.

Table 2.1 Domestic abuse arrests, Domestic Violence Protection Notices (DVPNs), domestic abuse prosecutions and domestic abuse-flagged rape prosecutions compared with DVDS disclosures, from 2017 to 2020

Year to 31 March	Domestic abuse arrests	% Change year on year	Domestic violence protection notices granted	% Change year on year	All CPS domestic abuse prosecutions E&W	% Change year on year	Domestic abuse-flagged rape prosecutions (E&W)	% Change year on year	DVDS disclosures, RtK and RtA, E&W	% Change year on year
2017	217, 607	n/a	3029	n/a	97,497	n/a	959	n/a	3410	n/a
2018	225, 714	+3.73	4219	+39.29	91,129	-6.53%	908	-5.32%	5649	+65.66
2019	214, 965	-4.76	4349	+3.08	81,035	-11.08%	542	-40.31%	6583	+16.53
2020	226, 385	+5.31	4468	+2.74	61,169	-24.52%	335	-38.19%	8715	+32.39

Sources: Ons.gov.uk (2020); Ons.gov.uk (2021); Cps.gov.uk (2020); Cps.gov.uk (2021)

2.3 Exploring 'Victim Vulnerability'

Policy interventions to protect (potential) victims of domestic violence are complex and multi-stranded; and they must be so, since, in the words of Ruth Lewis et al. (2000: 202), "arrest or protection orders cannot, alone, stop violent men". Police and wider criminal justice/governmental efforts to reduce and prevent levels of domestic violence are multi-faceted, and so it is difficult to make any connection over time between a growing use of the DVDS to make disclosures and any possible reductions in domestic violence offences reported, prosecuted or estimated in the longer term. It is appropriate at this juncture to explore the concept of victim vulnerability in more detail, however. The starting point in this book for a discussion of the vulnerability perspective on issues of victimisation through domestic violence is the work of Jonathan Herring. An academic lawyer, Herring takes the view that: "Properly understood, a rights-based response [to victimisation] mandates the state to take reasonable steps to protect victims of domestic abuse" (Herring, 2016: 134), but that "the hyper-autonomous, non-vulnerable man as the norm around which the law is developed is a fiction" (Herring, 2016: 9).

There are several implications of these two points from Herring for this research. Disclosures under the DVDS may be a component of a lawful response by the state to a risk of domestic violence. But a failure to consider the application of the policy principles upon which the DVDS is built, in the light of the particular vulnerabilities of victims of domestic violence, who can be drawn from any vulnerable section of society, may render the guidance on the operation of the Scheme overly simplified. In turn this could increase the vulnerability of some potential victims of domestic violence.

There is no doubt that preventing domestic violence may be the proper motivation for intervention on the basis of public policy, such as a DADS policy, that tries to protect vulnerable family members, even as other offending might be better dealt with through less intrusive regulatory or policy means. The primary motivation for putting domestic violence in a category of (potential) harms along with other serious offences that warrant a more proactive policing approach in policy and regulatory terms is, as Braithwaite acknowledges, the vulnerability of "less powerful members" of a family, household or relationship (Braithwaite, 1989: 182–183).

Ashworth and Zedner (2014) have theorised trends in 'preventive justice' in England and Wales, and in this vein Domestic Abuse Disclosure Schemes could be said to be a form of 'preventive justice'. DADS create a kind of preventive criminal offence, that is to say, the very situation of a person, namely a particular disclosure subject, being in a relationship or a domestic setting with a vulnerable victim. In terms of Ashworth and Zedner's taxonomy of preventive offences, a Disclosure Scheme will 'punish', through disclosure, this sort of situation is a 'crime of abstract endangerment' (Ashworth & Zedner, 2014: 102)—although all a disclosure subject may know of their 'punishment' is the recipient ending their relationship with them. Another, even more problematic way of using the concept of preventive justice to address 'Clare's Law' policies is that they are, in those terms, a means of correcting the behaviour of the recipients of disclosures. Potential victims in relationships with serial domestic violence perpetrators entail that those relationships are the basis for a crime of 'abstract endangerment'—requiring a "judgement about the degree of risk that is unacceptable" (Ashworth & Zedner, 2014: 102).

The current DVDS guidance is written with a considerable degree of neutrality towards a range of potential considerations of victim vulnerability, and this creates problems for the operation of the Scheme. Few victims of domestic violence, as a proportion, will be hyper-autonomous, non-vulnerable men and women. Instead the DVDS risks giving victims some false reassurances, in the form of 'nil returns', perhaps, about a potential violent perpetrator to whom they may then find themselves more vulnerable.

2.4 The Vulnerabilities of Minorities and of Children

This section addresses the enhanced vulnerabilities of those victims in same-sex relationships, as well as victims who are part of ethnic and cultural minorities, and children who are exposed to domestic abuse. Each of these groups are people who might need to feature under particular equality considerations any time the guidance and policy on a DADS is refreshed.

Disclosure Schemes and LGBTQ Relationships

While same-sex relationships of course suffer from domestic violence, LGBTQ victimisation is something that the DVDS guidance for England and Wales does not address, per se, simply remaining neutral in its stated language about the gender of victims of and potential perpetrators of domestic violence. This neutrality in the language of DVDS policy on issues of same-sex interpersonal violence is possibly a significant shortcoming of the Scheme guidance. As Lewis et al. have noted, a distinct approach to addressing the issue of violence in same-sex relationships is needed (Lewis et al., 2000: 202). In the sphere of the DVDS, it could be argued that as in the past the police in the UK were historically less likely to record or to take seriously issues of domestic violence between two men or two women in a relationship (Knight & Wilson, 2012), and same-sex partners were less likely to report being victims of domestic violence (Haynes, 2016); therefore, there would accordingly be less likelihood of a police record about violence demonstrated by one of the partners concerned (as cases would be less likely to be reported, to progress, and thus for convictions less likely to be secured etc.). These issues, if repeated over time, would result in LGBTQ serial domestic violence perpetrators (SDVPs) being under-assessed in terms of the risk they present, on the basis of the relative paucity of recorded information about their perpetration of abuse, on average. The DVDS guidance would potentially be improved if this possible issue was noted as a factor to be aware of in conducting a risk assessment as part of the process of screening an application of either kind under the Scheme. Equally, the same informational flaw in police recording systems, stemming from other cultural assumptions in the criminal justice system about the likelihood (or lack of it) of women being abusers, might apply to the manner in which heterosexual female SDVPs are risk-assessed as one-half of a relationship, for example.

Ethnic and Cultural Minorities

The CPS have caused a further informational flaw to be highlighted in the issue of recording the ethnicity of victims of violence, noting that while in 2018–19, the ethnicity of 65.1% of domestic abuse complainants was recorded, in previous years this had been lower, including just 52.9% in 2017–18 (CPS, 2019). This issue prompts consideration of the idea that the criminal justice system does not know enough about the perpetration of domestic violence from one particular racial and/or cultural community or context to another—while the current Scheme guidance is silent upon considerations of how culture in one ethnic group or setting might affect the receipt or efficacy of disclosures. Women from migrant and/or ethnic minority communities face intersectional, aggravating risk factors in terms of their vulnerability to domestic violence, and there are systemic problems that arise for police officers in working with women in those communities (Belur, 2008; Anitha, 2008; Femi-Ajao et al., 2020; Gill & Harrison, 2016). These have been argued and evidenced to include the risks of inadequate interpreting facilities, a relative lack of ethnic minority female officers, the psychology and legality of fragile immigration statuses, 'honour' violence arising from cultural stigma concerning the breakdown of relationships including marriage and a lack of specialised support services (Belur, 2008; Anitha, 2008; Femi-Ajao et al., 2020; Gill & Harrison, 2016). These issues *should*, as a result, be highlighted strongly in the guidance that regulates the operation of the Domestic Violence Disclosure Scheme in England and Wales. But these sorts of issues are not addressed at all by the DVDS guidance in place up to the summer of 2021 (Home Office, 2016b). In terms of potential victimhood, and aggravated risk factors, migrant women and women from BME communities are also not explicitly encapsulated by the DVDS guidance for England and Wales. Again, this is because a sort of victim neutrality appears to underpin the Scheme guidance: but it has been argued (Graca, 2017) that cultural factors may play a large role in the 'take up' (or not) of the Scheme in certain minority communities, and thus cultural factors may play a large role in the purported success of the DVDS in helping victims in those communities. 'Purported' success is a phrase used here because, as highlighted throughout this research at different points, the DVDS has not been widely or thoroughly evaluated, and certainly not from a critical perspective in terms of race or ethnicity, by HM Government, or police bodies themselves, as discussed later.

Language difficulties and cultural barriers to dealing with the police are however acknowledged by the Disclosure Scheme for Domestic Abuse (Scotland) (DSDAS) guidance as something Police Scotland officers should be conscious of in operating the Scheme:

> Members of the public with whom Police Scotland comes into contact with and who do not speak English as their first language and are potential victims of Domestic Abuse may be particularly vulnerable. … There may be additional cultural issues influencing their decision making (e.g. making it more difficult or stressful for them to go ahead with applying to the DSDAS) and/or the language barrier may discourage potential victims during Police contact. Every effort must be made to make Police contact as simple and comfortable as possible for these potentially vulnerable people. (Police Scotland, 2015: author copy, 17)

This particular section from the DSDAS guidance does go some way to addressing the concern, mentioned above in relation to work by Graca, that individuals from cultural minorities in the UK may be more likely to struggle to engage with a policy like a DADS due to some issues including a language barrier (Graca, 2017). Graca's point is also that women from ethnic and cultural minorities are likely to find it harder to utilise DADS disclosures should they secure one due to cultural or language barriers in accessing a support system for domestic violence victims that is often 'one size fits all'. However, guidance or such rejoinders on cultural and language barriers should be standard and explicit on all DADS policies.

Guidance on the DVDS in England and Wales, including statutory guidance in the future, has to be produced by the Home Secretary in such a way that it meets the public sector equality duty (PSED), which in this context requires 'due regard' to the need to prevent victimisation (through disproportionate levels of domestic violence) against women (as a group with a 'protected characteristic' of sex). This requirement under Section

149 of the Equality Act 2010, as it applies in this policymaking context, entails a duty, the courts have determined, on ministers to be 'properly informed' in their decision-making (see *R (Hurley and Moore) v Secretary of State for Business, Innovation and Skills* [2012] EWHC 201 (Admin)). The failure of the Home Office or national policing bodies to examine the overall *efficacy* of the Scheme across several iterations of guidance on it could be seen as evidence that the Home Secretary, in creating the most recent guide to the operation of the DVDS, was not so 'properly informed' in relation to intersectional issues of race/nationality and sex, and so, it could be argued, had not had 'due regard' to the PSED.

Disclosures Affecting Children

Neither guidance document on the DVDS nor DSDAS makes specific reference to standards from within the UNCRC as applicable law in the UK context, and so there is no explicit mention of the 'best interests of the child' test from the provisions of Article 3 of the United Nations Conventions on the Rights of the Child (UNCRC). But it is good to see that there is some detail in the DSDAS guidance, or 'Standard Operating Protocol', and the DVDS guidance from the Home Office on the issues involving children connected to the respective 'Power to Tell'/'Right to Know' strands of applications.

With particular regard to domestic abuse affecting children, Anglo-Welsh DVDS guidance does state the relevant force making a disclosure to an adult, where children may also be at risk, should consider taking steps to follow-up on these issues of particular victim vulnerability. As the DVDS guidance explains (Home Office, 2013b: 51–52):

> An appropriate follow-on plan should be agreed for the person receiving disclosure. This should give consideration to what action the person should now be advised to take to safeguard their child(ren). … The plan should note which agency is responsible for checking that the person follows advice to safeguard the child(ren) concerned.

The Standard Operating Procedure for the DSDAS also specifies that the welfare of children is of importance in the processes involving the DSDAS (Police Scotland, 2015: author copy, 4):

> Officers must be alert to the impact of Domestic Abuse on any children specified in the DSDAS application. The recognition of children who may be at risk (Domestic Abuse or otherwise) is the responsibility of all officers involved in each stage of the scheme. In circumstances where child protection matters are identified, a child protection concern form must be completed and appropriate agencies notified via the Interim Vulnerable Persons Database (IVPD).

On the point about compliance with the 'best interests of the child' test at the core of Article 3 UNCRC, on the other hand, the Domestic Violence and Abuse Disclosure Scheme (DVADS) guidance from the Department of Justice in Northern Ireland goes further in a positive move for the protection of children in the context of the operation of DADS in the UK (Department of Justice (Northern Ireland), 2018: 8):

> In applying the processes of the scheme, officers must be alert to the impact of domestic violence and abuse on any children specified in the DVADS application. The recognition of children who may be at risk (domestic violence and abuse or otherwise) is the responsibility of all officers involved at each stage. In circumstances where child protection matters are identified the information will be passed to the relevant Social Services Trust in written form as soon as possible. Article 3(1) of the UN Convention of the Rights of the Child, should also be observed.

The application of the UNCRC to the three UK Domestic Abuse Disclosure Schemes, and in particular how it may apply to the workings of the DVDS in England and Wales, is picked up again in Chap. 7 in an analysis of the extent to which the 'best interests of the child' should be foregrounded in the relevant Scheme guidance as a 'primary consideration', as per Article 3(1) UNCRC.

2.5 The Poor Policy Monitoring of the DVDS

Other than through the statistics I have compiled using freedom-of-information requests, discussed in Chap. 5, there has not been yet a longitudinal study of the vulnerability and victimisation of either Right to Ask or Right to Know applicants and disclosure recipients, or any study of the reoffending (if any) of those subjects about whom disclosures are made. As such it is impossible to know, based on the data that has been made available by the police or by government, whether or not disclosures under the DVDS have a real public protection effect. However, the Scheme was positively reviewed in a pilot review process, despite the fact that only a small number of potential victims of domestic violence could be relied upon to give a sense of how the receipt of a disclosure about their partner affected them in a positive manner (Home Office, 2013b). Just 4 out of the 23 disclosure-recipient respondents to the survey said that they would be more likely to seek help from an agency or support group post-disclosure (Home Office, 2013b: 10). The rate at which the 111 recipients of disclosures, in the 2012–13 pilot of the DVDS, were victimised by their partners in the longer term is unknown. Nor do we know anything as to the victimisation rates of the other 275 applicants in the pilot who did not receive a disclosure of any kind (Home Office, 2013b: 3).

As noted above in Chap. 1, and discussed in more detail in Chap. 5, the research for this book used freedom-of-information requests to try to build up a picture of the rate at which recipients of DVDS disclosures in the early months of the national operation of the Scheme were victimised by the very people they were warned about. An analysis of the responses to these requests allows for a suggestion that this is at least and quite possibly more than 45% of recipients. But Her Majesty's Inspectorate of Constabulary, Fire and Rescue Services (HMICFRS) certainly consider that the more successful police forces in using the DVDS for public protection purposes are, simply, those with higher levels of Right to Ask and Right to Know applications, and high rates of disclosures under the Scheme, *per capita*, in the force area concerned (HMICFRS, 2017: 86).

This degree of oversight by HMICFRS, in their inspection of forces to date in their procedural use of the Scheme, is far from a consideration or evaluation of whether the Scheme is actually effective in its public protection aims. There has been a lack of political challenge to police forces in England and Wales to demonstrate evidence that they are actually helping victims avoid harm using the Scheme. Recently this has started to change, albeit slowly. In 2019, the Chair of the Parliamentary Joint Committee on Human Rights, Harriet Harman MP, posed the question to Victoria Atkins MP and Edward Argar MP (then Home Office ministers) in correspondence over the Domestic Abuse Bill as it stood at the time, as to whether HM Government planned to review the efficacy of the DVDS, as currently operated, and whether it is "effective in protecting partners of known abusers" (Harman, 2019). The reply from the two ministers, in April 2019, made more of the way that the DVDS must be accepted as engaging the Article 8 ECHR rights of subjects of disclosures, and thus only deployed in cases where a disclosure is necessary and proportionate. Of the need for a review of the efficacy of the Scheme, the Home Office would only continue to 'monitor the operation of the Scheme' via the work of HMICFRS, while refreshed statutory guidance would be developed with the new Domestic Abuse Commissioner. The two ministers concluded this approach was enough in terms of regulation and evaluation of the Scheme, stating that "we do not believe a bespoke review of the [S]cheme is required at this time" (Atkins & Argar, 2019). However, it would appear that this position, and the rejection of a thorough review of the Scheme or its guidance, was shifting slightly by the time that the eventual Domestic Abuse Bill made its way through a Public Bill Committee in June 2020. Ministerial commitments were made to focus, in revising DVDS guidance, on key issues of risk assessments around children and the consistency of disclosure decision-making on the part of the police (Public Bill Committee, 2020)—something discussed later, and particularly in Chap. 7, on the legalities of disclosures.

Later chapters of this book give an overview of the weak effort by HMICFRS in 2017 and 2018 to hold individual police forces to account for the way they have used the DVDS. In 2019 the Inspectorate merely noted that police in Cumbria (HMICFRS, 2019a) and Leicestershire (HMICFRS, 2019b) made 'good use' of the DVDS. Durham Constabulary have also recently made, in the words of HMICFRS, a "clear commitment to Clare's Law being well used to protect potential victims of domestic abuse" (HMICFRS, 2019c: 19). This is hardly the equivalent of a full national evaluation of best use of the DVDS. However, the recent HMICFRS inspections of other forces have begun to show some greater introspection in relation to the rolling, monitoring and evaluation of the Scheme in those force areas, chiefly West Midlands Police (HMICFRS, 2019f) and Nottinghamshire Constabulary (HMICFRS, 2019e).

Across some parts of the country, there has been pressure from the families of victims of domestic homicide to reduce the recommended period of time for any eventual disclosures, from 35 days down to just 2 days or 48 hours. Rosie Darbyshire, for example, was killed in Preston by her boyfriend 11 days after making a 'Right to Ask' request, and her family have called for a reduction in the allowed amount of time in which forces can make disclosures (Harper, 2020). An issue with this as a focus for policy reform would be the legitimate expectation that new policy on a short deadline for DVDS processes would create, as a matter of public law. A shorter deadline would create new resource pressures, as well as new legal (and PR) liability arising from any stricter standard on time limits for the process of disclosures. As Lord Kerr explained in *re Geraldine Finucane* [2019] 3 All ER 191 at 62: "where a clear and unambiguous undertaking has been made, the authority giving the undertaking will not be allowed to depart from it unless it is shown that it is fair to do so". A shorter timeline for DVDS disclosures might put pressure on forces in a way that could not be readily met without significant investment in resources for the DVDS: the *Eastern Daily Press* reported FOI data in May 2021 which showed that out of a sample of 1609 'Right to Ask' requests made in 2020, as dealt with across 14 forces, the number of applications not resolved in the required 35 working days was 375 or 23.3% (Walsh, 2021). In relation to this area of concern, Norfolk Constabulary, HMICFRS have noted, undertook a peer review of their practices around the use of the DVDS, and when implementing the findings of this, have reduced the 'backlog of cases awaiting disclosure' (HMICFRS, 2019d: 19). However, the *Eastern Daily Press* investigation mentioned above found that Norfolk Constabulary made only 61% of its 'Right to Ask' disclosures within the required timescale (Walsh, 2021).

2.6 Problems with the Prediction of the Risk of Domestic Violence

Jane Monckton Smith sees Domestic Abuse Disclosure Schemes as simply "official recognition and acceptance of the risk of history" (Monckton Smith, 2019: 8). But predicting domestic violence in a relationship is fraught with difficulties. A key problem with trying to predict the risk of violence in a relationship in the future is that the prediction made obviously depends on the information about the past and the present, as known to the predictor at the time their prediction is made. This recorded information will not be a full record of violence in the past, in the case of many offenders. This problem has been theorised from a regulatory perspective by Julia Black (2001: 107), as the issue of the 'fragmentation of knowledge'. If no information is known to the police about a person who in truth is violent, or has been in the past, then a prediction by the police that he is not violent in the here and now might in time prove to be a kind of 'false negative' (Munro, 2004) that could be communicated to his current partner and potential victim, should he indeed transpire to be a violent and abusive partner in the future. By way of contrast, consider that telling the current partner of a second man, who has strived to turn his life around, that their partner was once violent, and had to be imprisoned, for example, might fracture that relationship and cause emotional pain and instability for both parties. This could be said to be a 'false positive' in the sense of an erroneous prediction of risk (Munro, 2004) if the second man were never to be violent with the current partner concerned. Jane Monckton Smith puts the DVDS forward as evidence of growing acceptance of the model of domestic violence as one of a progression over time (the 'coercive control discourse'), with intimate partner femicide as the last stage in some violent relationships, and "as part of a predictable process involving domestic abuse" (Monckton Smith, 2019: 2). A problem with evaluating the efficacy of prediction and possible disclosure under the Scheme is, of course, that we could never know how a future relationship would have unfolded for certain, were it for, or not for, a disclosure by the police.

Predicting domestic violence in a relationship is difficult to get right. People are not fully rational, nor might they be able to act rationally in response to risk. The personalities of antagonists in a relationship are going to be crucial. The controlling nature of many abusers means all too many victims are forced to be dependent on those very abusers—or to feel that they are—and this will affect how disclosures under DADS will be acted upon, or not (Duggan, 2018b). So how best to generalise as to the most effective circumstances when a disclosure might be made under a DADS, and how can crucial factors be anticipated or enlisted in trying to predict the best means and contexts in which to make such a disclosure, or when not to?

The nature of the DVDS presupposes two things about risk: firstly, that the police can correctly identify the risk posed by a subject of a potential disclosure to a particular potential victim of domestic violence, and secondly, that a recipient of the information contained in a disclosure can act effectively in order to prevent themselves from becoming/being further victimised. Further, the DVDS guidance does not place anywhere near as much emphasis on interventions to help the subject of a disclosure prevent their own offending behaviour. These elements of the DVDS reflect the broader concerns of Crowther-Dowey and Silvestri (2017) about the gendered nature of failures to anticipate risks in criminal justice setting, and who have highlighted that shortcomings in domestic abuse risk assessment are a human rights issue for many women.

There is of course a problem with the idea of trying to quantify a fluid concept such as the risk of domestic violence when it may have, in any individual scenario, a great amount of subjectivity in undertaking such an assessment, not to mention gaps in the knowledge of the situation from a police perspective. This is not only a problem with the basis of the DVDS, of course, but risk prediction in the business of public protection more generally (Crowther-Dowey & Silvestri, 2017). It is, however, no surprise that 'risk' emerged as a policy theme of the DVDS and its *travaux preparatoires* during the development of the idea of the Scheme by the Association of Chief Police Officers (ACPO) as described later. This section now examines 'risk' as a theme from the perspective of preventing the 'interpersonal' victimisation of individuals, chiefly women.

One example of the broader issue of difficulties predicting domestic violence would be the theory of crime 'displacement'. The police might more intensively patrol an area of a city known to be a drugs market, and the drug dealers might re-locate themselves and their operations to avoid greater police scrutiny (Wood et al., 2004). And, particularly relevant here, serial domestic abusers may leave one relationship when it becomes harder to control a (newly empowered) victim, only to later come to the attention of the police for abusing a new partner (Home Office, 2013b: 17). The Home Office policy impact assessment for the DVDS noted that if the Scheme were successful in its aim of informing potential victims of domestic abuse about the risks they faced, then there would indeed be a potential risk of the displacement of abuse, if an offender were not prevented from simply finding a new person to target in a violent relationship, following the successful 'breaking up' of a relationship as a result of a disclosure via the Scheme (Home Office, 2013b).

As a tragic confirmation of this concern about displacement of risk, the killing of Kerri McAuley led to a Domestic Homicide Review report which showed that while a disclosure of risk information to Kerri had been attempted by Norfolk Constabulary, the previous partner of her killer had been warned about his convictions for violence against women via the DVDS (Graham, 2018). In essence, one could re-tell the tale of Kerri McAuley's murder rather differently: she was killed by the violence of a man whom the DVDS had displaced from the life of another woman into her own. Kerri had been warned of her partner's violence against women by a friend before she was herself the victim of violence perpetrated by him against her (Graham, 2018). Perhaps she would have been too vulnerable to victimisation through domestic violence to have acted in an 'informed' manner on a disclosure properly made to her under the DVDS.

The Home Office impact assessment report produced prior to the adoption of the DVDS also explained in relation to risk displacement arising from disclosures, however, that the "police national database may mitigate this risk over time as perpetrators can be … made known to all police forces across England and Wales", while "appropriate data-sharing amongst agencies, appropriate support can be given to perpetrators to stop their offending" (Home Office, 2013a: 17). Unfortunately, no evaluation of any such data sharing amongst the police and other agencies has yet to take place with specific regard to the Scheme, and we have no evidence to show that DVDS disclosures are being linked with more support for perpetrators. Since the 2013 Home Office impact assessment on the DVDS was written, HMIC/HMICFRS have been very critical of the failures in police intelligence and information sharing in relation to protecting vulnerable people generally (HMIC, 2018). It must be noted, sadly, that such flagging of reports of domestic violence, and the secondary sharing of domestic abuse information concerning individual cases, is plainly not yet common from the content of the responses received to one of the nationwide freedom-of-information requests I made while conducting the research for this book; responses to my May 2018 FOI request sometimes cited difficulties with older recording systems that would prevent the ready and speedy access of data labelled as relating to domestic abuse incidents. Criticism can also be levelled at the notion that enough is in any way done with domestic violence perpetrators to help them stop their reoffending (Stevenson, 2017). There is certainly an issue with the nature of the Scheme as targeting resources at victims in terms of disclosures to try and make them more 'rational' about their partners, as opposed to resources being targeted, more appropriately, at serial domestic violence perpetrators and for their dissuasion from that serial offending.

A 'full risk assessment' under the DVDS guidance is one based upon the 'DASH' ('Domestic Abuse and Serious Harm') questionnaire. This is used under the DVDS guidance only where the 'Right to Ask' is drawn upon by a potential victim who approaches the police—as the police can then initially obtain information to feed into the risk assessment model directly from the potential victim of domestic violence themselves. However, the DASH model has its problems, as noted by some academics (Birdsall et al., 2017; Turner et al., 2019), because it does not readily take into account the personalities of controlling abusers and vulnerable victims, for example. However, at the same time, predicting domestic violence is going to be very difficult if we only focus on the personalities in a relationship. As Young (1992: 455) has noted, "one cannot explain transformations in wealth, weather, bankruptcy, biology, economic, medical or marriage forms by appeal to and only to the personal characteristics of the persons affected". Many societal and environmental factors may result in tendencies towards domestic violence in a relationship.

The DVDS of course presupposes a full agency for victims, and this recognition of agency is on one level correct, as it is "an understanding of women as active agents, engaged in a complex process of 'active negotiation and strategic resistance' both with their partners and with the range of helping agencies, in their struggle for safety and 'justice'" (Lewis et al., 2000: 180). However, this assumption should not be taken to mean, as identified above in relation to criticism of the DASH risk assessment model, that victims of domestic violence are always able to act as fully able agents who can easily remove themselves from relationships and so readily preclude the risk of violence a partner may pose to them. As Herring (2016: 9) has it, "the hyper-autonomous, non-vulnerable man as the norm … is a fiction". Matters are further complicated, from the perspective of whether the DVDS is an effective crime reduction tool, when we consider that there is some evidence that women in particular are at more serious risk of harm from abusive partners when they are in the process of leaving or have left those partners (Femicide Census, 2016: 21); bearing in mind that one assumption often made about the Scheme is that victims would end potentially dangerous relationships at a time and in a manner of their own choosing (Duggan, 2018a, 2018b). Marian Duggan has summarised these concerns about the DADS-type policies emerging globally, explaining that we must acknowledge the barriers faced by victims: insufficient access to housing, economic abuse from perpetrators and practicalities involving children from a relationship or in the household concerned (Duggan, 2018a, 2018b). However, nonetheless, 'Why doesn't she just leave?' persists as an attitude since the moral judgement of victims of domestic violence and their self-protection measures abounds in social cultures: "An innocent victim needs to watch where she goes, with whom she associates" (Madriz, 1997: 87).

2.7 Suggestions from Reported Cases That the DVDS Is 'Victim-Blaming'

The role of the DVDS in public protection and safeguarding work in England and Wales has come to augment the role of children's social care services. In a ground-breaking study, Kat Hadjimatheou conducted

32 interviews with police professionals in 14 forces who work with the DVDS as part of their safeguarding practices (Hadjimatheou, 2021). Hadjimatheou has been able to highlight the issue that because of reluctance on the part of some police forces to interpret DVDS guidance in such a way that would allow them to disclose older, 'spent' convictions, "children's social workers in many force areas can reveal criminal history information that is far more detailed and from much further back in the past, than can police" (Hadjimatheou, 2021: 12). Hadjimatheou (2021) also found that there was a distinct overlap between the public protection functions of the DVDS for several forces, with 'Clare's Law' forming a basis for trying to protect victims of domestic abuse but also forming the basis for greater child protection-oriented interventions with women at risk of violence from their partners. As Hadjimatheou notes (2021: 13), there is "a universal acceptance amongst police of their own moral and professional responsibility to report cases of children exposed to domestic abuse to social care". This entails, as Hadjimatheou notes (2021: 13), a distinct switch in the purported raison d'être of the DVDS, "from an emphasis on personal choice and autonomy to responsibilisation and implicit blame as soon as an ongoing risk to children is identified".

There are a pair of small case studies that can be observed concerning Clare's Law and work of child protection professionals, as drawn from two case law reports on care orders and child protection in the Family Court. Firstly, in *Tameside Metropolitan Borough Council v KU, DB and another* [2017] 8 WLUK 71, the DVDS was used to proactively disclose information to a pregnant woman and victim of violence perpetrated by the child's father (DB). It transpires (at para. 8) that this

> history was shared with KU, via Clare's Law, at an early stage in the pre-birth assessment in order that she could make informed choices regarding her relationship with him and demonstrate whether she could prioritise the needs of her child … [but it] subsequently became apparent that both parents withheld information in the pre-birth assessment process and did not share information regarding the extensive history of physical abuse which is now known.

Even assuming we accept the idea that a victim can be empowered by information to make informed choices and as a legitimate means of viewing victims, *KU, DB* is evidence of a (pregnant) vulnerable potential victim not only unable to act purposively in response to a disclosure but deciding, or being scared or coerced, into refraining from sharing with police or social services the abusive nature of her relationship. Disclosure in this example can be seen to do little or nothing to preclude 'victim vulnerability' here—but it is evidence of the way that a disclosure may achieve nothing *due to* the vulnerability of a victim. As for the use by a family court judge of the 'informed choice' mantra concerning the Scheme, as Patrick O'Connor QC might note, this is perhaps evidence of the way that a neo-liberal philosophy has suffused our society—allowing individual responsibility to be unfairly loaded upon the less fortunate 'customer' of the courts and social care system (O'Connor, 2018: 542). Presumably as a result O'Connor would despair of the way KU in her case is highlighted as being at fault, despite being the victim in her case. In Alberta, Canada, Professor Jennifer Koshan has observed that there may be "unintended consequences for women who perhaps get information about a partner who is violent but then still decide to stay with that person … they may then face adverse consequences when they try and use the justice system for other things" (Canadian Bar Association, 2020). We can see the very real risk of this in the case of KU.

In the second case involving the DVDS in its background context, *Northumberland County Council v LW, NW The Children* [2018] 2 WLUK 586, a mother of children who were subject to care orders was advised to seek information about the details of a 24-year-old conviction for rape possessed by her new partner (and which she had already learned the gist of from him), but did not do so. As the court explained (at 55), "the mother chose not to make a Clare's Law application to find out anything more about the details of his offence". This of course shows that a potential applicant may avoid drawing on the DVDS even when given very good reason to do so—and also that social workers and probation officers either did not seek a Right to Know disclosure in these circumstances, or, potentially, were not successful in demonstrating a 'pressing need' for disclosure to the police if they did indeed seek a Right to Know disclosure. As an aside, the notion that probation officers may sometimes fail to seek a Right to Know disclosure to a victim by the police, even where one may then result in a disclosure, is substantiated by a September 2018 inspection report by the HM Inspectorate of Probation. This report found that probation officers employed by Community Rehabilitation Companies, and therefore working with the majority of probationers convicted of domestic violence offences, "generally … did not understand the obligations and opportunities this legislation [sic] brings to help provide immediate protection to victims" (HMIP, 2018: 31).

2.8 Conclusions

So what to do? Even accepting risks of 'displacement' of domestic violence from some relationships into others, surely some kinds of interventions could be made with regard to the riskiest of new relationships. Why not proactively warn the new partners of, at the very least, known, serial domestic abusers that their past behaviour has been violent? There are some possible approaches to explore by way of comparators with the current operation of DADS.

First, the police could monitor and place under bureaucratic surveillance those strongly suspected or at least those already convicted of domestic violence on a kind of 'register' of domestic abusers. But this would, under the rule of law in the UK, require legislative effort to create a means by which the private life of such an offender could be interfered with 'in accordance with the law', and only when necessary and proportionate, due to the requirements of the Human Rights Act 1998 and Article 8 of the European Convention on Human Rights (1950) ('the ECHR'), which protect the right to respect for private life of the offender(s) concerned. However, this kind of statutory domestic abusers register is the approach that the Home Affairs Select Committee outlined in their October 2018 report on domestic abuse, when noting that expert witnesses to their inquiry had observed that "the Domestic Violence Disclosure Scheme ('Clare's Law') was dependent on an individual asking about an offender's history and recommended that the focus be changed so that offenders were tracked as a matter of course by police officers" (House of Commons Home Affairs Select Committee, 2019: 12), leading to their recommendation as a Committee that a "a national register of serial stalkers and domestic violence perpetrators … is introduced as a matter of urgency and that individuals placed on the register should, like registered sex offenders, be managed through multi-agency public protection arrangements (MAPPA)" (House of Commons Home Affairs Select Committee, 2019: 13). This would require new legislation (Oppenheim, 2020) and considerable investment in the management of offenders who are serial domestic violence perpetrators. The chance for this new legislative model was passed over by the Johnson government in passing the Domestic Abuse Act 2021 (Mason, 2021); instead a reform of offender monitoring guidance for MAPPA processes was promised without the actual creation of a new statutory offender registration regime for domestic abusers.

Second, the police could ensure that their warnings are only issued when a full package of emotional and logistical support is waiting for a woman (and her children) from an array of agencies and helpers, since the warning should preclude the relationship from continuing, in a perfectly rational world—since the police should know that the risk to a woman from an abuser is greatest at the point of a relationship coming to an end (Refuge, n.d.; Kelly, 2014). But this would entail putting the relevant and appropriate resources in place to secure this support for vulnerable women. Increasing the attention paid by the criminal justice system to victims of domestic violence would help the police, in particular, meet the challenge laid down to them in October 2018 by the Home Affairs Select Committee, who concluded that all too often, "there continue to be instances where victims' claims are not taken seriously or where there is an inadequate police response" (House of Commons Home Affairs Select Committee, 2019: 4).

Third, whatever approach is taken to this 'warning system', the police and their political masters in the Home Office could ensure that the pilot and initial national roll-out of a change in approach would be fully evaluated, in detail and from a variety of perspectives, and would be prepared to take radical steps to make the new approach work effectively, fairly and safely for victims. But this would entail putting a greater amount of resources and a stronger political priority on the assessment of a small piece of domestic violence policy whilst also conducting wider reforms to funding and policy priorities in the arena of policing more widely.

Instead of these three pragmatic steps, what has occurred to date with regard to the DVDS and the other UK DADS is a change of policy to produce a 'warning system' of sorts that depends as much on women coming forward to secure information for themselves as it does on the police protecting them proactively, inherently making some potential victims more responsible for their own safety because there was no specific legislation created to ensure greater proactivity by the police post-disclosure. This lack of joined up operational policy on the DVDS in England and Wales as a strand of police legal powers came about because the Scheme was designed in isolation from other such preventive powers in a policymaking process discussed in the next chapter of this book.

Disclosures under a statutory DVDS in England and Wales could have been enshrined in legislation, perhaps in the recent Domestic Abuse Act 2021, as something to be considered *only* when other offender monitoring or rehabilitative approaches are also deployed (perhaps curtailing the more victim-responsibilising 'Right to Ask'). This, from a vulnerable victim's perspective, would be a more coherent public protection policy development, but would necessarily entail more frequent and regular intrusions into the rights of subjects under the Scheme, as potential or actual serial domestic violence perpetrators. This would have admittedly greater policing costs, particularly if 'Right to Ask' applications were not also curtailed, and greater wider costs if support services such as women's refuges were to be better ready to deal with an increase in the number of dangerous relationships coming to an end. This is on top of the costs that Marian Duggan (2019) has identified in actually operating the DVDS in England and Wales, for example—mainly borne by the police but also other agencies, in advertising the DVDS, making or processing applications, advising on disclosures, recording decisions, and hopefully following up with disclosure recipients.

The combination of the development and roll-out and the media 'selling' of the DVDS by the police has coincided with an incoherent policy of cuts to services for women in a political climate as keen on austerity as it is on public protection. As Helena Kennedy has observed there is a "huge gulf between the best intentions of those in power, and their track record in in translating policy into practice" (Kennedy, 2018: 89). But as Crowther-Dowey and Silvestri might conclude, this is no surprise, since "senior policy makers in government seem reluctant to appreciate that their expectations about the degree of public protection that can be provided are essentially unrealistic and unobtainable in practice" (Crowther-Dowey and Silvestri, 2017: 12). In dealing with the disconnection between regulatory responsibility for vulnerable victims and policies on policing that push us towards responsibilising victims and making them take on their own risk management, with insufficient support for them in terms of services and practical and logistical help, it has been observed by Marian Duggan (2018a) that victims of domestic abuse might receive disclosures but also be unable to determine how best to act on them.

Foisting this kind of personal risk management on to vulnerable victims of serious violence is not the sort of risk management that would amount to good practice; in fact, this responsibilisation of domestic violence victims is quite possibly a risk that a sensible regulator would demand should be subject to mitigatory interventions. Close analyses may show that some practical changes can be made to policy and legal vehicles to better prevent domestic violence occurring in society (as this research does with DADS), while from a victim perspective the operation of the DVDS, for example, could be further reformed in order to be more coherent with wider aims of public protection policy by twinning it with initiatives on offender rehabilitation. Of course it can be argued, as Lewis et al. have noted, that the lawmaking or policymaking process could be too flawed to be a sole vehicle for positive change in preventing domestic violence, since "the law is so intrinsically gendered and has been so thoroughly implicated in previous injustices to women, that efforts to use it are misguided" (Lewis et al., 2000: 180). But these particular observations were made nearly 20 years ago, and it must be acknowledged that a degree of legal reform and victim-oriented progress has taken place in that time in England and Wales—in policy terms, if not in funding terms. Small changes to the 'soft law' operation of the DVDS could continue this work in a small part of this policy arena. There is a wider issue of the problematic nature of forecasting risk in public protection contexts, however—and this is in essence a fundamental challenge faced by the practitioners operating the DVDS, as "the scientific pretensions of risk assessment offer women limited protection from violent men and consequently their human rights are susceptible to being weakened" (Crowther-Dowey & Silvestri, 2017: 12).

The policy, guidance and the regulation of the DVDS could be amended to put the interests of different groups in society more at the heart of decision-making under the Scheme. This could be done in terms of the way the police should work to follow-up on the interests, for example, of children affected by domestic violence, where they come to police attention through the operation of the Scheme. It may also be that the Scheme needs to be re-posited as no longer gender-, culture- and sexuality-neutral in its Home Office guidance, but on the basis of a greater policing awareness in the prediction of risk posed by SDVPs to male, to BME and to LGBTQ victims. In a wider context of a prevention of domestic abuse, the overdue delivery by the Johnson government of the new Domestic Abuse Act 2021 will in time see a swathe of incrementally useful reforms adopted. These include the adoption of a new statutory definition for England and Wales of domestic abuse, a new Domestic Violence and Victims Commissioner and, most importantly perhaps, new and stricter Domestic Abuse Protection Orders, which the courts will issue on application from the police, and which will include requirements on the offender concerned to undertake some positive steps towards rehabilitation, such as attending behaviour management courses, or wearing GPS monitoring devices, on pain of committing a criminal offence in breaching the DAPO through a failure to engage with these requirements (Home Office, 2021). It can be argued that these additions to the armoury will all help the police and other criminal justice agencies (and policymakers) combat domestic violence more systematically.

This chapter has begun the process of undertaking a public policy analysis of Domestic Abuse Disclosure Schemes, in particular by giving an overview of the context of their operation (and very limited evaluation) to date. This initial policy assessment (which is followed by a much deeper dive into the background of the original Domestic Violence Disclosure Scheme in Chap. 3) has established a number of key issues connected to an emerging thematic finding, and crucial factor in the operation of DADS, in terms of victim vulnerability. Disclosures about the dangerousness of a partner based on information about their past may be regularly delivered to women who are ill-supported to put the information to 'rational' use and to leave their partners. This may particularly be the case because this change of national policy on sharing information about domestic abusers, embodied in the UK DADS, has come at a time of austerity (for policing, particularly) (National Police Chiefs' Council, n.d.), with a commensurate dwindling of police resources to support the women who stay in potentially risky relationships, dwindling probation resources to reach out and support likely (re)offenders (HM Inspectorate of Probation, 2018) and dwindling provision of support from refuges and other services for women who do want to leave their partners (McClenaghan & Andersson, 2017). Even government welfare policy has been noted as being seen as likely to contribute to problems with domestic violence: for example, the House of Commons Work and Pensions Committee, in a scathing report, argued that the payment of Universal Credit to a single householder by default would trap some vulnerable women in a situation of coercive control by a potential 'financial abuser' in the form of their partner who received the relevant payments (House of Commons Work and Pensions Select Committee, 2018).

Lastly, due to a tendency of the police to broadcast 'quick wins' to the press, since the DVDS became a national policy in England and Wales in March 2014, the public have been regularly informed that the new policy is working well by their trusted local newspapers (Grace, 2015). The new policy of the Scheme *might* be working very well in the sense of protecting individual, potential victims from serious harm in dangerous relationships. But unfortunately there is no persuasive quantitative or qualitative evidence that it is working in this manner, on any scale or level across England and Wales, because the Home Office, for one, is either yet to gather this evidence or to publish it in a way that is convincing. As Prof. Sandra Walklate has said, quoted by BBC News in an article in November 2018, and in a comment that would still ring true today, we have "no real way of knowing whether it's working or not" (Williams, 2018), meaning that the Home Office should have better studied the use of disclosures by women who receive them. It is essential to determine the efficacy of DADS in jurisdictions, like England and Wales, where their use is on a steadily rising trajectory over time. As noted already, the Femicide Census project reported at the end of 2016 that more than 586 women had been killed by men in 'intimate partner violence' cases between 2009 and 2015 alone, so the nature of the problem the Scheme purports to address is daunting and vitally important (Femicide Census, 2016). As will be explored later in this book there is an argument, however, that the operation of a DADS will be potentially risky for a victim of domestic violence, in the sense that an offender's knowledge that a disclosure has been made may elevate risk, or that a non-disclosure concerning a potential offender may give a problematic and false reassurance and sense of safety to a potential victim of domestic violence, thus increasing the sense that the DVDS may, in some circumstances, actually exacerbate victim vulnerability.

It is appropriate at this juncture in the book, having sketched some dimensions of the problems of victim vulnerability, to address how some of the problems mentioned above came to be 'baked in' to the design and operation of the DVDS as public policy in England and Wales. These issues began with 'Clare's Law' before it spread to other jurisdictions as a concept with public relations appeal. The next chapter (Chap. 3) addresses the problematic policy assumptions and positions taken in the process of creating the DVDS itself, while Chap. 4 examines the root causes of the current international DADS 'policy spiral' (Walker, 2018).

References

Anitha, S. (2008). Neither safety nor justice: The UK government response to domestic violence against immigrant women. *Journal of Social Welfare and Family Law, 30*(8), 189.

Ashworth, A., & Zedner, L. (2014). *Preventive justice*. Oxford University Press.

Atkins, V., & Argar, E. (2019, May 20). Letter to Harriet Harman MP (Chair of the Parliamentary Joint Committee on Human Rights). Retrieved 16 June 2020, from https://www.parliament.uk/documents/joint-committees/human-rights/correspondence/2017-19/190520_Letter_from_Edward_Argar_MP_and_Victoria_Atkins_MP_to_Chair_re_draft_Domestic_Abuse_Bill.pdf

Belur, J. (2008). Is policing domestic violence institutionally racist? A case study of South Asian Women. *Policing and Society, 18*(4), 426.

Birdsall, N., Kirby, S., & McManus, M. (2017). Police–victim engagement in building a victim empowerment approach to intimate partner violence cases. *Police Practice and Research, 18*(1), 75.

Black, J. (2001). Decentring regulation: Understanding the role of regulation and self-regulation in a 'post-regulatory world'. *Current Legal Problems, 54*(1), 103.

Braithwaite, J. (1989). *Crime, shame and reintegration.* Cambridge University Press.

Canadian Bar Association. (2020, April 20). Q&A with Jennifer Koshan. *CBA National.* Retrieved 29 June 2020, from https://www.nationalmagazine.ca/en-ca/articles/people/q-a/2020/qa-with-jennifer-koshan

Cps.gov.uk. (2020). *CPS data summary quarter 4 2019–2020 | The crown prosecution service.* [Online]. Retrieved Accessed 23 June 2021, from https://www.cps.gov.uk/publication/cps-data-summary-quarter-4-2019-2020

Cps.gov.uk. (2021). *Violence against women and girls data | The crown prosecution service.* [Online]. Retrieved 30 March 2021, from https://www.cps.gov.uk/publication/violence-against-women-and-girls-data

Crown Prosecution Service. (2019). *Violence against women and girls report: 2018–2019.* Retrieved 16 June 2020, from https://www.cps.gov.uk/sites/default/files/documents/publications/cps-vawg-report-2019.pdf

Crowther-Dowey, C., & Silvestri, M. (2017). The gendering of violent crime: Towards a human rights approach. *British Journal of Community Justice, 14*(3), 35–54.

Department of Justice (Northern Ireland). (2018, March 26). *Domestic Violence and Abuse Disclosure Scheme guidance.* Retrieved 8 November 2021, from https://www.justice-ni.gov.uk/publications/domestic-violence-and-abuse-disclosure-scheme

Duggan, M. (2018a). 'Idealising' domestic violence victims. In M. Duggan (Ed.), *Revisiting the ideal victim: Developments in critical victimology.* Policy Press.

Duggan, M. (2018b). Victim hierarchies in the domestic violence disclosure scheme. *International Review of Victimology, 24*(2), 199.

Duggan, M. (2019). Reflections on the domestic violence disclosure scheme (England and Wales). *Journal of Gender-Based Violence, 2*, 249–257.

Femi-Ajao, O., Kendal, S., & Lovell, K. (2020). A qualitative systematic review of published work on disclosure and help-seeking for domestic violence and abuse among women from ethnic minority populations in the UK. *Ethnicity & Health, 25*(5), 732.

Femicide Census. (2016). *Redefining an isolated incident—annual report on UK Femicides 2016.* Retrieved 19 June 2020, from https://1q7dqy2unor827bqjls0c4rn-wpengine.netdna-ssl.com/wp-content/uploads/2016/12/The-Femicide-Census-2016.pdf

Gill, A. K., & Harrison, K. (2016). Police responses to intimate partner sexual violence in South Asian Communities. *Policing: A Journal of Policy and Practice, 10*(4), 446.

Graca, S. (2017). Domestic violence policy and legislation in the UK: A discussion of immigrant women's vulnerabilities. *EJoCLI, 22*(1). Retrieved 16 July 2020, from http://webjcli.org/article/view/531

Grace, J. (2015). Clare's Law, or the national Domestic Violence Disclosure Scheme: The contested legalities of criminality information sharing. *Journal of Criminal Law, 79*(1), 36.

Graham, C. (2018, May). Norfolk County Community Safety Partnership. *Domestic Homicide Review Report: Review into the death of April in January 2017.*

Hadjimatheou, K. (2021). Social care 'told me I had to': Empowerment and responsibilization in the Domestic Violence Disclosure Scheme. *The British Journal of Criminology*, azab069. https://doi.org/10.1093/bjc/azab069

Harman, H. (2019, April 10). (MP and Chair of the Parliamentary Joint Committee on Human Rights), Letter to Victoria Atkins MP and Edward Argar MP. Retrieved 16 June 2020, from https://www.parliament.uk/business/committees/committees-a-z/joint-select/human-rights-committee/news-parliament-2017/domestic-abuse-letter-published-17-19/

Harper, P. (2020, August 1). Mum battered to death by boyfriend days after asking for info about him. *The Metro*. Retrieved 16 June 2020, from https://metro.co.uk/2019/08/01/mum-battered-to-death-by-boyfriend-days-after-asking-police-for-info-about-him-10501222/

Haynes, R. (2016). Violence is violence: comparing perceptions of intimate partner violence in homosexual and heterosexual relationships. *Journal of Applied Psychology and Social Science, 2*(2), 1.

Herring, J. (2016). *Vulnerable adults and the law*. Oxford University Press.

HM Inspectorate of Probation. (2018, September). *Domestic abuse: The work undertaken by community rehabilitation companies (CRCs).*

HMICFRS. (2017, November). *A progress report on the police response to domestic abuse*. Retrieved 29 June 2020, from https://www.justiceinspectorates.gov.uk/hmicfrs/wp-content/uploads/progress-report-on-the-police-response-to-domestic-abuse.pdf

HMICFRS. (2019a). *PEEL: Police effectiveness, efficiency and legitimacy 2018–2019—An inspection of Cumbria Constabulary*. Retrieved 16 June 2020, from https://www.justiceinspectorates.gov.uk/hmicfrs/wp-content/uploads/peel-assessment-2018-19-cumbria.pdf

HMICFRS. (2019b). *PEEL: Police effectiveness, efficiency and legitimacy 2018–2019—An inspection of Leicestershire Police*. Retrieved 16 June 2020, from https://www.justiceinspectorates.gov.uk/hmicfrs/wp-content/uploads/peel-assessment-2018-19-leicestershire.pdf

HMICFRS. (2019c). *PEEL: Police effectiveness, efficiency and legitimacy 2018–2019—An inspection of Durham Constabulary*. Retrieved 16 June 2020, from https://www.justiceinspectorates.gov.uk/hmicfrs/wp-content/uploads/peel-assessment-2018-19-durham.pdf

HMICFRS. (2019d). *PEEL: Police effectiveness, efficiency and legitimacy 2018–2019—An inspection of Norfolk Constabulary*. Retrieved 16 June 2020, from https://www.justiceinspectorates.gov.uk/hmicfrs/wp-content/uploads/peel-assessment-2018-19-norfolk.pdf

HMICFRS. (2019e). *PEEL: Police effectiveness, efficiency and legitimacy 2018–2019—An inspection of Nottinghamshire Police*. Retrieved 16 June 2020, from https://www.justiceinspectorates.gov.uk/hmicfrs/wp-content/uploads/peel-assessment-2018-19-nottinghamshire.pdf

HMICFRS. (2019f). *PEEL: Police effectiveness, efficiency and legitimacy 2018–2019—An inspection of West Midlands Police*. Retrieved 16 June 2020, from https://www.justiceinspectorates.gov.uk/hmicfrs/wp-content/uploads/peel-assessment-2018-19-west-midlands.pdf

Home Office. (2013a). *Domestic Violence Disclosure Scheme pilot: Guidance (Revised March 2013)*. Home Office.

Home Office. (2013b). *Domestic Violence Disclosure Scheme (DVDS) pilot assessment*. Home Office.

Home Office. (2016a). *Domestic Violence Disclosure Scheme (DVDS): One year on—Home office assessment of national roll-out*. Home Office.

Home Office. (2016b). *Domestic Violence Disclosure Scheme (DVDS) guidance*. Retrieved 16 June 2020, from https://www.gov.uk/government/uploads/system/uploads/attachment_data/file/575361/DVDS_guidance_FINAL_v3.pdf

Home Office. (2021). *Domestic abuse protection notices/orders factsheet*. [Online]. Retrieved 23 June 2021, from https://www.gov.uk/government/publications/domestic-abuse-bill-2020-factsheets/domestic-abuse-protection-notices-orders-factsheet

House of Commons Home Affairs Select Committee. (2019). *Domestic abuse-ninth report of session 2017–2019*. HC 1015.

House of Commons Work and Pensions Select Committee. (2018). *Universal credit and domestic abuse, seventeenth report of 2017–2019*. HMSO.

Kelly, L. (2014, December 10). Domestic abuse: 'You're most at risk of being killed when you try to leave. *The Guardian*. Retrieved 19 June 2020, from https://www.theguardian.com/society-professionals/2014/dec/10/domestic-abuse-risk-trying-leave-housing-community

Kennedy, H. (2018). *Eve was shamed: How British justice is failing women*. Penguin.

Knight, C., & Wilson, K. (2012). Domestic violence and abuse in same-sex relationships. In *Lesbian, gay, bisexual and trans people (LGBT) and the criminal justice system*. Palgrave Macmillan.

Lancashire Post. (2018, November 14). Violence against Lancashire men: Figures show worrying drop in men coming forward to report abuse. *Lancashire Post*. Retrieved 16 June 2020, from https://www.lep.co.uk/news/crime/violence-against-lancashire-men-figures-show-worrying-drop-in-men-coming-forward-to-report-abuse-1-9444233

Lewis, R., et al. (2000). Protection, prevention, rehabilitation or justice? Women's use of the law to challenge domestic violence. *International Review of Victimology, 7*(1), 179.

Madriz, E. (1997). *Nothing bad happens to good girls: Fear of crime in women's lives*. University of California Press.

Mason, G. (2021). *Ministers challenge domestic abuse cases being subject to MAPPA | UK Police News—Police Oracle*. [Online]. Policeoracle.com. Retrieved 23 June 2021, from https://www.policeoracle.com/news/Ministers-challenge-domestic-abuse-cases-being-subject-to-MAPPA-_107076.html

McClenaghan, M., & Andersson, J. (2017, October 16). Revealed: Thousands of women turned away as refuge funding is cut. *The Bureau of Investigative Journalism*. Retrieved 19 June 2020, from https://www.thebureauinvestigates.com/stories/2017-10-16/a-system-at-breaking-point

Merchant, L. V., & Whiting, J. B. (2018). A grounded theory study of how couples desist from intimate partner violence. *Journal of Marital and Family Therapy, 44*(4), 590–605.

Monckton Smith, J. (2019). Intimate partner Femicide: Using Foucauldian analysis to track an eight stage progression to homicide *Violence Against Women, 26*, 1267–1285. Retrieved 20 July 2020, from https://doi.org/10.1177/1077801219863876

Munro, E. (2004). A simpler way to understand the results of risk assessment instruments. *Children and Youth Services Review, 26*(9), 873.

National Police Chiefs' Council (NPCC). (n.d.). Chief constable Dave Thompson: Policing is at the tipping point—and we've got to move on from here. Retrieved 19 June 2020, from https://news.npcc.police.uk/releases/

chief-constable-dave-thompson-policing-is-at-the-tipping-point-and-weve-got-to-move-on-from-here

O'Connor, P. (2018). Neo-liberalism and human rights. *European Human Rights Law Review, 6*, 541.

Office for National Statistics. (2016, February). *Intimate personal violence and partner abuse*. Retrieved 16 June 2020 from https://www.ons.gov.uk/peoplepopulationandcommunity/crimeandjustice/compendium/focusonviolentcrimeandsexualoffences/yearendingmarch2015/chapter4intimatepersonalviolenceandpartnerabuse

Office for National Statistics. (2019a). *Domestic abuse and the criminal justice system, England and Wales: November 2019*. Retrieved 16 June 2020, from https://www.ons.gov.uk/peoplepopulationandcommunity/crimeandjustice/articles/domesticabuseandthecriminaljusticesystemenglandandwales/november2019

Office for National Statistics. (2019b). *Domestic abuse victim characteristics, England and Wales: Year ending March 2019*. Retrieved 16 June 2020, from https://www.ons.gov.uk/peoplepopulationandcommunity/crimeandjustice/articles/domesticabusevictimcharacteristicsenglandandwales/yearendingmarch2019

Ons.gov.uk. (2020). *Domestic abuse in England and Wales overview—Office for national statistics*. [Online]. Retrieved 23 June 2021, from https://www.ons.gov.uk/peoplepopulationandcommunity/crimeandjustice/bulletins/domesticabuseinenglandandwalesoverview/november2020

Ons.gov.uk. (2021). *Domestic abuse and the criminal justice system—Appendix tables—Office for national statistics*. [Online]. Retrieved 30 March 2021, from https://www.ons.gov.uk/peoplepopulationandcommunity/crimeandjustice/datasets/domesticabuseandthecriminaljusticesystemappendixtables

Oppenheim, M. (2020, June 8). Use domestic abuse bill to stop serial perpetrators abusing multiple women, government urged. *The Independent*. Retrieved 19 June 2020, from https://www.independent.co.uk/news/uk/crime/domestic-abuse-bill-serial-perpetrators-register-a9555126.html

Police Scotland. (2015). *DSDAS guidance and operational protocol*. Author Copy.

Public Bill Committee on the Domestic Abuse Bill. (2019–2020). 8th sitting minutes, PBC (Bill 96) 2019–2021.

Raine, A. (2014). *The anatomy of violence*. Penguin Books.

Refuge. (n.d.). Barriers to leaving. Retrieved 19 June 2020, from http://www.refuge.org.uk/about-domestic-violence/barriers-to-leaving/

Sharp-Jeffs, N. (2020). Understanding the economics of abuse: An assessment of the economic abuse definition within the Domestic Abuse Bill. *Journal of Gender-Based Violence, 5*, 163–173.

Stevenson, L. (2017, September 19). Not enough focus on perpetrators in domestic abuse cases inspectors say. *Community Care*. Retrieved 19 June 2020, from http://www.communitycare.co.uk/2017/09/19/enough-focus-perpetrators-domestic-abuse-cases-inspectors-say/

Turner, E., Medina, J., & Brown, G. (2019). Dashing hopes? The predictive accuracy of domestic abuse risk assessment by police. *British Journal of Criminology, 59*, 1013–1034.

Walker, C. (2018). Counter-terrorism and counter-extremism: The UK policy spirals. *Public Law, 725*(4).

Walsh, P. (2021). *Abuse victims 'must have power to put safety measures in place'*. Eastern Daily Press. Retrieved 22 June 2021, from https://www.edp24.co.uk/news/crime/norfolk-abuse-charity-says-disclosure-vital-7993902

Williams, F. (2018, November 29). Clare's Law: The women who risk their lives by refusing information. *BBC News*. Retrieved 19 June 2020, from https://www.bbc.co.uk/news/uk-england-42920020

Wood, E., et al. (2004). Displacement of Canada's largest public illicit drug market in response to a police crackdown. *Canadian Medical Association Journal, 170*(10), 1551.

Young, T. R. (1992). Chaos theory and human agency: Humanist sociology. *Humanity and Society, 16*(4), 441.

3

Policy Origins of the Domestic Violence Disclosure Scheme

3.1 Introduction

This chapter explores the policy origins of the Domestic Violence Disclosure Scheme (DVDS) in England and Wales. In this way, it gives an account of why the DVDS was allowed to become the root of the eventual 'policy spiral' (Walker, 2018) demonstrated over the next set of chapters. The last few chapters will examine some of the problems or complexities of the Scheme in operation, but this chapter takes a deeper look at how those problems and complexities originated in policy terms. In particular, it begins to build up the argument for DADS globally as a criminal justice 'policy spiral', that is:

> a policy which lacks *clear initial purpose* or subsequent direction, progression, control and reflection. A policy spiral is therefore susceptible to *unresolved contradictions or gaps*, dramatic direction changes, and *uncertain outcomes*. As a result, policy spirals arise from *inexact and contested meanings, objectives*, and mechanisms. (Walker, 2018: 726) [Emphases added]

This chapter will focus on the elements of Walker's definition that concern a lack of 'clear initial purpose' of the DVDS in England and Wales

J. Grace, *Domestic Abuse Disclosure Schemes*,
https://doi.org/10.1007/978-3-030-89039-1_3

as something which supposedly aims to reduce the risk of domestic violence and yet focuses on managing victims' behaviour. It will also discuss the 'inexact and contested meanings' and objectives of the DVDS when it comes to its method of boosting the degree to which a victim makes 'informed choice' about their own management of risk of intimate violence. Later chapters detail the regulation of the Scheme with regard to its growth and policymakers' 'progression, control and reflection' of the UK DADS, and DADS more widely.

This chapter also presents the development of Scheme-related policy as an ongoing process in the jurisdiction of England and Wales. As noted earlier, the DVDS has evolved, after all, from being a 'pure' policy proposal (ACPO, 2009; Home Office, 2013c), put first under public consultation (Home Office, 2012), and then to a pilot in four police force areas in England and Wales in 2012–13 (Home Office, 2013b); then to a national Scheme for England and Wales from March 2014; and to being rolled out in Scotland after a pilot there in 2015; as well as being consulted upon in Northern Ireland in 2016, and ultimately adopted there too in 2018. The Scheme in England and Wales was evaluated at the end of its pilot phase in just four police force areas (Home Office, 2013b); then examined 'one year on' from its national roll-out (Home Office, 2016a), and then re-founded on a tweaked set of policy guidelines in 2016 (Home Office, 2016b).

In terms of its classification as a matter of developing public policy, the DVDS in England and Wales is a nationwide project or programme that has the capacity to impact upon the lives of vulnerable victims or potential victims of domestic violence, and their children or other dependents. Whether that impact is beneficial, efficacious or properly scrutinised, at the least, is in question throughout this book—but some of the lack of oversight of the Scheme has come from a lack of public recognition by policymakers and policing regulators that the Scheme was founded and predicated on some assumptions, tensions and difficulties. Home Office policymakers have made assumptions that victims will be safer once they are better informed about a perpetrator's past (when actually there is a concern that the breakdown of an already abusive relationship can worsen violence, as the Home Office are well aware (Home Office, 2012: 9)). There are also tensions between the need to protect the most vulnerable potential victims and the ongoing need to rehabilitate offenders, together with practical difficulties such as the partial record of domestic violence that any system of police intelligence can provide. As a result, there are grounds for suggesting that such a policy position must be revisited.

The DVDS has since inception looked to help victims of domestic violence, and reduce harms to them arising from the criminality of repeat domestic violence perpetrators. The relevant Home Office policy impact assessment took pains, in outlining why the DVDS should be introduced, to make it clear that:

> The three main objectives of the [DVDS] policy are:
>
> 1. Reduce incidents of domestic violence and abuse;
> 2. Reduce the health and criminal justice related costs related to domestic violence and abuse;
> 3. Strengthen the ability of the police and other multi-agency partnerships to provide appropriate protection and support to victims at risk of domestic violence and abuse. (Home Office, 2013c: 1)

However, no Home Office review of the Scheme (neither the pilot assessment published in 2013 (Home Office, 2013b) nor the 'one year on' evaluation following the national roll-out of the DVDS in England and Wales (Home Office, 2016a)) actually determines whether these objectives have been met in any substantive way. This chapter now examines the process of policy development for the DVDS by looking at key policy actors' work in influencing the founding ethos of the Scheme, and the way that secondary policy actors, particularly the police and media, have had a great influence on the way the Scheme is utilised and deployed in practice.

3.2 Policy Considerations in Developing the Scheme: From Pilot to National Roll-out

In 2009, the Association of Chief Police Officers (ACPO, now the National Police Chiefs' Council, or NPCC) published a report ('the ACPO report' (ACPO, 2009)), written for a Home Office and wider policymaking audience, which, amongst other recommendations, argued for a stronger focus on repeat or serial domestic violence perpetrators as a significant group of offenders within the body of domestic violence perpetrators generally. The report argued that these high-risk offenders warranted better monitoring or 'tracking'. The ACPO report also concluded that repeat victims of domestic violence could be better identified and supported by the police as particularly at-risk individuals.

Furthermore, the ACPO report acknowledged that the police had common law powers to disclose information to members of the public for public protection purposes—as well as statutory powers to share information as part of their work in facilitating 'Multi-Agency Public Protection Arrangements'. As such, the ACPO report ultimately did not fully conclude that the creation of new police statutory powers to share domestic violence-related criminality information was required for a shift in police practice in the area now purportedly addressed by the Scheme. Instead, ACPO observed that in order to "assist the operation of a disclosure regime, a provision equivalent to that in S.140 of the [Criminal Justice and Immigration Act 2008, which amended the Criminal Justice Act 2003 to create the Child Sex Offender Disclosure Scheme] could be enacted in primary legislation" (ACPO, 2009: 27). However, the ACPO report retreats quickly from this position, observing that their own "research suggests that there is sufficient existing legislation/guidance and stated cases to allow MARAC and MAPPA to be used as a vehicle for disclosure to potential victims" (ACPO, 2009: 27). As a result, the scope of the Scheme, as well as its fundamental rationale, and its legal footing (as a practice based only upon the common law), all began to be forged five years before the Scheme became national criminal justice policy for England and Wales.

The Home Office report on responses to a 2012 public consultation on the prospect of a DVDS, following the ACPO report in 2009, noted that several respondents felt the Scheme, though it could operate on the basis of common law powers of the police to disclose information for public protection purposes, would be used more consistently in a wider legal framework (of data protection, public protection and human rights laws) if it had a specific statutory basis. The Committee for the Centre for Child and Family Law Reform, as well as the Safe Durham Partnership, for example, felt that a statutory 'right to ask' strand of any Scheme would "formalise the current position [of the common law] by creating a regularised framework for the disclosure of this type of information by the police", and would "ensure clear guidelines and rules [were] available to the police", respectively (Home Office, 2012: 8–9). The follow-up Home Office impact assessment (Home Office, 2013b), however, did not then indicate any possibility of the Scheme being put on a statutory footing to better articulate its operation in the midst of this wider legal framework. This is perhaps because there was also some opposition to a statutory footing for the Scheme in the consultation responses received by the Home Office. A statutory footing for the Scheme had been consulted upon, but the high-profile campaign group Liberty refuted the need for a statutory-based Scheme, arguing that instead of being used on operating a DVDS, police resources should and could be better deployed in using conventional means of monitoring, detecting and otherwise bringing to justice domestic violence perpetrators (Home Office, 2012). The two well-known anti-domestic violence campaign groups, Refuge and Women's Aid, were both insistent that the Scheme need not be created with an explicit statutory basis. However, this was mainly because they were opposed to the creation of a DVDS at all, as explored below (Home Office, 2012).

There was considerable opposition to the introduction of the Scheme on a more practical basis, during the span of the Home Office consultation over the introduction of the Scheme, which took place at a formative stage for the DVDS as a policy as a whole (Strickland, 2013). Total responses to the Home Office consultation on the Scheme included a strong majority, collectively speaking, in favour of either a 'Right to Ask' policy basis for a Domestic Violence Disclosure Scheme, or a 'Right to

Know' policy basis, or both aspects of the eventual Scheme (Home Office, 2012). But Refuge and Women's Aid both felt that there did not need to be more emphasis on facilitating disclosures to women at risk, and that police resources would be better directed to improving general police responses to domestic violence (Strickland, 2013).

The eventual founding of the DVDS on a non-statutory basis, as a piece of national policy, and operated on the basis of pre-existing police common law powers, is, as a result, highly problematic as a 'middle ground' outcome of sorts, when we consider the inconsistent application of the DVDS as a policy regulating disclosures of perpetrators' histories across police forces in England and Wales. A clear statutory basis for the processes involved in the Scheme, and the relevant threshold tests for and parameters of disclosures, might have closed down some of the possible inconsistencies in operating the DVDS from the outset. As Jean L. Cohen has observed, "Law has its own efficacy, and the mode of legal regulation matters very much indeed … [since] subject[s] before the law and even the harm being redressed are in part legally constructed" (Cohen, 2002: 126).

Definitions of perpetrators and victims, intimate partners and former partners, as well as *what* can be disclosed and *when*, within the ambit of the Scheme in England and Wales, and for the purpose of the operation of the 'Right to Know' and the 'Right to Ask', were left to Home Office policy alone. Recent FOI-based research has begun to show, however, that considerable discrepancies exist between police forces in England and Wales in terms of how they operationalise risk assessments in relation to potential disclosures and their contents (Hadjimatheou & Grace, 2020). A lack of consistency in terms of policy logic in the DVDS is something that was anticipated prior to the full national roll-out of the Scheme. In the public consultation phase of the development of the Scheme as a matter of public policy, Refuge in particular had concerns about the 'victim-blaming' nature of the Scheme. Their consultation response noted "concerns about the underlying premise of the 'Right to Ask' scheme", and were sceptical that "knowing about a partner's history of domestic violence will somehow empower a woman to leave him and seek safety", while noting that "women are at greatest risk of homicide at the point of separation or after leaving a violent partner" (Home Office, 2012: 9).

There has been some limited journalistic coverage of the Scheme from a civil liberties perspective, criticising the Scheme as an unacceptable policy-based intrusion into the private lives of individuals and their relationships (Gittos, 2013). Early academic criticism of the Scheme has however centred on the following four aspects of the Scheme: Firstly, there is a degree to which the Scheme can be said to (inappropriately) 'responsibilise' potential and actual victims of domestic violence, potentially feeding into a culture of 'victim blaming' (Duggan, 2012). The latter concern could be said to arise since under the 'right to ask' strand of the Scheme, potential victims are encouraged to approach the police, and if they do not do so, despite having suspicions or fears about their partner, this could (unfairly) be offered up as a criticism of their own complicity in victimisation (Grace, 2015). This is nothing new, sadly, in policy terms. In 1997 Esther Madriz concluded that:

> Ideologies of crime and the fear of crime have helped to foster a conservative moral agenda in which women are told to protect themselves and their children … by adhering to specific standards of behaviour that are considered appropriate. (Madriz, 1997: 92)

Secondly, there has been criticism that the Scheme is not a policing service which some women, particularly, from certain BME and/or immigrant communities would find culturally easy to engage with (Graca, 2017). (The Home Office impact assessment in 2013 had already noted that there were potential equality-related issues concerning the operation of the Scheme, such as in relation to issues of first language; potential risks of so-called honour-based violence; a need for police outreach work in particular communities in relation to the Scheme; the importance that the Scheme was perceived as gender neutral; and the involvement of carers in disclosures, where relevant (Home Office, 2013c).) Thirdly, there has been criticism of the (lack of an) extent to which the Scheme provides proper protection for the procedural rights of 'subjects'—the (alleged or suspected) repeat domestic violence perpetrators themselves (Grace, 2015). Fourthly, and finally, the Scheme has not been shown to be objectively efficacious in preventing domestic violence due to the poor availability of data about the precise operation of the Scheme and any clear trends in its effect on the lives of potential victims of domestic violence (Fitz-Gibbon & Walklate, 2017).

As criticisms of the operation of the Scheme, these four concerns were not amongst those other, more pragmatic concerns listed among the findings of the Home Office evaluation report that assessed the pilot phase of the Scheme undertaken by police forces in Wiltshire, Warwickshire, Gwent and Greater Manchester (Home Office, 2013c). This Home Office study did identify a number of practical and policy issues with the pilot Scheme, however, such as a perceived vague nature of the 'pressing need' test which is a core legal threshold in decision-making in relation to potential disclosures under the Scheme. The Home Office study also identified that the Scheme as piloted seemed to overlap, in the minds of public protection professionals, with MAPPA arrangements, and placed an emphasis on police and social work coordination that had been less well anticipated or planned for than would have been ideal. But ultimately, the study went on to recommend that the Scheme could be adopted across England and Wales as a whole, without any additional legislative measures or policy amendments to support it, though noting a number of ways in which the Scheme needed to improve in operation. At least, this was how the Home Secretary at the time, Theresa May, chose to interpret the findings and recommendations of this report—declaring to Parliament that the Scheme had been adopted across England and Wales on the 8 March 2014—International Women's Day (May, 2014). This policy announcement was made without discussing any potential for a change of legal footing for the Scheme, and without simultaneously updating and clarifying the Scheme guidance (an arguable 'regulatory failing') (Grace, 2015). As a result, the Scheme was initially rolled out across England and Wales on the basis of the same, untouched Home Office guidance document which underpinned the pilot phases of the Scheme (Home Office, 2013a).

Given that the Home Office evaluation of the pilot phase of the Scheme highlighted that the legal tests for disclosures as articulated in the Scheme guidance were hard to interpret consistently (Home Office, 2013b), it is interesting to note some information which was made available about the operation of the Scheme in early 2015. Freedom-of-information requests by the Press Association first showed that the disclosure rates under the Scheme, expressed as a proportion of the total number of combined 'Right to Ask' and 'Right to Know' applications received, varied considerably from force area to force area—between 11% in Merseyside and 60% in Greater Manchester (BBC News, 2015). This would appear to support the point expressed in the pilot evaluation that the Home Office should have addressed legal tests for disclosures that were difficult to apply consistently. These disparities in disclosure rates have generally continued, as shown in Table 1.2 (Chap. 1).

By 2017, the Scheme was into its third year of national operation, and its third set of non-statutory guidance materials (issued in December 2016); though the latter did little to amend in detail the Home Office interpretation of the legal tests for disclosures (Home Office, 2016b). Furthermore, the Home Office evaluation of the DVDS 'one year on' from national roll-out in England and Wales highlighted (again) that the legal tests for disclosures as articulated in the current Scheme guidance are difficult to interpret consistently, meaning disclosure rates continue to vary considerably across force areas in England and Wales (Home Office, 2016a). Of course, one cannot forget that while the DVDS is an intervention as a policy in England and Wales that purports to safeguard victims, there is added complexity about 'Clare's Law'. As well as the need to safeguard victims, another consideration must be the right to respect for private life, and the rights to rehabilitation, owed to previously violent perpetrators of domestic abuse under Article 8 ECHR and the (qualified) right to respect for private and family life. In responding to a summary of consultation submissions on the original development of the DVDS, the Home Office highlighted important questions over the lawfulness of wider-scope disclosures of criminal histories data on Scheme subjects. Consultation respondents had informed the Home Office that there were concerns over the legality of the scope of disclosures under the Scheme, observing that (Home Office, 2012: 12):

> greater clarity was required on the safety planning, privacy, proportionality and data protection issues concerning disclosure before firm decisions on the scope of disclosure could be made. Respondents also highlighted the

need for appropriate safeguards to be built into any disclosure process to prevent malicious allegations and stigmatisation from occurring.

In terms of what could, or should, be deemed to be reliable material for disclosure, the Home Office (2012: 12) noted that:

> on extending disclosure beyond convictions to include intelligence, respondents recognised that many alleged perpetrators would not have convictions, thus strengthening the argument to extend disclosure to include intelligence. However, respondents wished to ensure that such intelligence was robust and reliable to guard against malicious and unfounded allegations that would otherwise stigmatise an innocent person.

So from its very inception as a Home Office policy, there were concerns over the complexities of operating the DVDS not just in an effective manner but in a balanced and careful one too. Unfortunately, the police in England and Wales have allowed the media narrative over the Scheme to be driven by an assumption of the effectiveness of the DVDS as a policy and policing approach to protecting victims of domestic violence, when it may do far less of the sort—worryingly unevaluated as it is.

3.3 The Press and the Scheme

Local press media coverage of the Scheme shows that police forces across England and Wales are promoting the Scheme widely and proactively in their own areas, with a variety of degrees to which the success of the Scheme is represented, or, arguably, misrepresented (Grace, 2015). This is of course at least partly attributable to journalistic licence, we might assume, but it is concerning for the sake of transparency that some local newspaper articles (or the police press teams that feed them press releases) might conflate the number of disclosures made under the Scheme with the number of individuals who have been definitively protected or 'saved' from the risk of domestic violence. For example, in one local newspaper article from September 2014 (Baker, 2014), notably titled 'Domestic abuse scheme working', Ian Johnston, Police and Crime Commissioner for Gwent, was reported as commenting that:

> Whether it's male or female victims of domestic abuse, when used properly, the Domestic Violence Disclosure Scheme can provide people with the information they need to escape an abusive situation before it's too late. … [The Scheme] can play a vital role in ensuring that more people can make an informed decision about their relationship.

But on the sole basis of the Home Office pilot evaluation, the evidence for the actual intended effect of the Scheme—that (principally) women are made sufficiently aware of the risks of a partner or potential partner that they effectively limit or end their contact with that person—was actually rather sparse (Home Office, 2013b). It would be hard to state, objectively, that the Scheme as operated by the police in Gwent was 'working' in the *true* sense of protecting victims by helping them know to leave or avoid their partners, without resulting in any harm to their well-being, as opposed to 'working' in the *literal* sense of being operated according to Home Office policy. Certainly, like nearly all forces in England and Wales when I asked them using an FOI request in May 2018, Gwent did not produce any evidence that they had ever evaluated the effectiveness of the DVDS as it was operated in their own force area.

Some further (and some rather leading) headlines from the local press, and which convey the presumption that greater use of the Scheme will increase public safety, are, for example:

- "Ending the fear: Clare's Law saves almost 280 people from domestic abuse in just TWO years" (Cowlishaw, 2014)
- "GMP: Inaction DID leave Katie Cullen to be murdered by ex but we were muzzled before Clare's Law" (Wilson, 2014)
- "Notts: 'Groundbreaking' new domestic violence law could save lives, say Police" (The Newsroom, 2014)
- "Clare's Law has saved more than 300 Greater Manchester people in three years since introduction" (Scheerhout, 2015)
- "Revealed: How Clare's Law is helping people in Leicestershire escape violent partners" (Fagan, 2018)

- "Domestic killings fall as women use Clare's Law to check partners" (France, 2020)

Many local news headlines about the DVDS are less presumptuous, or show less journalistic licence, than the examples above, of course. But the kind of local news headlines cited above will reinforce a perception by the public that the introduction of 'Clare's Law' was an effective policy move by the Home Office. This may in time be proven to be the case—and many local news articles will take at least some care to be accurate about the fundamental difference between a disclosure under the Scheme versus a life being 'saved' by the Scheme. It could be argued that the most objective media reports about the DVDS are likely to be those that in their headlines acknowledge that the operation of the Scheme is 'changing lives' (Pirate FM, 2015). And there has been some scepticism from media profiles of the Scheme as to its actual efficacy, and concerns from those quarters about the 'victim blaming' qualities of the Scheme (Reed, 2011). However, media pieces that are critical of the DVDS are few and far between—and any critical public media discourse of the Scheme is weak overall. This is salient, in terms of explaining one reason why the DVDS in particular has gone without considerable evaluation as to its effectiveness for over four years, and without statutory codification since its inception. As Adam White (2016: 185) has explained, "where critical public discourse is weak and piecemeal, the state is more likely to respond with weak regulation".

Of course, police forces do not present, in public or to the media, the kind of qualitative or quantitative data that would allow us to see, in an actuarial sense, how an individual life is saved through a disclosure under the Scheme, or explain whether an individual woman has left their partner without moving on to a relationship with another abuser, or without suffering retaliation from the partner she left. It is of course very much possible that police forces have nowhere near this level of detailed understanding of the lives of (potential) victims of domestic violence in their area, in a longitudinal sense. So it is troubling when one can readily encounter a study like that of the Femicide Census project, which identified that 200 women out of at least 586 killed between 2009 and 2015 had been killed by *former* partners (Femicide Census, 2016: 21). In essence, a relationship that has ended is not a risk of harm avoided.

So a policy focus on the DVDS as a conveying mechanism for information that empowers a person to end a relationship will by no means keep potential victims of domestic violence safer by virtue of having helped them end their relationship per se. We are left with the conclusion, perhaps, that a better focus of police resources used on the DVDS could be on joining with other agencies in encouraging offenders to desist in perpetrating domestic violence, through making enabling or more therapeutic or restorative interventions—but this is hardly a policy shift that would create the 'right' kind of headlines according to the 'politics of public protection' (Nash, 2010). Indeed, Phil Scraton is critical of the manner in which the police operate strategically with an eye on headlines, arguing that "it is often difficult to tell police press officers and local journalists apart" (Scraton, 2016: 169).

Local media reports working with the police press release 'machine' could well be a cheap way of securing greater public confidence in the role of the police in protecting the public. The national figures for lives lost to acts of domestic violence are horrendous, and while any attempt to reduce this number each year is welcome and important, there could be the concern that unquestioning media support for the Scheme could lend weight to an idea that the police are pioneering and improving in their work to improve on this most vital measure of success in preventing (fatal) harm arising from domestic violence. Police resources are after all, finite, and the media promotion of the operation of the scheme may be cost-effective if what is being measured is public uptake of the Scheme—but this still incurs an associated cost for policing resources that could be better devoted to other modes of policing domestic violence, which in turn could be more effective still. This leads us to a discussion of another of the core themes of the policy production process in relation to the DVDS: the costs of the Scheme itself.

3.4 The Issue of Costs of the DVDS

One further issue which recurs in the policy analyses presented in this book is the issue of costs. An issue is that the cost of operating the most prominent DADS, the Domestic Violence Disclosure Scheme, and its resulting burden on police resources, is already outstripping the initial Home Office estimates made when the policy was designed—with more than twice as many applications (under both strands of the Scheme combined) being made per year, and with nearly three times as many disclosures being made per year compared to the numbers of each that were initially predicted (Home Office, 2013c: 15). Cost, and a reduction in the cost of domestic violence perpetration to the operation of the criminal justice system and beyond, was a key feature of the policy rationale of adopting a mixed-model for the DVDS that included both a Right to Ask and a Right to Know strand of the policy, respectively. The initial Home Office policy impact assessment on the implementation of the DVDS had noted the savings to be made only on a superficial view of the potential effects of the Scheme, observing that: "Every homicide related to domestic violence and abuse costs the CJS approximately £180,000 and bears an overall cost to society of approximately £1.8m" (Home Office, 2013c: 10). What we do not yet know, of course, is how many homicides the DVDS could be said to have directly prevented, something noted by researchers interested in the DVDS and its national operation to date (Fitz-Gibbon & Walklate, 2017: 274).

The relevant Home Office policy impact assessment explained that for an approach to the DVDS that included both a Right to Ask and a Right to Know, total costs were "estimated at £3.18m, the largest component of which is attendance at the Decision Making Forum" (Home Office, 2013c: 15), while a "reduction in domestic violence and abuse [would] have to reduce total cost of domestic violence and abuse by 0.02% to break even, equivalent to preventing domestic violence and abuse in around a third of cases going through the [DVDS]" (Home Office, 2013c: 5). Home Office policymakers, from a purely costs perspective, would be glad that data presented in Chap. 5, produced using a series of FOI requests, show that in a best-case scenario the use of the DVDS in

England and Wales might reduce or preclude domestic violence in 55% of cases *where disclosures are made.*

3.5 An Institutional Account for the Spread of DADS Policies

One thing this book explores in later chapters is the extent to which there is a variety versus a similarity of approaches to DADS between forces in different jurisdictions in the UK (and in implementing the DVDS in England and Wales), as well as the manner in which different executive bodies, as policy actors and regulators, do, or do not, implement DADS at all. These patterns or groupings of institutional responses to regulation can be seen as a result of different strengths of varying forms of institutional policy 'isomorphism'. As Halliday has explained:

> organisations within the same field become more alike in their structures and operations. … Coercive isomorphism occurs when organisations are put under pressure from other organisations on which they are dependent. … However, mimetic isomorphism occurs when organisations copy other organisations, often because of uncertain conditions. Further, normative isomorphism occurs when organisations adopt and apply norms that are shared in wider cultural forums, particularly professional associations. (Halliday, 2013: 319–320; citing DiMaggio & Powell, 1983: 150)

These forms of isomorphism are identified in the spread of the DADS across different common law jurisdictions inside and outside of the UK, as discussed later in this book. It is worth noting at this juncture, however, that within the three UK jurisdictions of England and Wales, Scotland and Northern Ireland, DADS spread as a policy in that order, without initial and genuine evaluation of the efficacy of the DVDS in England and Wales, prior to the adoption of the DSDAS in Scotland or the DVADS in Northern Ireland. This state of not knowing, institutionally, about the true efficacy or otherwise of the DVDS became fertile ground for the prerequisite 'uncertain conditions' needed for mimetic isomorphism to occur, in terms of the policy spread of DADS, in the UK and elsewhere.

Police organisations in those jurisdictions with a DVDS-type disclosure scheme have never once spontaneously developed a DADS policy entirely of their own volition; as Chap. 4 explores, such policy development of DADS, in each of the jurisdictions where they are to be found, is very much in the remit of government bodies that are 'coercively isomorphic' developers of public protection policies—such as the Home Office, with its overall responsibility for public protection policy, and complement of ministers who can steer relevant legislation through Parliament. There is an observable trend, again explored in Chap. 4, for government agencies in common law jurisdictions to borrow the idea of DADS from one another, regardless of the relative lack of evaluation of the effectiveness of DADS concerned, quite likely due to what Mike Nash has termed 'the politics of public protection' (Nash, 2010). The 'politics of public protection' means that resources are sometimes channelled not towards interventions that assist public protection work and reduce reoffending better than 'tougher' interventions, but instead are channelled disproportionately towards interventions that are gimmicky, or punitive, and quite possibly both. Public perception of government 'softness' on violent crime is a significant driver in the 'politics of public protection'. Indeed, some politicians, such as those in official opposition in Queensland in Australia (Ryan, 2017), have campaigned on the political capital of a promise to introduce the policy of a DADS despite, or perhaps because of, strong policy opposition from the sitting government.

Given the reluctance of policymakers to want to take on any share of blame for policies in the 'politics of public protection' that are not working, it is in many ways entirely unsurprising that there has to date been a failure to properly evaluate any DADS globally for their effectiveness in preventing harm, as opposed to their efficiency in operation in process, time and resources terms. This failure to evaluate the DADS is a regulatory failure on the part of a number of regulators, but is also an exercise in potential blame avoidance or minimisation in a scenario where reputations must be protected. It is a brave policymaker who admits in public to an avoidable mistake. As Christopher Hood has observed, "governments and public managers put in a great deal of effort and investment to stress the positive aspects of their performance and achievement in the face of critics accentuating the negatives" (Hood, 2007: 199). Put simply, the *creation* of Clare's Law is worth a degree of political capital to the policymakers who oversaw its creation, and failing to create one can be made to seem like carelessness or negligence; while the *operation* of a Clare's Law policy that is known to be only *partially* effective is something that will only attract blame.

For policymakers, while an evaluation of the effectiveness of the DADS in the UK may actually show a distinct success in reducing the victimisation of *some* recipients of disclosures, simply leaving the dominant media narrative of Clare's Law as an unmitigated success for *any* recipient of a disclosure is a far better bet (or "policy strategy"). This is the only sound approach, in some respects, in the media-driven game of blame avoidance; except that this 'blame game' has, in terms of the proliferation of DADS in a 'policy spiral', covered up the extent to which the Home Office and other prominent policymakers and criminal justice regulators have failed to get to the bottom of the questionable efficacy of the operation of such Schemes.

3.6 The Relevance of the 'Right to Rehabilitation'

Disclosures of criminal histories under DADS are an ongoing potential for interference by the police with the privacy and private life of (past) domestic violence offenders. This treats these (mainly) men as unreformed and dangerous—and some of them will be—however, some will not pose the risk that others do. These lower or low-risk offenders, albeit with a high-risk past, might consider themselves as 'rehabilitated'—certainly where their personal relationships are concerned. However, there are substantial problems defining 'rehabilitation' in policy terms and as a term of legal construction. The UK justice system certainly struggles with a lack of a concrete legal definition of what 'rehabilitation' means, or who can be labelled a 'rehabilitated person', as the discussions later in this book (Chap. 7) of the problems in consistently regulating the (possible) disclosure of spent convictions under the UK DADS can be seen to show. However, 'rehabilitation' is not just about the concept of a person's series of convictions or cautions and so on all being spent or not: it is the issue of a fluid concept of good character and desistance from offending, that is problematic to translate into an actionable or defensible legal right. Certainly the European Court of Human Rights has provided the basis for a general (albeit qualified) right to rehabilitation in its case law, observing that "the emphasis on rehabilitation and reintegration has become a 'mandatory factor' that member states need to take into account when designing their penal policies" (*Khoroshenko v. Russia*, 30 June 2015, at 121), therefore becoming a positive obligation on the part of the contracting state (and as acknowledged in *Murray v. The Netherlands*, 26 April 2016, at 104). As Sonja Meijer has highlighted: "Recognising rehabilitation as a positive obligation—grounded in human dignity—is important, because it makes clear that rehabilitation is at all times to be taken into account and cannot be set aside by other concerns" (Meijer, 2017: 161).

There is also an element of the literature on the essence of what 'rehabilitation' might mean, as a concept, which is problematic when it comes to Domestic Abuse Disclosure Schemes. Disclosures under such Schemes must be proportionate, in the European human rights law sense, and so there might be a practical approach to time-limiting the disclosure of certain pieces of criminality information about a person, but as will be explored in detail in Chap. 7, even older, 'spent' convictions, under UK law, are not absolutely barred from disclosure through the three main UK DADS in current operation, not to mention intelligence information such as arrest records. Yet, as Hebenton and Thomas have explained, rehabilitation is the process designed "to help the offender return to and remain as a full member of society, with the status and obligations which that membership confers", while if "offenders are not rehabilitated in this sense when formal punishment ends, then de facto punishment persists" (Hebenton & Thomas, 1993: 113). There is then the issue that some ('former') domestic violence perpetrators will be subject to (from their point of view) an ongoing, non-linear and seemingly arbitrary risk of an unusual punishment: the encroachment of the state into their personal relationship with a new partner, and, therefore, potentially no "personal 'year zero' to be the springboard for better times" (Hebenton & Thomas, 1993: 1).

One would hope that, in time, probation organisations, Her Majesty's Prison and Probation Service, and ultimately the Ministry of Justice, would become as responsible for the operation of the DVDS in England and Wales, for example, as clusters of policing bodies and the Home Office. In the longer term this will be essential—as if the goal of DADS is ultimately public protection and/or homicide prevention, then the impact of any DADS on offender rehabilitation becomes an essential policy consideration, perhaps largely overlooked, to date.

3.7 Conclusions

So the DVDS can readily be seen to be a particular policy response to the social and criminological problem of serial domestic violence perpetrators (Strickland, 2013), as opposed to a contribution to the field of rehabilitation work. But how did the Scheme come to be such a steadfast and indeed, rapidly adopted policy measure, quite so quickly? The view expressed in this book is that the reason is threefold: firstly, the Scheme was relatively cheap and straight-forward to implement as an initial idea which suited a Home Office conscious of cost savings to be made. As highlighted elsewhere in this book, the actuarial approach taken in the relevant Home Office policy impact assessment meant that the view was adopted that for the DVDS to 'break even' each year, domestic violence would need to cease in only one-third of the relationships that were the subject of a disclosure under the Scheme, based on the estimates made in 2013 as to how many applications would be made to the Scheme, and of the costs of domestic violence to the criminal justice system as a whole. Secondly, the DVDS policy found favour in purportedly targeting a vulnerable group of people in society (victims of domestic violence) for support, and was purportedly offering them knowledge and empowerment; and thirdly, it was a policy to be adopted in the world of policing in England and Wales: a top-down, hierarchical structure well-suited to policy being implemented (at least on paper) with efficiency and uniformity. As we have seen from responses to the 2012 DVDS consultation by the likes of Refuge and other charities, the Home Office and the police in England and Wales are only some of the policy actors that have, in a process which is still ongoing, helped to shape the manufacture of DVDs policy. This is nothing unusual. As Page (2009: 790) has put it, "policy is better seen as a production process involving people at all levels adding different bits to the overall product, although it is hardly a linear process that starts with agreement on principle which is followed by elaboration of detail".

As noted above, Clive Walker (2018: 726) has observed that: "policy spirals arise from inexact and contested meanings, objectives, and mechanisms". In addition, Cairney has explained that while "policy processes are complex and often unpredictable", a "division of policymaking into stages helps us analyze the process [of policymaking] … with reference to … five pillars of explanation: institutions, networks, ideas, socio-economic factors and choices" (Cairney, 2012: 288–289). This chapter has begun to explore the *institutions* and *networks* that have helped to shape *ideas* about DADS in the UK, with a primary focus on the DVDS in England and Wales, and the responses of the Home Office to other policy actors, like Refuge, and ACPO/the NPCC. This policy development-mapping continues in respect of the other two UK DADS, in Scotland and Northern Ireland, in the next chapter. This chapter has also explored the *socio-economic factors* or costs of the DVDS, and the range of *choices* that have been made over DVDS policy development. However, this chapter has shown that the potential for a 'policy spiral' in relation to DADS in many parts of the common law world has been created by institutions pressing for a DVDS in England and Wales, and in using a choice of 'inexact and contested' ideas, objectives and mechanisms—creating the potential, in short, for a DADS 'policy spiral'.

At this juncture in this book, it can now be stated that the very idea of a DADS, as something that 'operationalises' victim responsibilisation, is controversial. This chapter has discussed how the shaping of the DVDS in England and Wales was a conscious choice. To avoid the use of statutory codification, and to avoid placing the onus on organisations responsible for offender management, the DVDS was always posited as something the police would use with (potential) victims of domestic violence, rather than as something that probation services, as institutions equally involved in public protection, could establish as their own. This was a natural result, perhaps, of the ownership the police have traditionally assumed over records-keeping concerning offenders. The chosen 'network' for the delivery of Clare's Law in England and Wales was thus the police as a service—and not merely as an equal partner in a new policy process for the whole of the 'public protection network' (Magee, 2008) to follow. This was a choice of political organisation for the sake of policy expediency. ACPO had formulated a case for something like the DVDS as early as 2009; and as a policing oversight body had the ear of the Home Office on the DVDS by 2012. This chapter has made plain that the institutions which have shaped the development and operation of DADS more than any other are the national-level policymakers and regulators, in the form of the Home Office for the DVDS, and as will be seen, the Northern Irish Department of Justice and the Scottish Government for the DVADS and DSDAS respectively (as discussed in Chap. 4).

As to whether the spread of DADS constitutes a 'policy spiral', this chapter has laid the foundations for later conclusions as to whether this is the case. This chapter has also shown a number of contradictions or gaps in DADS policy, as well as inexact or contested objectives. For one thing, the risk in a violent relationship might peak when it is coming to an end, and DADS seek, ultimately, to convince victims with the necessary autonomy to bring a relationship to an end. Secondly, for women in a violent relationship, being 'responsibilised' through receipt of a disclosure under a DADS, austerity policies under UK governments in the last 12 years mean that there are less support services available to assist her. As a result, DADS in the UK have 'spiralled', in the sense Walker would mean in terms of a 'policy spiral', above—and no less so since DADS in the UK have 'uncertain outcomes'. The three main UK DADS have never been thoroughly evaluated, after all, in terms of their effectiveness at reducing victimisation—only their efficacy in terms of the process of managing an application or referral to the DADS concerned. This clear lack of 'control and reflection' to date, in no way halting the spread of DADS across the UK and to overseas common law jurisdictions, is the subject of the next chapter.

References

Association of Chief Police Officers (ACPO). (2009). *Tackling perpetrators of violence against women and girls: ACPO review for the Home Secretary.*

Baker, K. (2014, September 24). Domestic abuse scheme working. *South Wales Argus*. Retrieved March 14, 2015, from http://www.southwalesargus.co.uk/news/11492624.CRIME_FILE__Domestic_abuse_scheme_working/

BBC News. (2015, January 26). Clare's Law: 1,300 domestic abuse disclosures made. *BBC News*. Retrieved March 14, 2015, from http://www.bbc.co.uk/news/uk-30977759

Cairney, P. (2012). *Understanding public policy: Theories and issues*. Palgrave Macmillan.

Cohen, J. L. (2002). *Regulating intimacy: A new legal paradigm*. Princeton University Press.

Cowlishaw, D. (2014, September 4). Ending the fear: Clare's Law saves almost 280 people from domestic abuse in just TWO years. *Mancunian Matters*. Retrieved June 19, 2020, from http://www.mancunianmatters.co.uk/content/040970505-ending-fear-clares-law-saves-almost-280-people-domestic-abuse-just-two-years

DiMaggio, P., & Powell, P. (1983). The iron cage revisited: Institutional isomorphism and collective rationality in organizational fields. *American Sociological Review, 48*, 147.

Duggan, M. (2012). Using victims' voices to prevent violence against women: A critique. *British Journal of Community Justice, 10*(2), 25.

Fagan, K. (2018, December 26). Revealed: How Clare's Law is helping people in Leicestershire escape violent partners. *Leicester Mercury*. Retrieved June 19, 2020, from https://www.leicestermercury.co.uk/news/leicester-news/revealed-how-clares-law-helping-2357796

Femicide Census. (2016). *Redefining an isolated incident—Annual Report on UK Femicides 2016*. Retrieved June 19, 2020, from https://1q7dqy2unor827bqjls0c4rn-wpengine.netdna-ssl.com/wp-content/uploads/2016/12/The-Femicide-Census-2016.pdf

Fitz-Gibbon, K., & Walklate, S. (2017). The efficacy of Clare's Law in domestic violence law reform in England and Wales. *Criminology & Criminal Justice, 17*(3), 284.

France, A. (2020, February 21). Domestic killings fall as women use Clare's Law to check partners. *London Evening Standard*. Retrieved June 16, 2020, from https://www.standard.co.uk/news/crime/domestic-killings-fall-as-women-use-clare-s-law-to-check-partners-a4367966.html

Gittos, L. (2013, November 28). Clare's Law: A violation of our private lives. *Spiked*. Retrieved March 14, 2015, from http://www.spiked-online.com/newsite/article/clares_law_a_violation_of_our_private_lives/14352

Graca, S. (2017). Domestic violence policy and legislation in the UK: A discussion of immigrant women's vulnerabilities. *EJoCLI, 22*(1). Online. Retrieved July 16, 2020, from http://webjcli.org/article/view/531

Grace, J. (2015). Clare's Law, or the national Domestic Violence Disclosure Scheme: The contested legalities of criminality information sharing. *Journal of Criminal Law, 79*(1), 36.

Hadjimatheou, K., & Grace, J. (2020). 'No black and white answer about how far we can go': Police decision making under the domestic violence disclosure scheme. *Policing and Society*. https://doi.org/10.1080/10439463.2020.1795169

Halliday, S. (2013). The governance of compliance with public law. *Public Law*. 312.

Hebenton, B., & Thomas, T. (1993). *Criminal records: State, citizen and the politics of protection*. Avebury.

Home Office. (2012). Domestic Violence Disclosure Scheme: A consultation—Summary of responses. Retrieved June 19, 2020, from https://www.gov.uk/government/uploads/system/uploads/attachment_data/file/157807/consultation-responses.pdf

Home Office. (2013a). *Domestic Violence Disclosure Scheme pilot: Guidance (Revised March 2013)*. London: Home Office.

Home Office. (2013b). *Domestic Violence Disclosure Scheme (DVDS) pilot assessment*. London: Home Office.

Home Office. (2013c). Domestic Violence Disclosure Scheme impact assessment. Retrieved June 16, 2020, from https://www.gov.uk/government/uploads/system/uploads/attachment_data/file/260899/DVDS_IA.pdf

Home Office. (2016a). *Domestic Violence Disclosure Scheme (DVDS): One year on—Home Office assessment of national roll-out*. Home Office.

Home Office. (2016b). *Domestic Violence Disclosure Scheme (DVDS) guidance*. Retrieved June 16, 2020, from https://www.gov.uk/government/uploads/system/uploads/attachment_data/file/575361/DVDS_guidance_FINAL_v3.pdf

Hood, C. (2007). What happens when transparency meets blame avoidance? *Public Management Review, 9*(2), 191.

Madriz, E. (1997). *Nothing bad happens to good girls: Fear of crime in women's lives*. University of California Press.

Magee, I. (2008). *Review of criminality information: Executive summary and recommendations*. Review of Criminality Information.

May, T. (Home Secretary). (2014). Written statement to Parliament: Domestic violence protection orders and domestic violence disclosure scheme. Retrieved May 29, 2014, from https://www.gov.uk/government/speeches/domestic-violence-protection-orders-and-domestic-violence-disclosure-scheme

Meijer, S. (2017). Rehabilitation as a positive obligation. *European Journal of Crime, Criminal Law and Criminal Justice, 25*, 145.

Nash, M. (2010). The politics of public protection. In M. Nash & A. Williams (Eds.), *Handbook of public protection*. Willan.

Page, E. C. (2009). Their word is law: Parliamentary counsel and creative policy analysis. *Public Law*, 790.

Pirate FM News Team. (2015, March 14). Claire's Law is 'Changing lives' in cornwall. *Pirate FM*. Retrieved June 19, 2020, from https://www.piratefm.co.uk/news/latest-news/1555993/claires-law-is-changing-lives-in-cornwall/

Reed, L. (2011, July 22). Why Clare's Law won't prevent domestic violence. *The Guardian*. Retrieved June 19, 2020, from https://www.theguardian.com/society/2011/jul/22/why-clares-law-wont-prevent-domestic-violence

Ryan, E. (2017, November 14). Lawyer slams 'pig-headed' policy. *Lawyers Weekly*. Retrieved June 23, 2020, from https://www.lawyersweekly.com.au/sme-law/22253-lawyer-slams-pig-headed-policy

Scheerhout, J. (2015, September 6). Clare's Law has saved more than 300 Greater Manchester people in three years since introduction. *Manchester Evening News*. Retrieved June 19, 2020, from http://www.manchestereveningnews.co.uk/news/greater-manchester-news/clares-law-saved-more-300-9999679

Scraton, P. (2016). *Hillsborough: The truth*. Mainstream Publishing.

Strickland, P. (2013). (House of Commons Library Standard Note), 'Clare's Law: The Domestic Violence Disclosure Scheme', House of Commons Library.

The Newsroom. (2014, December 29). Notts: 'Groundbreaking' new domestic violence law could save lives, say Police. *Chad*. Retrieved June 19, 2020, from http://www.chad.co.uk/news/notts-groundbreaking-new-domestic-violence-law-could-save-lives-say-police-1-7024494

Walker, C. (2018). Counter-terrorism and counter-extremism: The UK policy spirals. Public Law. 725.

White, A. (2016). Private security and the politics of accountability. In S. Lister & M. Rowe (Eds.), *Accountability of policing*. Routledge.

Wilson, T. (2014, November 14). GMP: Inaction DID leave Katie Cullen to be murdered by ex but we were muzzled before Clare's Law. *Mancunian Matters*. Retrieved June 19, 2020, from http://www.mancunianmatters.co.uk/content/141171652-gmp-inaction-did-leave-katie-cullen-be-murdered-ex-we-were-muzzled-clares-law

4

A 'Policy Spiral' in Common Law Jurisdictions

4.1 Introduction

This chapter examines the development of DADS in a range of common law jurisdictions, with arguably similar standards on personal legal rights and mutually recognisable policymaking processes. DVDS-model policies have been adopted, using a variety of processes, in parts of Canada and Australia, as well as in New Zealand, the Isle of Man and even the Channel Island of Jersey (BBC News, 2014), where a 'Clare's Law' policy was used to make two disclosures in just under a year after it was introduced in April 2014 (ITV News, 2015). However, there is as yet no 'Clare's Law' policy in the Republic of Ireland. In December 2019, in giving an answer to a written question in the Dáil, the Irish Minister for Justice and Equality, Charlie Flanagan TD, ruled out the adoption of a specific policy or legislative reform for a Domestic Violence Disclosure Scheme in the Republic, explaining that the policy was not necessary at that time (Dáil Éireann, 2019).

The idea of Domestic Abuse Disclosure Schemes (DADS) has arguably caught on with policing policymakers across the Commonwealth before the practices concerned have been consistently or thoroughly evaluated,

J. Grace, *Domestic Abuse Disclosure Schemes*,
https://doi.org/10.1007/978-3-030-89039-1_4

in a manner that accords with Walker's concerns about policy 'spirals' (Walker, 2018). The defining characteristic of a 'policy spiral' is policy proliferation with unclear or competing priorities and objectives, and where that proliferation takes place with little review or reflection. Jane Wangmann (2016) (while not using the term 'policy spiral') has noted that issues of cost-effectiveness are particularly pertinent when in the wider context the prevention of domestic violence is relatively under-funded, and issues of *overall* effectiveness of DADS are again very pertinent when one considers that any potential beneficiaries of their operation are a tiny fraction of the number of women abused by their partners in any one jurisdiction—and even then the evidence of the effectiveness of the disclosures that are made is in short supply.

All legal systems have the function of regulating comparative social phenomena, including regulating violence against women. However, we might expect there to be both (a) broad similarities between the legalities of the policing of domestic violence between states on opposite sides of the globe that are nevertheless part of the same common law 'family', and yet (b) micro-differences in the way that Domestic Abuse Disclosure Schemes are operated on the ground in different jurisdictions, albeit ones in the same common law 'family' (Dannemann, 2006). To a comparative law theorist such as Dannemann (2006), a 'macrocomparison' of these members of the common law family should, over a period of years, show the development of similar laws (and policies including those on DADS) to combat domestic violence. But from a policy analysis perspective, the hasty adoption of a policy like a DADS in a jurisdiction that can do so readily and speedily due to possessing a similar constitutional structure and body of law(s) does not mean this is a welcome prospect; instead it could be evidence of a 'policy spiral' (Walker, 2018: 276). As this chapter explores, the 'policy spiral' of DADS across common law jurisdictions starts with a straightforward, outward burst of 'policy transfer' between civil servants, political leaders and policy advocates and campaigners (Dolowitz & Marsh, 1996). This policy transfer takes place at a range of different levels; both transnationally because of supranational umbrella bodies, and inter-organisationally between policy actor bodies at the national level (Evans & Davies, 1999).

Nearly all criminal justice systems in the world need to strike a fair balance between potential risks to victims versus maintaining adequate privacy protection for 'rehabilitated' offenders. The operation of any criminal records disclosure system with public protection purposes is one that every such jurisdiction, including those that operate DADS in the common law world, would need to conduct with regulatory care and precision. This is particularly so where intrusions into personal privacy must be proportionate in order to avoid unlawful arbitrariness in disclosures. Privacy can be asserted as a fundamental right, after all, albeit one with qualifications and limitations built into it as a concept. As Marion Oswald has observed (2013: 8), "those tasked with the protection of the vulnerable may well be concerned that premature deletion, or suppression, of intelligence will hamper their ability to use information to make connections". The same could be readily said about decisions to share information for public protection purposes as much as for decisions as to deleting such information, too. As a result, with the policy question of how best to share information for public protection purposes through DADS becoming an increasingly global one, there is a need to look comparatively at DADS as they have developed around the globe, and as they have spread both inside and outside of the UK.

There are four different Domestic Abuse Disclosure Schemes in use in the UK today; in England and Wales; in Jersey, in Northern Ireland, and in Scotland. Additionally, at the time of writing, the Isle of Man has now introduced a statutory basis for a policy scheme to regulate the disclosure of police-held information "for the purposes of preventing and mitigating the effects of domestic abuse", under Section 44 of the Domestic Abuse Act 2020. Each of the existing UK DADS is subtly but importantly different in their policy framing and legal operation. These differences, as this chapter and later chapters will explore, have important regulatory ramifications. For example, the DVDS in England and Wales is currently based on the common law power of the police to share information to protect members of the public where there is a 'pressing need' to do so (Home Office, 2013b), and more recently on the basis of (forthcoming) statutory guidance under Section 77 of the Domestic Abuse Act 2021, which will refresh the procedure on "the disclosure of police information by police forces for the purposes of preventing domestic abuse".

But in Scotland, the Disclosure Scheme for Domestic Abuse Scotland (DSDAS) is purportedly based upon the provisions of the Police and Fire Reform (Scotland) Act 2012. However, these relevant provisions of this Act of the Scottish Parliament are somewhat vague. This supposed statutory nature of the DSDAS is something that was in the understanding of Police Scotland but had not been publicly linked to the 2012 Act until a freedom-of-information request I submitted in 2017 saw the release into the public domain of the text of the DSDAS 'Standard Operating Procedure' (Police Scotland, 2015). The DVADS in Northern Ireland is also purportedly based, in part, on broad statutory provisions rather than specific legislation controlling the application of the use of a 'Clare's Law'-type policy by the Police Service of Northern Ireland (Department of Justice (Northern Ireland), 2018a).

Despite some commentary on known inconsistencies in police practice in making disclosures emerging in 2017 (Her Majesty's Inspectorate of Constabulary, 2017: 86), and some 'known unknowns' around the effectiveness of the DVDS in actually protecting victims (or helping them to protect themselves) being flagged up by academic researchers (Grace, 2015; Duggan & Grace, 2018; Hadjimatheou & Grace, 2020), the notion of a DVDS has become politically popular with policing policymakers in the common law world. Outside of the national operation of the Scheme in England and Wales, the DSDAS was piloted in Ayrshire and Aberdeen, before being rolled out across all areas of Scotland in 2015 (Police Scotland, n.d.), as well as being adopted in Northern Ireland in the spring of 2018, following a public consultation in early 2016 (Department of Justice (Northern Ireland), n.d.-a). Further afield in New South Wales, Australia and more recently in South Australia, Domestic Violence Disclosure Schemes have also been piloted and rolled out. A DVDS-model policy has also been adopted in New Zealand (New Zealand Police, n.d.). Versions of the policy have been adopted in provinces in Canada, too. These developments are explored in sections of this chapter. The aim is to seek out comparative lessons in how the different DADS concerned have been established as pieces of public policy, and from a regulatory point of view. It will be seen that some regional governments in Australia, in particular, are more thorough in their oversight of the introduction of DADS than UK authorities have been.

4.2 The Disclosure Scheme for Domestic Abuse (Scotland)

Before turning to examine how the Disclosure Scheme for Domestic Abuse (Scotland) (DSDAS) came to be founded in public policy, and the variations in its operation with the DVDS in England and Wales, it must be noted that it has begun to make a considerable contribution to the overall activity involving DADS in the UK. By October 2018 the DSDAS had been in operation across all of Scotland for three full years, resulting in nearly 1600 disclosures from 3500 applications under both the 'Right to Ask' and 'Power to Tell' strands of the Scottish Scheme (BBC News (Scotland), 2018). In April 2020, Police Scotland released some statistics on the use of the DSDAS by members of the public over the previous two years. Police Scotland had recorded 1596 applications to both strands of the DSDAS in 2018–19, and this increased by 66% to 2648 in 2019–20; while 1240 disclosures were made in 2019–20, an increase of 40% on 886 disclosures, therefore, in 2018–19 (Picken, 2020). A total of 1240 disclosures from 2648 applications to the DSDAS in 2019–20 is a disclosure rate for that year of 46.8%. This means that Police Scotland were able and willing to make disclosures more readily than the average force in England and Wales: where the disclosure rate in the year ending March 2020 had dipped to 43.4% from a high of 51.5% in the year ending March 2018 (see Table 1.1, in Chap. 1). Put another way, Police Scotland were responsible for more than an eighth of the comparative number of disclosures that took place in England and Wales in the year to March 2019, and nearly a seventh of the proportion in the year to March 2020, albeit in relation to a population in Scotland only around one-eleventh of the size of the population in England and Wales (ONS, 2021). Put in context then, it should be noted that 2648 applications to both strands of the DSDAS in 2019–20 is a significant amount of work for Police Scotland, in terms of their responsibilities to deal with domestic abuse, as Police Scotland "recorded 60,641 incidents of domestic abuse in 2018–2019, an increase of 2% compared to the previous year" (Gov.scot, 2020). The following year, in 2019–20, the Crown Office and Procurator

Fiscal Service (COPFS) reported 30,178 charges as relating to domestic abuse in Scotland (COPFS.gov.uk, 2020).

The policy of a 'Right to Ask' and a 'Power to Tell', in shaping the DSDAS, was formulated swiftly following the national roll-out of the DVDS in England and Wales from March 2014. Notably, therefore, this Scottish policymaking process took place before the DVDS in England and Wales was subject to a larger-scale, albeit more procedural, evaluation, as came from the Home Office by the end of 2016 (Home Office, 2016a). In Scotland, the Disclosure Scheme for Domestic Abuse (Scotland) (DSDAS) was announced as a pilot scheme in August 2014, before being trialled in Aberdeen and Ayrshire for six months from the spring of 2015. Scottish Justice Secretary Kenny MacAskill was reported in August 2014 as commenting, on the announcement of the start of a DSDAS policy, as follows:

> It is right that people in relationships should have the opportunity to seek the facts about their partner's background if, for example, they have concerns that their partner has a history of violence and I am particularly interested in the results of the pilot to assess how effective it can be. … The scheme has already proved successful in England and Wales and it is important that the practical implementation is tested to ensure that it is suitable for Scotland's unique justice system. (Scottish Government, 2014)

A key issue with MacAskill's position in August 2104 was that a closer reading of the Home Office policy on and evaluation of the DVDS as it operated in England and Wales was that any evidence for the true effectiveness of the original Scheme was very thin or non-existent, in relation to the pilot evaluation in four force areas south of the border. It is true that the Home Office had rolled out the Scheme across all of England and Wales in March 2014; but that is a sparse meaning of 'success'. This is clear evidence of a component of Walker's 'policy spiral' (Walker, 2018): a lack of proper reflection on the implementation of a policy.

MacAskill may have been personally interested in the results of the pilot and its effectiveness—but as a Scottish justice minister he certainly did not achieve, as a policymaker, the step of making public the resulting evaluation of the pilot. Given the mixed findings of the pilot evaluation, discussed below, it is no surprise that the study was not made public by his successor as Scottish justice secretary, Michael Matheson. Matheson made another policy announcement on the DSDAS in November 2014: "It is important that the practical implementation of the Disclosure Scheme for Domestic Abuse in Scotland, or Clare's Law, is tested to ensure that it is suitable for Scotland's unique justice system" (BBC News (Scotland), 2014). Matheson also failed to ensure that the findings of the 'testing' of the DSDAS pilot was made public or that the DSDAS was subject to any public consultation prior to introduction across Scotland.

Even if the findings were not initially made public, the pilot DSDAS *was* in fact evaluated by unknown academics at the University of Glasgow by the September of 2015 before the DSDAS was rolled out nationally in Scotland in October 2015. This audit by the University of Glasgow ('the Glasgow study') was not publicly available until I obtained it using a freedom-of-information request under the Freedom of Information (Scotland) Act 2002, having spotted a reference to the evaluation report being passed on by Police Scotland to the Queensland Law Reform Commission, who in 2017 had produced a report on the possibility (which they recommended against) of a DADS in that Australian jurisdiction (Queensland Law Reform Commission, 2017). The FOI response from Police Scotland that supplied me with a copy of the Glasgow study (University of Glasgow, 2015) highlighted that the audit itself, which examined small DSDAS pilot areas, was used to inform the Scottish national roll-out of the DSDAS.

Overall, the Glasgow study concluded that the DSDAS was considered by the officers who had worked on it as a pilot in Scotland to be a useful policy as it allowed for the greater knowledge of potential victims with regard to the risks of remaining with their partners (University of Glasgow, 2015). Clearly, this evaluation of the DSDAS pilot had picked up on the point now often repeated about DADS by government policymakers that they help victims make better life choices and better protect themselves from harm and domestic abuse, all for being more aware of the risks they face. However, reported claims by officers in the pilot areas that the very existence of the Scheme in Scotland could have a deterrent effect on any offenders with regard to preventing their domestic violence offending (University of Glasgow, 2015) frankly seem far-fetched. As discussed above, if the chief aim of a DADS is to empower and inform victims, so that they might end potentially violent relationships before they become violent, this is at odds with the evidence that relationship break-down can be a trigger for domestic violence—something picked up on by the focus groups of Scottish officers involved in the pilot themselves (see below).

The Glasgow study's authors did find that the focus groups of police officers from Aberdeen and Ayrshire, where the DSDAS had been piloted, raised a number of other worrying concerns about the Scheme overall: that disclosures might trigger violence in a relationship due to changing behaviours on the part of the victim post-disclosure, or that some disclosures would not be well-received—and crucially, that there was no mandatory follow-up or parallel procedure for safeguarding victims (University of Glasgow, 2015). Lastly, the focus groups for the Glasgow study felt that there could be an undermining of the right to rehabilitation as an effect of disclosures under the DSDAS, and noting that there was a trend towards not consulting or informing the subject of a disclosure (University of Glasgow, 2015). Certainly, the Scottish Government and Police Scotland do not appear to have given much weight to the concerns of their officers involved in the DSDAS pilot, given the move to make the DSDAS a national policy for Scotland. The tension revealed by the Glasgow study as to the contrasting views of police officers in the pilot DSDAS areas aligns consistently with the arguments made for and against the introduction of what became the Domestic Violence and Abuse Disclosure Scheme in Northern Ireland, as will be shown in the section below.

4.3 The Domestic Violence and Abuse Disclosure Scheme in Northern Ireland

The DVADS in Northern Ireland was introduced in the spring of 2018 following a public consultation operated by the Department of Justice for Northern Ireland in the spring of 2016 (Department of Justice (Northern Ireland), n.d.). The summary of responses to the consultation was published by the Department of Justice in the summer of 2016 (Department of Justice (Northern Ireland), n.d.). The summary of responses identifies what might, in terms of the development of this book, feel like a typical array of concerns and expectations for the creation of a new domestic abuse disclosure scheme. The responses touched upon issues of victims from some cultures not being as able to approach the police; the dangers of disclosures coming too slowly; the problem of gaps in the knowledge possessed by PSNI about offenders; an impact on the privacy of the subject of the disclosure; and possible increased risks to potential victims after a disclosure is made (Department of Justice (Northern Ireland), n.d.: 36–37). Furthermore, the summary of responses published by the Department of Justice noted:

> A number of respondents considered that current arrangements with regard to PSNI common law powers may not be effective as the decision to disclose information is solely at the PSNI's discretion. They stated that there may be inconsistency and disclosures may vary across the service. It was highlighted that some officers may be reluctant to disclose as they may not fully understand their powers or the circumstances in which they should/could be used. … It was noted that there is no data published with regards to the use and effectiveness of current disclosure arrangements in relation to public protection and PSNI common law powers. It was also proposed that potential and actual victims are unaware that the police had these common law powers. (Department of Justice (Northern Ireland), n.d.: 17)

Overall, however, the summary of responses maintained the standard line on Domestic Abuse Disclosure Schemes that is generally preferred, it would seem, by policymakers—that is each decision to disclose will depend upon the facts, but that there is a duty to empower victims where possible should the circumstances indicate a 'pressing need' to do so. As the summary of responses in Northern Ireland put it, "a well-managed and proportionate domestic violence disclosure scheme could be beneficial in reducing offending and supporting people to make informed choices" (Department of Justice (Northern Ireland), n.d.: 35).

Of course, given the prevailing 'politics of public protection' (Nash, 2010) around the combatting of domestic violence, as discussed elsewhere in this book, it was in fact the case that despite consultation respondents' concerns, the Domestic Violence and Abuse Disclosure Scheme for Northern Ireland began operation in the spring of 2018 (Meredith, 2018), garnering 70 applications under the 'right to ask' strand of the DVADS by July 2018 (McCann, 2018). Interestingly, the summary of responses to the consultation operated by the Department of Justice for Northern Ireland also highlighted that, in the view of respondents, "a robust central collection of data would allow effective monitoring of the enquiries, disclosure and outcomes" (Department of Justice (Northern Ireland), n.d.: 18–19).

The Department for Justice for Northern Ireland publicly stated its intention to monitor and review the Domestic Violence and Abuse Disclosure Scheme in partnership with the Police Service of Northern Ireland by March 2019, as a particular element of its seven-year strategy to better address and prevent domestic and sexual violence and abuse (Department of Justice (Northern Ireland), 2018). This commitment was refined in a later action plan to entail a continuation of a multi-media campaign to raise awareness of the DVADS in Northern Ireland, and a further commitment to "evaluate it (ensuring feedback is sought from all agencies involved) and bring forward any necessary modifications, with PSNI continuing to work with partner agencies to ensure effective delivery" (Department of Justice (Northern Ireland), n.d.-b: 4–5). However, details of any evaluation, first slated for March 2020, were not published at the time of finalising the research for this book in the summer of 2021.

Done properly, with a focus on whether the DVADS actually helped to protect victims after its implementation, this sort of review would be good evidence that policy leadership, performance management and governance values were thriving in the regulation and oversight of any DADS. A merely procedural examination, or process review, of the DVADS, while useful on some measures, would not be a true measure of the (dis)benefits of introducing it. So far, all that has been released into the public domain in terms of a measure of the effectiveness of DVADS is simply some figures from the Criminal Justice Inspectorate of Northern

Ireland (CJINI) to show it is in operation: with 336 applications in 2018–19, down to 317 applications in 2019–20 (CJINI, 2021: 20). Overall, the degree of public transparency and the degree of control and review around the operation of the DVADS are so far commensurate with that around the DVDS and DSDAS.

4.4 The Family Violence Information Disclosure Scheme in New Zealand

The Family Violence Information Disclosure Scheme (FVIDS) in New Zealand is the domestic abuse disclosure scheme about which the least information is publicly available to date. Operating from the end of 2015 (NZFVC, 2015), the FVIDS was not created by new legislation in New Zealand, but operates on a common law basis (although Section 9 of the New Zealand Policing Act 2008 defines crime prevention as a policing function). FVIDS disclosures are regulated in practice by statutory checks and balances through the interpretation and application of the New Zealand Privacy Act 1993. The New Zealand Police website states that: "The ... Privacy Act already enable[d] Police to disclose family violence information about an individual. Disclosure of information will be considered on a case-by-case basis. Police can only provide information if the relevant legislation permits" (New Zealand Police, n.d.).

Section 6 of New Zealand's Privacy Act 1993, as amended by section 5(2) of the Privacy Amendment Act 2013, creates a number of 'information privacy principles'. Principle 11 ('Limits on disclosure of personal information') requires, amongst its provisions, that

> An agency that holds personal information shall not disclose the information to a person or body or agency unless the agency believes, on reasonable grounds ... that the disclosure of the information is necessary to prevent or lessen a serious threat ... to ... the life or health of the individual concerned or another individual.

On this legal basis, in around seven months, from the launch of the FVIDS in December 2015 to early July 2016, there were 38 referrals for disclosures under the Scheme, with a disclosure made after 21 of those 38 referrals (New Zealand Law Society, 2016). For context, New Zealand Police have seen a steady and worrying increase, recently, in their recorded levels of 'family harm investigations': from 118,926 in 2016 to 121,762 in 2017 and then to 133,022 in 2018, the last data available (New Zealand Police, 2019). Detailed and up-to-date information on the uptake or use of the FVIDS is not publicly available—and the picture from the New Zealand courts is also unhelpful, as in New Zealand there is an absence of reported case law on the substantive issues of whether or how disclosures are made under the FVIDS in a particular manner.

4.5 The Fragmented Approach Between States in Australia

The approach to adopting DADS in Australia, across its federal state jurisdictions, is somewhat fragmented, with differing legal frameworks relating to privacy rights across those states, for example, and with local political and policy priorities playing out in relation to determining the question as to whether a disclosure scheme of some sort should be adopted. Both New South Wales and South Australia have operated pilots of a DADS-model policy, with a view to rolling them out across those federal Australian states; Tasmania on the other hand has explored a feasibility study (Hodgman, 2019). However, state governments in both Queensland and Victoria have initially taken a position, after investigation, *against* the adoption of a disclosure scheme as state policy; while opposition political parties (particularly the Liberal National Party (LNP) coalition) have attempted to make political capital out of this reluctance on the part of the current governments in Queensland and Victoria to follow New South Wales and South Australia in piloting the adoption of a DADS in those jurisdictions too.

New South Wales

In New South Wales, a pilot of a Domestic Violence Disclosure Scheme took place from April 2016, and initially had a two-year pilot period in which time more than 50 people received disclosures of information (New South Wales Government, 2018). The New South Wales pilot was the first of its kind in Australia, and was introduced following a public consultation (and a report recommending the adoption of the Domestic Violence Disclosure Scheme and a pilot Scheme as public policy) in 2015 (Urbis, 2020). The Scheme in New South Wales was extended on an interim basis and ran until June 2019, although still only in four pilot areas of New South Wales as a whole (New South Wales Government, 2018). As Jane Wangmann has observed the NSW Scheme does not formally include a 'Right to Know' strand, only a 'Right to Ask' strand (Wangmann, 2016), although under Section 18 of the Privacy and Personal Information Protection Act 1998, regardless of the stated parameters of the Scheme by the NSW Government, police in NSW can make disclosures where it would be "necessary to prevent or lessen a serious and imminent threat to the life or health of the individual concerned or another person". Interestingly, the New South Wales pilot did, though, ostensibly have a more fundamental statutory basis of sorts, given the existence of a core police function in New South Wales of the "protection of persons from injury or death", under Section 6 of the relevant Police Act of 1990.

The government of New South Wales were initially careful, and transparent, about how they planned to evaluate the two-year pilot of the Domestic Violence Disclosure Scheme, stating that a contracted-out evaluation would "consider implementation of the Scheme, the level of demand, impacts and outcomes for people applying for and receiving disclosures, impacts on the service sector, strengths and limitations of the model, and lessons learned for rollout of the Scheme" (New South Wales Government, 2016: 3). By promising some analysis on the "impacts and outcomes for people applying for and receiving disclosures", we might have expected some detail of the substantive *effectiveness* of the New South Wales pilot. The results of the New South Wales pilot programme evaluation were published in April 2019, but were not particularly insightful on the issue of the effectiveness of the initiative. A total of 105 people made an application in the NSW pilot, and 39% of those received disclosures by the end of the pilot period, but only 12 could be interviewed in depth about what they did (or did not do) as a result of receiving information about the convictions of their partners in the past.

The Urbis researchers appeared split over the efficacy of the Scheme in NSW, noting that although the "number of DVDS applications is modest, there are early indications that the DVDS is proving of value to individual applicants who are taking safety actions"; yet also summarising their research as showing "no information to indicate whether applicants are safer as a result of using the DVDS" (Urbis, 2020: 6). Following this piloting of the disclosure scheme in New South Wales for two years, and the following, underwhelming report on its evaluation, the policy was dropped (Dillon, 2021). While this would suggest a strong degree of policy reflection and control in New South Wales, acting as a counter-turn to the DADS 'policy spiral' (Walker, 2018) globally, the poor return of the pilot in New South Wales has not acted as a break on DADS policymaking in South Australia and parts of Canada, as discussed below.

South Australia

In South Australia, a public consultation in 2016 on policy reforms to address domestic violence placed a possible Domestic Violence Disclosure Scheme as its first point for discussion out of eight policy points (South Australia Government, 2016); while in a parallel development, a domestic abuser watchlist set up in 2015 in South Australia now has almost 6300 men registered on it (Novak, 2021a). The public consultation in 2016 eventually led to the South Australian government confirming in October 2017 that a Domestic Violence Disclosure Scheme was something they would pursue as a policy for the state (SBS News, 2017), and to then, in June 2018, announce that from October 2018 there would be a year-long pilot of a Domestic Violence Disclosure Scheme for the state, with support not just from police and government officials but also crisis and support services (ABC News, 2018). By the end of July 2019, nearly

200 requests to the Scheme in South Australia had been made in an eight-month period (Mirage News, 2019)—and by July 2021 this number had grown to more than 900 requests in total (Novak, 2021c). What we know of the operation of the Scheme in South Australia confirms what we know to be the twin weakness of DADS—namely, a possible shortage of information recorded about dangerous partners (the 'false negative' in terms of risk) and the inability of a disclosure to act as an effective intervention with a violent abuser in and of itself. South Australia Police found that in the six months to July 2021, of 221 people who were the subjects of requests for information, while more than 100 subjects had recorded information to disclose, 98 had no recorded information about domestic violence to disclose—but some subjects were very high risk: of the 221 subjects concerned, 15 had four or more previous victims recorded (Novak, 2021c).

Towards the onset of the COVID-19 pandemic, in June 2020, the Marshall Liberal state government announced that it would continue to fund the DVDS in South Australia for a further year, to the tune of A$500,000, noting that the DVDS in South Australia in total had cost A$900,000 up to that point, since October 2018 (nineteen months). The Marshall Government (Marshall, 2020) explained that:

> Of the 455 applications the DVDS has received since the scheme began on October 2, 2018 … 317 were deemed eligible for further consideration, with 18 applicants deemed to be at imminent risk … 136 disclosure meetings were completed with a further 22 approved to take place … 62 per cent of applications came from people at risk of domestic and family violence and 38 per cent from someone concerned about another person being at risk … 58 per cent of applications involved children … 39 per cent were from regional areas and 61 per cent from the metropolitan area … 440 applicants were women with a male partner, 11 applicants were men with a female partner and four applicants were men with a partner of the same gender … 61 per cent of applicants had not previously received support from a domestic violence service.

These figures mean that the disclosure rate in the first phase of the DADS in South Australia was 49.8%, and that the overwhelming majority of applicants for disclosures would have been women with male partners (96.7%). It is an interesting and valuable piece of information that 61% of these applicants had not previously drawn on domestic violence services, showing the policy reaching a new audience amongst the public. This does show how a DADS can have a tangible albeit indirect public protection benefit—and which could be boosted, in terms of that benefit, so long as the policing and/or social work and victim-support resources were in place to appropriately and meaningfully deal with this 'new business'. A South Australian Government minister argued (Marshall, 2020) that:

> The results really speak for themselves. … The fact that at least 18 applicants were deemed to be at imminent risk and more than half of applications had not previously received support from a DV service really highlights this trial is very worthwhile and a potential life-saver. … The volume of disclosure scheme applications continues to demonstrate there are people at risk of experiencing domestic and family violence in South Australia and this scheme is an important way to help take control of their situation, and possibly provide a safer environment for themselves and their children.

This phrasing at the end of this summary from the South Australian government minister is very telling: the Scheme *possibly* provides a safer environment for recipients of disclosures, and their families—and perhaps in time a further evaluation will show that in South Australia this is indeed the case. On the other hand, further evaluation may show what the New South Wales pilot evaluation by Urbis showed: that there is no sufficiently persuasive evidence that the Scheme actually works (Urbis, 2020: vi).

Despite this seeming gap in evidence as to the efficacy of the policy in South Australia, in February 2021, the South Australian government announced new funding for the prevention of domestic violence in the state, including "$1.9 million to fund the Domestic Violence Disclosure Scheme for the first time in South Australia—and so it can continue until mid-2024" (Lensink & Power, 2021). The South Australian state government are now considering adding a 'mandatory' 'Right to Know' strand to the DVDS in South Australia, as the policy was originally conceived and implemented without one. In the words of state Attorney General Vickie Chapman, this would "mandate proactive disclosures to those deemed to be at risk" (Novak, 2021b).

Victoria

The Victorian state government in Australia instigated a Royal Commission report on domestic violence which explored the possibility of a domestic violence 'perpetrator register' that could be used for the basis of disclosures to potential victims, in the manner of the kind recommended by the Home Affairs Select Committee and for adoption in England and Wales. However, the Royal Commission report concluded, and in recommending against a DVDS-model approach being adopted, that the "effect of such a scheme on increasing women's safety has not been demonstrated", and that "under such a scheme the onus remains on the victim to keep herself safe" (note the gendered use of *herself* here), while such a scheme is "usually limited to those perpetrators who have a criminal history"—which is of course a most significant limitation to the practical impact of any model of DVDS-style intervention policy (Government of Victoria, 2016: 145). The Liberal National Party (LNP) coalition manifesto for the November 2018 Victoria state elections made a commitment to move ahead with a pilot of a Family Violence Disclosure Scheme (Fair Agenda, 2018), but the LNP were defeated by the Labor party.

Western Australia

As with the Royal Commission report in Victoria in 2016, which rejected the notion of a 'Clare's Law' policy because of concerns about the onus for public protection (Government of Victoria, 2016: 145), a major report in Western Australia also recommend that overall a domestic abuse disclosure scheme was an unwise move. The Law Reform Commission of Western Australia reported their "significant unease about the introduction of a public disclosure scheme for family and domestic violence and [a] view that such [a] scheme is fraught with potential difficulties" (Law Reform Commission of Western Australia, 2014: 180). At the time of the publication of the report by the Law Reform Commission of Western Australia, the DVDS in England and Wales had not been in national operation for very long, just for a handful of months in the second quarter of 2014. Despite a stated intention (Law Reform Commission of Western Australia, 2014: 180) to monitor the way that the national DVDS might be evaluated in England and Wales over time, policymakers and police in Western Australia have yet to return to the option of a disclosure scheme policy at the time of writing.

Queensland

The Queensland Law Reform Commission report in 2017 was scathing of the idea of a domestic violence disclosure scheme for the state, and notable for the degree to which criticisms of the DVDS in England and Wales were precursors to that criticism. The QLRC concluded that given the complex causes, dynamics and risks of abusive relationships, then simply a "disclosure (or a non-disclosure) of information under a DVDS would not address these issues" (QLRC, 2017: 130–131). Furthermore, the Queensland Law Reform Commission were also critical of the initial Home Office attempts to evaluate the effectiveness of the Domestic Violence Disclosure Scheme in England and Wales, commenting that these "reviews were limited to assessments of how the scheme process was working in practice; they did not consider the impact of the scheme on the incidence of domestic and family violence, or analyse its 'value for money'" (QLRC, 2017: 143–144). Interestingly, and on the question as to whether a Domestic Violence Disclosure Scheme in Queensland was even necessary as a specific novel public policy from the perspective of needing a new legal footing, the Queensland Law Reform Commission was sceptical. The QLRC highlighted that the sharing of criminality information for public protection purposes already had a statutory basis through the Information Privacy Act 2009 (Qld) (QLRC, 2017: 131).

In Queensland, the Liberal National Party coalition would have pushed for the eventual adoption of a domestic violence disclosure scheme (*Brisbane Times*, 2017), despite the recommendations of the Queensland Law Reform Commission (QLRC) report (QLRC, 2017), should the party have won the November 2017 state elections in Queensland. The LNP were defeated in those elections (Wiggins, 2017), however, and so the decision of the Queensland government in Brisbane in October 2017 not to press ahead with a disclosure scheme policy still stands (Caldwell, 2017). The obstinacy of the LNP to include a DVDS in their election manifesto in the face of the QLRC recommendation against such a Scheme for Queensland had attracted strong criticism from some Queensland family lawyers (Ryan, 2017). This was no surprise: in fact, a disclosure scheme had not featured amongst any of the 140 recommendations made concerning the prevention of domestic and family violence in the Queensland domestic violence task force report *Not Now, Not Ever*, first published in 2015 (Mitchell-Whittington, 2016).

The QLRC report discussed here, and its conclusion to reject the adoption of a DADS, shows an unusually high degree of resistance to the general DADS 'policy spiral'; even compared with other jurisdictions in Australia. Globally, this 'policy spiral', by October 2017, when the QLRC report was published, had seen 'Clare's Law'-type policies spread to Scotland, from England and Wales, as well as to New South Wales (in pilot form), while a scheme had been confirmed as policy in South Australia, with another under consultation prior to introduction in Northern Ireland. The 'policy spiral' has then continued, however, despite the approach taken by the QLRC, in relation to the spread of DADS policies in Canadian provinces.

4.6 'Clare's Law' in Canada

In Canada, and in relation to duties on the police, "[t]he law is clear that in certain circumstances, the police have a duty to warn citizens of foreseeable harm … [t]he obvious purpose of the warning is to protect the citizens", as Moldover J explained in *Jane Doe v. Board of Commissioners of Police for the Municipality of Metropolitan Toronto* [1990] O.J. No.

1584 (Div. Ct.). In *Metropolitan Toronto*, Moldover J also said that in relation to *a decision not to warn* a woman of a predatory rapist committing offences in her neighbourhood, "I would go further and suggest that even if the decision not to warn was one of policy and was responsibly made, it may have carried with it an enhanced duty to provide the necessary resources and personnel to protect the plaintiff and others like her". This suggests that in Canada, there would be legal consequences of not better supporting those individuals in some way where a disclosure is decided against, after that point in time.

The policy development of domestic abuse disclosures schemes has begun to spread across different provinces in Canada, from Saskatchewan to Alberta, more recently. There has arisen what has come to be the normal criticism from identifiably feminist academic lawyers and criminologists due to the 'unintended consequences' for victims of domestic violence (Koshan & Wiegers, 2019) that have already been explored in this book to a degree earlier.

Saskatchewan

The province of Saskatchewan was the first in Canada to have introduced an Interpersonal Violence Disclosure Protocol, following the passing of an *Interpersonal Violence Disclosure Protocol (Clare's Law) Act 2019*. Section 3(3) of the 2019 Act indicates that: "A local police service may provide disclosure information to an individual who has been determined to be a person at risk in accordance with the Interpersonal Violence Disclosure Protocol". The relevant Protocol, now published, explains in para. 10 that Clare's Law as enacted in Saskatchewan is "focused on an assessment of risk taking into account any relevant convictions, warnings, charges, or diversions for violent or abusive offences; and/or information held about B's behaviour which *reasonably leads the police service to believe that B poses a risk of harm to A*" [Emphasis added]. The Justice Minister and Attorney General for Saskatchewan, Don Morgan, has claimed that if the police in that province "are able to identify risk and inform those at risk, we hope to help protect people in Saskatchewan from violent and abusive behaviour by a partner" (Saskatchewan Department of Justice, 2018).

The Saskatchewan Department of Justice (2018) also stated that: "Work will continue with police services and organizations helping survivors of domestic violence on the protocol in the coming months". There was however no sense that the Saskatchewan model of 'Clare's Law' would be piloted (and hopefully evaluated for its efficacy) as the newest Domestic Abuse Disclosure Scheme in the common law world at the time. Journalists in Saskatchewan picked up on the issue that, in the UK, 'Clare's Law'-type policies and the DADS they put into practice are operated 'patchily' and variably between forces in England and Wales and elsewhere in the UK (McKenna, 2018). Furthermore, when the Protocol was brought into force in Saskatchewan in the summer of 2020, to begin the operation of a 'Clare's Law'-model DADS in the province, this was accompanied by an immediate concern that the Royal Canadian Mounted Police (RCMP) would not be part of the operation of the Protocol in Saskatchewan province, since the records it held, as a federal-level policing organisation, were not covered by the regional Protocol—and which would not displace any operation of federal-level privacy protections over criminality information about domestic abuse perpetrators (Paul, 2020). Despite this initial legal uncertainty that would potentially limit the effectiveness of the DADS concerned, there was insufficient scrutiny of the adoption the Interpersonal Violence Disclosure Protocol in Saskatchewan.

In Saskatchewan, only six requests were made under the Domestic Violence Disclosure Scheme (DVDS), between June 2020 and January 2021 (Taylor, 2021), a very small number of requests for six months or more in a region with a population of more than a million people. Taylor (2021) has reported that a lack of participation by the Royal Canadian Mounted Police (RCMP), the federal police force that operates as the sole police presence in much of rural Saskatchewan, was a principal reason for this low number of applications. However, by the end of March 2021, the RCMP were able to begin involvement in the DVDS in Saskatchewan. C/Supt. Alfredo Bangloy, Acting Commanding Officer for the Saskatchewan RCMP, was reported as stating that: "In order to participate in Clare's Law, changes were required to federal regulations, which we have worked diligently to obtain" (Kurz, 2021). As a result of this reflective practice on the part of the Saskatchewan RCMP, reforms were made to the RCMP Regulations 2014 to allow for information disclosures under 'Clare's Law'-type legislation, including under the relevant Interpersonal Violence Disclosure Protocol Act in Saskatchewan in force from June 2020. RCMP detachments across Canada were empowered by new provisions, in s. 57.5 and s.57.6 of the 2014 Regulations, to provide "information that is to be disclosed under the Clare's Law that is applicable in the province in which the disclosure is to be made" (S.57.5), and where the RCMP "is the police force for a province in which Clare's Law is in force, or for a municipality in such a province, a member who is a peace officer may provide disclosure information" (S.57.6). Correcting this regulatory oversight in less than a year is strong steering practice amongst police leaders and policymakers in Canada at the federal level, based on feedback on a policy problem at a provincial level, and shows that the 'policy spiral' (Walker, 2018) in relation to Clare's Law in Canada may be under better control than in some other jurisdictions. What will be crucial is whether evaluation as to the effectiveness of the disclosure scheme in Saskatchewan will follow, when more applications and disclosures have been made.

Alberta

In the Canadian province of Alberta, the DVDS, operating under the Disclosure to Protect Against Domestic Violence (Clare's Law) Act 2020, came into force on 1 April 2021 (Government of Alberta, 2019; Government of Alberta, 2020), albeit with the "support and full participation" of the RCMP in the province (Smith, 2021). Criticisms of the DADS in Alberta have already been forthcoming. As Jenna Robinson has argued: "Alberta's adoption of Clare's Law places a great deal of trust in judicial systems and police agencies that routinely fail DV survivors; police agencies and judicial systems continue to neglect the severity of domestically violent relationships and have frequently favour the abuser" (Robinson, 2020: 9). Nonetheless, between April and July 2021, 39 applications for disclosures were made in Calgary, the largest city in Alberta (Lasuik, 2021).

Newfoundland and Labrador

Government authorities in Newfoundland and Labrador are to introduce the DVDS in the second half of 2021 (Taylor, 2021)—although there have been media reports that there are policymaking delays over exactly how disclosure regulations might be able to take into account subjects' privacy interests (Antle, 2021).

4.7 Conclusions

The general attitude towards DADS amongst policymakers, when compared across a range of different jurisdictions, is more collectively aligned in the UK than in any other large jurisdiction in the common law world: five different Domestic Abuse Disclosure Schemes are now in operation in England and Wales, Scotland, Northern Ireland, Jersey and the Isle of Man. Their legal bases are somewhat different, however, and this chapter has put some inconsistencies of the precise legal decision-making involved under the guidance on each of the three UK DADS into a sharper focus (a comparative analysis that is continued in Chap. 7). In Australia, there is less political unity amongst government bodies at the state level over whether a Domestic Abuse Disclosure Scheme is a positive move in public policy terms—with New South Wales and South Australia pushing ahead with such Schemes, and Victoria, Western Australia and Queensland having rejected them, for now. In a broader international context, meanwhile, in China, a database has been launched in the eastern city of Yiwu, which will allow couples set to marry an opportunity to determine whether their prospective partner has a history of domestic abuse, where any such offences have been recorded across China since 2017 (Oppenheim, 2020).

The most salient point in this chapter, which can inform the later chapters in this book, is with regard to the Australian federal state jurisdictions and their DADS policies. There, the New South Wales pilot of a Domestic Violence Disclosure Scheme was extended to more than three years in terms of its total length; yet the relevant evaluation report produced no overall evidence of improvements to public protection through the operation of a DADS (Urbis, 2020)—and the policy in New South Wales now appears to have been abandoned (Dillon, 2021). (Contrast this with the position in Western Australia, Queensland and Victoria, where state-level policymakers even more pragmatically considered the (lack of) evidence of the effectiveness of Domestic Abuse Disclosures Schemes and applied a brake to the otherwise accelerating 'spiral' of DADS policies across the common law world.) However, the relative lack of compelling evidence as to the effectiveness of the DVDS in New South Wales must be set against the point made by policymakers about one effect of the DVDS observed in South Australia—namely that 61% of South Australian applicants in the pilot of the Scheme had not previously drawn on domestic violence services (Marshall, 2020)—a potentially very important way of assessing the contribution of any 'Right to Ask' policy to public protection work.

The disparate nature of the precise operation of the UK DADS, and the extent, described above, of the adoption of DADS by federal states and provinces in Australia and Canada, respectively, and to varying degrees, actually highlights Paul Cairney's view of the fragmented manner in which public policy can sometimes spread across jurisdictions in non-linear ways (Cairney, 2012: 261). With sets of disparities between different DADS established in relation to domestic abuse disclosure schemes from two sides of the globe, the next chapter considers the extent to which information about the actual efficacy of such schemes currently exists in the public domain.

References

ABC News. (2018, June 15). SA to bring in Clare's Law for partners to get access to domestic violence criminal history. *ABC News*. Retrieved 20 June 2020, from http://www.abc.net.au/news/2018-06-15/sa-to-bring-in-clares-law-for-partners-to-find-dv-convictions/9873890

Antle, R. (2021, June 14). N.L. again pushes back timeline to enact Clare's Law | CBC News. *CBCnews*. https://www.cbc.ca/news/canada/newfoundland-labrador/nl-clares-law-nl-protocol-regulations-1.6064114.

BBC News. (2014). *Jersey brings in 'Clare's Law' domestic abuse scheme*. [Online]. Retrieved 22 June 2021, from https://www.bbc.co.uk/news/world-europe-jersey-26840231

BBC News (Scotland). (2014, November 25). Clare's Law pilot introduced in Aberdeen and Ayrshire. *BBC News*. Retrieved 23 June 2020, from https://www.bbc.co.uk/news/uk-scotland-30191757

BBC News (Scotland). (2018, August 1). Hundreds told of partner's abusive past. *BBC News*. Retrieved 20 June 2020, from https://www.bbc.co.uk/news/uk-scotland-45697807

Brisbane Times. (2017, November 7). LNP to name and shame domestic abusers. Retrieved 23 June 2020, from https://www.brisbanetimes.com.au/queensland-election-2017/lnp-to-name-and-shame-domestic-abusers-20171107-p4ywvf.html

Cairney, P. (2012). *Understanding public policy: Theories and issues*. Palgrave Macmillan.

Caldwell, F. (2017, October 25). Queensland rules out domestic violence disclosure scheme. *Brisbane Times*. Retrieved 23 June 2020, from https://www.brisbanetimes.com.au/politics/queensland/queensland-rules-out-domestic-violence-disclosure-scheme-20171025-p4ywnc.html

Copfs.gov.uk. (2020). *Domestic abuse and stalking charges in Scotland, 2019–2020*. [Online]. Retrieved 7 May 2021, from https://www.copfs.gov.uk/media-site-news-from-copfs/1902-domestic-abuse-and-stalking-charges-in-scotland-2019-20

Criminal Justice Inspectorate of Northern Ireland (CJINI). (2021). No excuse: A follow-up inspection of the recommendations. Retrieved 8 November 2021, from https://www.cjini.org/TheInspections/Action-Plan-Reviews-Inspection-Follow-Up-Revie/2021/April-June/No-Excuse

Dáil Éireann Debate, Tuesday—17 December 2019 Question 274.

Dannemann, G. (2006). Comparative law: Study of similarities or differences? In M. Reimann & R. Zimmermann (Eds.), *Oxford handbook of comparative law*. OUP.

Department of Justice (Northern Ireland). (2018). *Stopping domestic and sexual abuse and violence strategy—draft year 3 action plan*. Retrieved 23 June 2020, from https://www.justice-ni.gov.uk/sites/default/files/publications/justice/draft-year-3-action-plan-aug-18.pdf

Department of Justice (Northern Ireland). (n.d.-a). Domestic Abuse Offence and Domestic Violence Disclosure scheme—A consultation: Summary of responses. Retrieved 23 June 2020, from https://www.justice-ni.gov.uk/sites/default/files/consultations/justice/domestic-abuse-offence-domestic-violence-disclosure-scheme-summary-of-responses.pdf

Department of Justice (Northern Ireland). (n.d.-b). *Stopping domestic and sexual abuse and violence strategy—draft year 4 action plan*. Retrieved accessed 23 June 2020, from https://www.justice-ni.gov.uk/sites/default/files/publications/justice/Year%204%20draft%20Action%20Plan%20Stopping%20Domestic%20and%20Sexual%20Violence%20and%20Abuse%20Strategy.pdf

Dillon, M. (2021, July 24). Victoria reviews approach to domestic violence as family of Alicia Little calls for action. *ABC News*. Retrieved 17 August 2021, from https://www.abc.net.au/news/2021-07-25/domestic-violence-disclosure-scheme-victoria-south-australia-/100291906

Dolowitz, D., & Marsh, D. (1996). Who learns what from whom: a review of the policy transfer literature. *Political Studies, 44*(2), 343–357.

Duggan, M., & Grace, J. (2018). Assessing vulnerabilities in the Domestic Violence Disclosure Scheme. *Child and Family Law Quarterly, 2*, 145.

Evans, M., & Davies, J. (1999). Understanding policy transfer: A multi-level, multi-disciplinary perspective. *Public Administration, 77*(2), 361–385.

Fair Agenda. (2018). Where do the parties stand on domestic violence? Retrieved 23 June 2020, from https://www.fairagenda.org/blog_2018vicelection

Gov.scot. (2020). *Domestic abuse: Statistics 2018–2019—gov.scot*. [Online]. Retrieved 7 May 2021, from https://www.gov.scot/publications/domestic-abuse-scotland-2018-2019-statistics/pages/2/

Government of Alberta. (2019). Informing those at risk of domestic violence. Retrieved 23 June 2020, from https://www.alberta.ca/release.cfm?xID=646535E511EDA-90AF-F086-0613C9D66E3E6810

Government of Alberta. (2020). Disclosing history of domestic violence. Retrieved 23 June 2020, from https://www.alberta.ca/disclosing-domestic-violence-history.aspx

Government of Victoria. (2016). *Royal commission into family violence: Report and recommendations*. Retrieved 18 April 2016, from http://www.rcfv.com.au/Report-Recommendations

Grace, J. (2015). Clare's Law, or the national Domestic Violence Disclosure Scheme: The contested legalities of criminality information sharing. *Journal of Criminal Law, 79*(1), 36.

Hadjimatheou, K., & Grace, J. (2020). 'No black and white answer about how far we can go': Police decision making under the domestic violence disclosure scheme. *Policing and Society, 31*, 834–837. https://doi.org/10.1080/10439463.2020.1795169

Her Majesty's Inspectorate of Constabulary. (2017, March). *PEEL 2016: Police effectiveness 2016—A national overview*. Retrieved 16 June 2020, from https://www.justiceinspectorates.gov.uk/hmic/wp-content/uploads/peel-police-effectiveness-2016.pdf

Hodgman, W. (2019, July 1). Family and sexual violence plan receives record funding. Retrieved 02 March 2021, from http://www.premier.tas.gov.au/releases/family_and_sexual_violence_plan_receives_record_funding

Home Office. (2013b). *Domestic Violence Disclosure Scheme (DVDS) pilot assessment*. Home Office.

Home Office. (2016a). *Domestic Violence Disclosure Scheme (DVDS): One year on—Home Office assessment of national roll-out*. Home Office.

ITV News. (2015). Police tell women your partner has violent past. *ITV News*. [Online] Retrieved 22 June 2021, from https://www.itv.com/news/channel/2015-03-10/police-tell-women-your-partner-has-violent-past

Koshan, J., & Wiegers, W. (2019). *Clare's Law: Unintended consequences for domestic violence victims?* University of Calgary. Retrieved 23 June 2020, from https://ablawg.ca/2019/10/18/clares-law-unintended-consequences-for-domestic-violence-victims/

Kurz, L. (2021). Sask. RCMP now allowed to participate in Clare's Law due to regulatory changes. *MooseJawToday.com*. [Online]. Retrieved 16 April 2021, from https://www.moosejawtoday.com/local-news/sask-rcmp-now-allowed-to-participate-in-clares-law-due-to-regulatory-changes-3592822

Lasuik, S. (2021, July 27). Alberta domestic assault survivors urge women to take advantage of Clare's Law. *660CityNews*. Retrieved 17 August 2021 from https://www.660citynews.com/2021/07/27/alberta-domestic-assault-survivors-clares-law/

Law Reform Commission of Western Australia. (2014, June). *Enhancing family and domestic violence laws—final report*. Project No. 104. Retrieved 17 August 2021, from https://www.parliament.wa.gov.au/publications/tabledpapers.nsf/displaypaper/3912246a89ee9b3e1def188448257d71002ad571/$file/2246.pdf

Lensink, M., & Power, C. (2021). *Record domestic violence funding in SA*. Premier of South Australia. [Online]. Retrieved 30 March 2021, from https://www.premier.sa.gov.au/news/media-releases/news/record-domestic-violence-funding-in-sa

Marshall, S. (2020). (Premier of South Australia), '$600,000 boost to extend DV disclosure scheme and life-saving app. Retrieved 23 July 2020, from https://www.premier.sa.gov.au/news/media-releases/news/$600,000-boost-to-extend-dv-disclosure-scheme-and-life-saving-app

McCann, M. (2018, July 6). Seventy domestic violence checks under new 'right to ask' scheme. *BBC News (Northern Ireland)*. Retrieved 23 June 2020, from https://www.bbc.co.uk/news/uk-northern-ireland-44724641

McKenna, R. (2018, December 11). Law that allows domestic violence records to be released 'patchy' in the U.K. *City News*. Retrieved 23 June 2020, from https://www.citynews1130.com/2018/12/11/law-that-allows-domestic-violence-records-to-be-released-patchy-in-the-u-k/

Meredith, R. (2018, March 26). Domestic violence: Clare's Law equivalent begins in NI. *BBC News*. Retrieved 23 June 2020, from https://www.bbc.co.uk/news/uk-northern-ireland-43533426

Mirage News. (2019, July 31). Domestic Violence Scheme offers support to South Australians at risk. Retrieved 23 June 2020, from https://www.miragenews.com/domestic-violence-scheme-offers-support-to-south-australians-at-risk/

Mitchell-Whittington, A. (2016, September 23). Not now, not ever report made 140 recommendations. What happened?. *Brisbane Times*. Retrieved 23 June 2020, from https://www.brisbanetimes.com.au/national/queensland/not-now-not-ever-report-made-140-recommendations-what-happened-20160923-grncyy.html

Nash, M. (2010). The politics of public protection'. In M. Nash & A. Williams (Eds.), *Handbook of public protection*. Willan.

New South Wales Government. (2016). *Factsheet: NSW Domestic Violence Disclosure Scheme*, p. 3. Retrieved 23 June 2020, from http://www.domesticviolence.nsw.gov.au/__data/assets/pdf_file/0008/371195/dvds-fact-sheet.pdf

New South Wales Government. (2018, May 1). NSW Domestic Violence Disclosure Scheme to continue. Retrieved June 23, 2020, from https://www.facs.nsw.gov.au/about/media/releases/nsw-domestic-violence-disclosure-scheme-to-continue

New Zealand Family Violence Clearinghouse (NZFVC). (2015, December 15). Police introduce family violence disclosure scheme. Retrieved 17 August 2021, from https://nzfvc.org.nz/news/police-introduce-family-violence-disclosure-scheme

New Zealand Law Society. (2016, July 6). Family Violence Information disclosure details released. *NZ Law Society*. Retrieved 23 June 2020, from https://www.lawsociety.org.nz/news-and-communications/latest-news/news/family-violence-information-disclosure-details-released

New Zealand Police. (2019). *Our data—you asked us*. Police.govt.nz. [Online]. Retrieved 7 May 2021, from https://www.police.govt.nz/sites/default/files/publications/our-data-you-asked-us-web.pdf.

New Zealand Police. (n.d.). Family Violence Information Disclosure Scheme (FVIDS). Retrieved 20 June 2020, from http://www.police.govt.nz/advice/family-violence/family-violence-information-disclosure-scheme-fvids

Novak, L. (2021a, April 24). DV shock: Thousands of SA men added to abuser watchlist. *Sunday Mail (South Australia) Online*.

Novak, L. (2021b, May 1). Police could be compelled to warn potential DV victims. *The Advertiser Online*.

Novak, L. (2021c, July 11). SA's worst abusers' shocking violent pasts unmasked. *The Advertiser Online*.

Ons.gov.uk. (2021). *Domestic abuse and the criminal justice system—Appendix tables—Office for National Statistics*. [Online]. Retrieved 30 March 2021, from https://www.ons.gov.uk/peoplepopulationandcommunity/crimeandjustice/datasets/domesticabuseandthecriminaljusticesystemappendixtables

Oppenheim, M. (2020, June 24). Domestic abuse database for couples contemplating marriage launched in China. *The Independent*. Retrieved 25 June 2020, from https://www.independent.co.uk/news/world/asia/china-domestic-abuse-database-marriage-yiwu-a9583121.html

Oswald, M. (2013). Joining the dots—intelligence and proportionality. *P. & D.P., 13*(5), 6.

Paul, R. (2020, June 30). RCMP opt out as Saskatchewan becomes first province to enact Clare's Law. *The Star*. Retrieved 17 July 2020, from https://www.thestar.com/news/canada/2020/06/30/rcmp-opt-out-as-saskatchewan-becomes-first-province-to-enact-clares-law.html

Picken, A. (2020, April 29). Coronavirus: Rise in requests to reveal partners' abusive pasts'. *BBC Scotland News*. Retrieved 16 June 2020, from https://www.bbc.co.uk/news/uk-scotland-52444555

Police Scotland. (2015). *DSDAS guidance and operational protocol*. Author Copy

Police Scotland. (n.d.). Disclosure scheme for domestic abuse Scotland. Retrieved 20 June 2020, from http://www.scotland.police.uk/contact-us/disclosure-scheme-for-domestic-abuse-scotland

Queensland Law Reform Commission. (2017, June). *Domestic violence disclosure scheme*. Report No. 75. Retrieved 23 June 2020, from http://www.qlrc.qld.gov.au/__data/assets/pdf_file/0010/541189/qlrc-report-no-75.pdf

Robinson, J. (2020). Clare's legacy travels to Alberta: Undesired consequences and repercussions of bill 17. *INvoke*, p. 6.

Ryan, E. (2017, November 14). Lawyer slams 'pig-headed' policy. Lawyers Weekly, Retrieved 23 June 2020, from https://www.lawyersweekly.com.au/smelaw/22253-lawyer-slams-pig-headed-policy

Saskatchewan Department of Justice. (2018, November 5). Interpersonal Violence Disclosure Protocol Act—Clare's Law—introduced in Saskatchewan.

SBS News. (2017, October 7). SA to introduce new domestic violence laws. *SBS News*. Retrieved 23 June 2020, from https://www.sbs.com.au/news/sa-to-introduce-new-domestic-violence-laws

Scottish Government. (2014, August 18). *Domestic abuse pilot areas announced*. Scottish Government. Retrieved 20 June 2020, from https://news.gov.scot/news/domestic-abuse-pilot-areas-announced

Smith, A. (2021). Alberta's version of Clare's Law to come into effect next month | Calgary Herald. *Calgaryherald.com*. [Online]. Retrieved 16 April 2021, from https://calgaryherald.com/news/local-news/albertas-version-of-clares-law-to-come-into-effect-next-month

South Australia Government. (2016). Summary: Domestic violence discussion paper. Retrieved 23 June 2020, from https://www.agd.sa.gov.au/sites/g/files/net2876/f/dvdiscussionpaper_web_final.pdf?v=1490754880

Taylor, S. (2021). Clare's Law in Saskatchewan used handful of times; RCMP review their role. *Global News*. [Online]. Retrieved 30 March 2021, from https://globalnews.ca/news/7669407/clares-law-saskatchewan-2/

University of Glasgow. (2015, September). *Audit of the Disclosure Scheme for domestic abuse (Scotland)*. Author's Copy obtained via freedom-of-information request.

Urbis. (2020). NSW Domestic Violence Disclosure Scheme evaluation and crisis assistance service review pilots—final report. Retrieved 23 June 2020, from https://www.women.nsw.gov.au/__data/assets/pdf_file/0004/670009/Domestic-Violence-Disclosure-Scheme-Pilot-Evaluation-and-Crisis-Assistance-Scheme-Review-Final-Report.pdf

Walker, C. (2018). Counter-terrorism and counter-extremism: The UK policy spirals. *Public Law, 725*(4).

Wangmann, J. (2016). Has he been violent before? Domestic violence disclosure schemes. *Alternative Law Journal, 41*(4), 230.

Wiggins, N. (2017, December 8). Queensland election: LNP's Tim Nicholls concedes defeat, quits LNP leadership. *ABC News*. Retrieved 23 June 2020 from http://www.abc.net.au/news/2017-12-08/queensland-election-tim-nicholls-concedes-defeat/9239930

5
The Effectiveness of Domestic Abuse Disclosure Schemes

5.1 Introduction

This chapter reviews the available evidence for the effectiveness of Domestic Abuse Disclosure Schemes, and in particular looks to add a fresh empirical perspective on the issue of the effectiveness of the DVDS in England and Wales. It is argued here that this effectiveness can best be measured in terms of what we can discern about the contribution by DADS to public protection work, gauged by the proportion of potential or actual victims of domestic abuse who are recipients of a DADS disclosure, but who do not go on to be (re)victimised by the subject of that disclosure. A notable benefit from evidence about DADS, stemming from work by police in South Australia, is that the majority (61%) of DVDS applicants there were members of the public who had not used a domestic violence service before (Marshall, 2020). But the Urbis report on the NSW pilot found a relative lack of evidence of effectiveness, in terms of whether disclosures actually helped keep victims of domestic violence safer overall (Urbis, 2020: 6).

In the context of England and Wales, a starting point is actually to acknowledge the shortage of substantive reviews of the effects of Clare's

J. Grace, *Domestic Abuse Disclosure Schemes*,
https://doi.org/10.1007/978-3-030-89039-1_5

Law (Duggan & Grace, 2018; Hadjimatheou & Grace, 2020). As discussed earlier in this book, there has been a distinct lack of detailed reviews either by central government bodies, or by national or regional policing bodies, of the way that the UK DADS operate in relation to the *effectiveness* of the public protection contribution that they might make. As the Queensland Law Reform Commission have observed, while the Home Office initially scrutinised the implementation of 'Clare's Law', these reviews of the DVDS were problematic, as these were both procedural "reviews [that] were limited to assessments of how the scheme process was working in practice; they did not consider the impact of the scheme on the incidence of domestic and family violence, or analyse its 'value for money'" (QLRC, 2017: 143–144). Indeed, the reviews by government of the workings of DADS in the UK have not met the key test of proper regulation and evaluation of criminal justice policy in failing to determine whether the DVDS or the other UK DADS have a positive effect on victim safety when it comes to preventing domestic abuse.

The Home Office impact assessment of the DVDS policy was undertaken in October 2013 (Home Office, 2013b) following an evaluation (published in November 2013 (Home Office, 2013a)) of the 14-month pilot scheme that ran in 2012–13. The pilot saw 111 disclosures from 386 applications (a disclosure rate of 29%). The impact assessment established the policy options for what was launched as the national policy of a Domestic Violence Disclosure Scheme for England and Wales in March 2014. This impact assessment stated that the first 'main objective' of any final DVDS policy would be to "[r]educe incidents of domestic violence and abuse" (Home Office, 2013b: 1); but what was undertaken in the course of the pilot evaluation, which took place prior to the impact assessment process, did not really try and measure this first main objective of the DVDS.

The pilot assessment report explains the methods of the evaluation very clearly: it used "pilot police force monitoring data, focus groups with practitioners who delivered the scheme and a small number (38) of questionnaires completed by those who had applied for and/or received a disclosure" (Home Office, 2013a: 2). The pilot evaluation report, however, also highlighted that the pilot evaluation "aimed to understand: the nature of cases going through the scheme, including the volume and characteristics of applications and disclosures; perceptions of police officers and partner agencies involved in implementing the scheme, to capture lessons learnt; and experiences of those who requested and/or received a disclosure" (Home Office, 2013a: 2). The pilot evaluation used questionnaire data from 38 disclosure applicants and recipients to try and gauge their experience of the process, as well as focus groups with police officers and other professionals. However, the authors of the evaluation report were clear that this "assessment focused on capturing views of the disclosure process and was not designed to assess any impact of the pilot scheme for victims or perpetrators of domestic abuse (for example, changes in potential domestic abuse victimisation or recidivism)" (Home Office, 2013a: 9). In this way, there was a misalignment between the first 'main objective' of the DVDS, as considered by Home Office policymakers (to 'reduce incidents of domestic violence and abuse'), and the remit and design of the pilot evaluation itself. Although the questionnaire was completed by 38 respondents, only 23 of these were disclosure recipients (there were 111 disclosure recipients in the 14-month pilot in total), the rest being disclosure applicants only (Home Office, 2013a: 10). We are also told that "officers used their professional judgement and risk assessment tools to ensure victim safety was not compromised by completing questionnaires" (Home Office, 2013a: 10). This is a useful methodological insight into the pilot assessment process. However, while the authors of the evaluation report note that "most questionnaires were completed with a police officer present, rather than completed directly by the respondent which may affect the content and candour of responses" (Home Office, 2013a: 10), this screening through the use of professional judgement might mean that disclosure recipients who were at a higher risk of victimisation were more likely to be excluded from the questionnaire process on the basis of risk.

The Home Office pilot assessment evaluation would have been strengthened if, by the time it was published in November 2013, it had been augmented to include an analysis of police-held data to see how many of the 111 disclosure recipients had reported or had been reported in police intelligence as being victimised by their partner in the interim. What the pilot assessment report did establish through the use of questionnaires with a mix of 38 applicants and disclosure recipients, at least, was that:

> The majority of respondents who had received disclosures stated that the information the police had given them had helped them to make more informed choices about their relationship. As a result of the information disclosed, respondents stated they would be more likely to keep a closer look out for signs of domestic abuse in their relationship and seek support from family and friends. A small number of respondents (4) reported that they were likely to seek support from support services following the disclosure. (Home Office, 2013a: 14)

This is pretty thin evidence of a public protection benefit from disclosures. However, the focus groups with police officers and other professionals did at least allow the pilot evaluation report authors to conclude that there was a public protection benefit from the DVDS, since "[i]n some cases, [applications] had brought potential victims and perpetrators of domestic abuse to the attention of the police and other agencies for the first time—for example in cases where the potential victim alleged their partner was abusive but the police had no prior intelligence about this" (Home Office, 2013a: 14). There are echoes of this benefit of the nature of DADS in the context of South Australia's pilot assessment of the DVDS, too (Steven Marshall (Premier of South Australia), 2020).

Unfortunately, the Home Office 'one-year-on' assessment was likewise "not designed to consider any impact [the] DVDS may have had on domestic violence and abuse victims" (Home Office, 2016a: 3), drawing as it did on relatively superficial data: that is, on numbers of applications and disclosures from all 43 policies forces in England and Wales. While a number of focus group workshops were conducted for this 'one year on' review, and these included a total of 29 criminal justice practitioners (though mainly police officers), there was a missed opportunity here to undertake any more questionnaires with disclosure recipients, or to undertake a review of police intelligence data to estimate post-disclosure victimisation rates for both applicants and disclosure recipients. The 'one-year-on' study by the Home Office therefore was, as a result, even less of a substantive review of the Scheme, and as much a procedural or 'light touch' review as the pilot assessment. Nevertheless, these workshops did allow the Home Office authors to highlight "some inconsistency in information given in disclosures and variation in the service provided to victims" (Home Office, 2016a: 5); concerns that remain about the Scheme (Duggan & Grace, 2018; Hadjimatheou & Grace, 2020).

Nazir Afzal QC is of the view that "Clare's Law was a great success but it was only half the job with the burden of finding out if your partner has a history of violence falling entirely on the potential victim" (Bunyan, 2020). While this view underplays the 'Right to Know' strand of the DVDS, the coronavirus 'lockdown' periods have certainly seen the 'Right to Ask' strand of the DVDS see a rise in prominence. In London, the Metropolitan Police recorded 955 'Clare's Law' requests between March and December 2020 (while a figure for the Met for the year to March 2020 is not available from the ONS, but in the whole year to March 2019, they recorded only 682 DVDS applications), and the force were using social media applications like WhatsApp to make disclosures about partners (Dearden, 2020). For Essex Police, there were 422 Right to Ask applications between January and September 2020, the highest annual level of Right to Ask applications under the DVDS in that period since the start of the Scheme (Bryson, 2020). As a result of what is likely to be a rise in the use of the DVDS and similar Schemes in other jurisdictions since the coronavirus pandemic started and the response of 'lockdown' began, it is as important as ever to try and gauge the effectiveness of 'Clare's Law' disclosures themselves, as contributions to public protection work. As such, this chapter turns in its next section to a consideration of the evidence that exists in the public domain as to the effectiveness of the Scheme, and in the light of the main academic criticisms outlined earlier. One principal aim of this chapter is to communicate the extent to which police forces and police regulators, chiefly in England and Wales, show a troubling lack of 'organisational learning' (Thomas, 2014) around the operation of the DVDS—a policy measure which, in evidence terms, is struggling to assert itself as a consistently valuable policing practice in combatting domestic violence—even while it enjoys tremendous media and PR 'cut through'.

5.2 The Evidence Published by Regulators as to the Operation of the Scheme

In considering the evidence published by regulators as to the operation of the Scheme, our starting points are the first HMICFRS inspection reports following the publication of the Home Office 'one year on' evaluation of the DVDS (Home Office, 2016a). However, the HMICFRS National PEEL report for 2017 actually makes no mention of the DVDS, which means no true review of effectiveness by the policing inspectorate, and no review of the great variation in disclosure rates nationally (the 'postcode lottery' outlined in Chap. 1) (Her Majesty's Inspectorate of Constabulary, 2018). HMICFRS did conclude in the report that more consistency is needed in terms of using police powers to protect victims of domestic abuse, while the Inspectorate still "have concerns about the extent to which police officers keep domestic abuse victims safe and bring their offenders to justice" (Her Majesty's Inspectorate of Constabulary, 2018: 22). HMICFRS also found in their 2017 national report on policing in England and Wales that, in general, those options and powers available to the police, to be used to protect victims of domestic abuse, could be used more rigorously. Around 40% of forces had seen a recent fall in the number of Domestic Violence Protection Orders they were obtaining from the courts against abusers. The national rate of arrests for domestic abuse offences was also falling slightly even as the rate of such crimes nationally rose by 18% in 2016–17. Additionally, the rate of conditional bail used to protect victims from perpetrators and even the rate of prosecutions in relation to the number of reported domestic abuse offences were both falling at the time the report was written (Her Majesty's Inspectorate of Constabulary, 2018: 22–23).

Moving on to consider *force-level* inspection reports from HMICFRS for 2017, which were the first to capture the operation of the DVDS in England and Wales under the newer Home Office guidance from 2016, a troubling theme develops when looking at how the DVDS is presented in those reports. HMICFRS is not taking thorough regulatory responsibility for its role in relation to the oversight of the DVDS that it performs (see Chap. 6). Force-level commentary by HMICFRS tends to be scant when it comes to the opportunity to really press for an evaluation of whether the DVDS is truly effective at preventing offending, or increasing victim safety, as opposed to monitoring whether it is administered smoothly. Sometimes mention is made in force-level reports that use of the DVDS is subject to some kind of innovation or improvement. In Avon and Somerset, for example, HMICFRS noted that: "Officers and staff in the safeguarding co-ordinating units process domestic violence disclosure scheme applications. … The force makes good use of this scheme" (HMICFRS, 2018a: 17). But there is no accompanying explanation of what constitutes 'good use' of the Scheme. Similarly vague plaudits are offered for slight improvements in the use of the DVDS in other force areas, without HMICFRS actually specifying their measures for the 'good' use of tools to prevent domestic violence. HMICFRS offer these vague assurances in relation to Northumbria, where it deems that: "The force is good at using its legal powers to protect vulnerable people" (HMICFRS, 2018h: 18). In relation to Cheshire and in Hertfordshire, HMICFRS wished those force areas to use the DVDS more frequently (HMICFRS, 2018b: 14, 2018c: 16).

However, in relation to some force areas, reports by HMICFRS take pains to highlight something that a force is doing, or has demonstrated, which suggests that the forces concerned are in some way considering the effectiveness of DVDS disclosures. In relation to Lancashire, for example, HMICFRS commented that (HMICFRS, 2018d: 13):

> The constabulary's use of the legal powers under the domestic violence disclosure scheme are among the highest for police forces in England and Wales. … In order to protect victims from further abuse, the constabulary considers the effectiveness of the use of such powers before making an application and looks for an alternative. This could include participation in a domestic abuse perpetrator programme in an attempt to address the causes of the offending.

On Lincolnshire, HMICFRS noted that (HMICFRS, 2018e: 19):

> The force promotes the use of domestic violence protection orders (DVPOs) and the domestic violence disclosure scheme, known as Clare's Law, and reports that officers are more aware and confident now about completing an application. The force intends soon to require officers to complete a new

> public protection notice when attending incidents involving vulnerable victims, which will also help to identify repeat offenders. This replaces the 'stop abuse' form and will automatically pass referrals to different agencies more quickly.

As an aside, it must be noted that the effectiveness of DVPNs and DVPOs is hard to judge. Blackburn and Graca (2020: 11) report a breach rate of only 8% from a sample of more than 250 DVPNs and DVPOs in their study using Metropolitan Police data. However, the two authors of course acknowledge that some breaches of these types of protective order will not be reported by victims (Blackburn & Graca, 2020: 11), which would make these orders look more effective than they are in reality. Blackburn and Graca (2020) also note that Kelly et al. (2016: 3), in their study of DVPO outcomes for the Home Office, found a 16% breach rate for the orders. In the context of this chapter on the policy monitoring of DADS, this work by Kelly et al. (2016) for the Home Office is notable. While the Home Office were clearly interested in the question of how often DVPOs might be breached, as a measure of their substantive effectiveness, the Home Office were not as interested in measuring the substantive effectiveness of DVDS disclosures, as the measure of victimisation of disclosure recipients is missing from the 'one year on' Home Office study of the DVDS (Home Office, 2016a).

HMICFRS might not be clear in its inspection reports as to what constitutes 'good' or even 'effective' use of the DVDS, but it still takes forces to task regardless. In relation to London and the work of the Metropolitan Police Service, HMICFRS:

> identified in [a] 2016 inspection that the force was failing to make full use of wider powers available to it which could help in its efforts to prevent domestic abuse and protect victims. … There is also limited use of 'Clare's Law' disclosures. In the 12 months to 30 June 2017, 121 disclosures were made under the scheme. The force needs to be more proactive in these disclosures; it is currently reliant on responding when people exercise their 'right to ask', with very limited disclosure under 'right to know'. It is disappointing that more progress has not been made in using these wider powers, especially in the light of the rising levels of domestic abuse crime. (HMICFRS, 2018i: 21–22)

HMICFRS however does not provide any evidence for its confidence in the DVDS as something that "could help in its efforts to prevent domestic abuse and protect victims". However, it is plain from some of its inspection reports for 2017 that HMICFRS do consider that there are merits, and best practices, emerging from the use of the DVDS in England and Wales, particularly where the policing of domestic abuse is 'proactive', 'appropriately skilled', or emphasised or highlighted within the force. In North Yorkshire, for example, HMICFRS noted that:

> The force is an active user of the domestic violence disclosure scheme. … The force also encourages people to ask for disclosure under Clare's Law. … During our inspection, HMICFRS found that domestic abuse officers are proactive in their approach to identifying when new relationships start between either victims or perpetrators, and that they consider use of the scheme to protect domestic abuse victims or those in new relationships with domestic abuse perpetrators. (HMICFRS, 2018g: 18)

In South Yorkshire:

> the force has a low rate of use of the 'right to ask' and 'right to know' legislation [sic] … compared to the rate in England and Wales. It could do more to publicise the 'right to ask' and be more proactive in its own disclosure under the 'right to know'. (HMICFRS, 2018j: 24)

While in relation to Suffolk:

> We found that the use of Clare's Law is one of the specific considerations included within the secondary assessment of DASH risk forms, which is carried out by the domestic abuse teams. This results in a high number of cases being submitted to the MASH for consideration of disclosure under Clare's Law 'right to know' provisions. … We found that the force provided timely disclosures by using appropriately skilled officers and staff throughout the force with support from the three domestic abuse teams throughout the county. (HMICFRS, 2018k: 14)

Of the police in Sussex, HMICFRS reported that: "the force is actively trying to increase its use of powers to safeguard victims, such as Clare's

Law, by highlighting it within the force" (HMICFRS, 2018l: 20). And of Wiltshire Constabulary, HMICFRS noted: "The force makes appropriate use of legal powers to protect people from harm. … A domestic violence disclosure scheme co-ordinator is bringing renewed emphasis on this important legislation" (HMICFRS, 2018m: 12).

In reviewing these particular DVDS-focused inspection findings from HMICFRS, it is possible to see there was a body of knowledge of best practices about the DVDS in existence by 2017–18, yet it was 'fragmented' (Black, 2001: 107) from a regulatory perspective. Certainly the Home Office could have gone one better than HMICFRS and might have chosen to require forces to self-evaluate the DVDS in England and Wales, and with particular regard to the effectiveness of the disclosures to help safeguard vulnerable victims in a given force area, yet have not. Overall, we do not have the ability to conclude that HMICFRS could be said to have a good regulatory grasp of the DVDS in 2017–18, when they made their first solid attempts to understand forces' use of the Scheme, given the number of forces where they have either not commented on the use of the Scheme by that force, or gave only general commentary and no regulatory requirements in the relevant inspection report. We can conclude that HMICFRS is overall not as interested as it could be in answering key questions of efficacy when it inspects forces on how they use the DVDS in England and Wales. This is problematic because the Inspectorate is a key regulator in relation to maintaining standards in policing (see Chap. 6) and in particular the requirements to safeguard victims of abuse.

5.3 Evidence of Force-Level Self-evaluation of the Scheme Conducted by Forces Themselves

It would seem that, *prima facie*, HMICFRS were shown evidence in 2017 by certain forces as to the effectiveness of the DVDS in relation to protecting victims from domestic abuse. Given the extent to which *some* forces were commended in the extracts from HMICFRS reports presented above, one might expect that there would be a careful internal evaluation of the effectiveness of the DVDS going on in those forces at that time. In fact, the opposite appears to be true, as this chapter section demonstrates. There is an issue arising from the freedom-of-information research for this research that belies the idea that there was any kind of self-evaluation of effectiveness of the use of the DVDS, other than for a small minority of forces, and this self-evaluation often focused on compliance with Home Office policy in terms of DVDS processes, as opposed to trying to investigate the contribution the DVDS actually made to their domestic violence prevention practice. However, some forces have begun to address the challenge set by HMIC in 2016 to monitor processes and evaluate data in relation to "ensure that they are making best use of these powers to safeguard victims of domestic abuse" (Her Majesty's Inspectorate of Constabulary, 2017: 86); and case studies on these forces and their own evaluations (and the shortcomings of these) are presented in the chapter sections below.

FOI Requests About DVDS Self-evaluation

When I submitted an FOI request to all police forces in England and Wales in April 2018, asking about the existence of any kind of internal review of the operation and effectiveness of Clare's Law in each force, there were few meaningful responses. All but one force (Cleveland Constabulary, 2018) responding to this FOI request had not reviewed DVDS disclosures for their effectiveness in anything approaching a systematic way. (A case study on Cleveland Constabulary, in part based on their 2018 FOI response, is featured below). In terms of other partial but useful responses to this particular FOI request in May 2018:

- Durham Constabulary provided an action plan produced in 2015, which detailed the need for greater internal awareness raising for officers in the force, and the need for training on what would be an appropriate process for using the DVDS, but produced no updates or detail of work on this, however (Durham Constabulary, 2018).
- West Mercia and Warwickshire provided a joint response, including an extract of an internal report highlighting the need for more research and training on the DVDS in the force, which stated that "[a]rguably,

Right to Know should be a first consideration by all officers when they become aware that a repeat or serial perpetrator is becoming involved in a new close relationship" (West Mercia Police and Warwickshire Police, 2018a: 3). The two forces also provided an extract from a memo on the need for a secure online application portal for their DVDS processes (West Mercia Police and Warwickshire Police, 2018b).
- Hertfordshire Constabulary provided their entire domestic abuse action plan for 2016–19, which noted that more information is needed on the Scheme in the 'welcome pack' for new officers in the force (Hertfordshire Constabulary, 2016: 4).
- Northumbria Police produced a report on internal DVDS processes, such as timescales, but this contained nothing in terms of data or commentary on the outcomes or the effectiveness of those disclosures (Northumbria Police, 2018a).

When I repeated this exercise in April 2021, using FOI requests to police forces in the UK about any report or evaluation they had undertaken into the effectiveness of their operation of the DVDS, there was a marked difference. The number of forces responding to this FOI request with few or no details were still very much in the majority, but there were a larger number of examples of self-evaluation, overall, than had existed in 2018. The significance for the issue of prompting forces to self-regulate on their use of the DVDS and common law powers of disclosure is clear: the police service in England and Wales, at force level, had little overall interest in seeing if their use of Clare's Law could be said to meet its objectives; but some forces have led the way in trying to investigate the way that the DVDS is operated in their force area—and even its effects on disclosure applicants and recipients. There is clearly some innovation and serious reflection going on in a minority of forces in England and Wales with regard to the DVDS. Details of the less comprehensive, but still substantive responses to my FOI request in April 2021 are as follows:

- Dorset Police reported that they had undertaken a review of their operation of the DVDS, and found that "a percentage of applicants to the scheme were the victim of domestic related offences during the time it took to process the applications", where the "perpetrator was the subject of that application" (Dorset Police, 2021: 1); although the force did not report the percentage of applicants who has been victimised. Dorset have now created a system for flagging the subjects of ongoing DVDS applications to senior officers, so that officers responding to domestic abuse incidents can be more easily advised to make urgent or immediate disclosures (Dorset Police, 2021).

- Lancashire Constabulary reported in their response that they had now introduced a new DVDS triage process to determine whether an urgent disclosure was needed within 24 hours (Lancashire Constabulary, 2021).
- South Yorkshire Police (SYP) reported that they undertook a dip sample of 15 disclosure cases in the summer of 2019, and found that there was a great variety of styles and lengths and levels of details in the wording of disclosures made; the force reported that they are making efforts to both simplify and standardise the wording of disclosures (South Yorkshire Police, 2021). SYP also reported that from a dip sample of 105 'Right to Know' disclosures by the force in the autumn of 2019, 11 of these files (10.5%) lacked recorded detailed safety plans for people at risk (South Yorkshire Police, 2021). SYP also explained that where "a legal basis exists, consideration of a Clare's Law disclosure should take place for all applicable detainees for domestic abuse … as an early intervention mechanism and a way of informing potential victims before they become too embedded in an abusive relationship" (South Yorkshire Police, 2021: 4).
- Staffordshire Police responded to explain that they had undertaken a review of their DVDS processes in July 2020 in order to preclude the processing of what they felt was a 'high volume' of 'unsuitable applications' from individuals no longer in a relationship and no plans to renew that relationship (Staffordshire Police, 2021: 1), or no plans to enter into a new relationship with a person; or where an applicant is a member of a family that is engaging with social services, and where social work professionals might make disclosures instead. Since December 2020 a new process drawing on this review of the suitability of disclosures has been in place, resulting in a decrease in 'unsuitable applications' (Staffordshire Police, 2021: 1).

- West Midlands Police (2021) explained that they had created a dedicated process to centralise the process of DVDS applications and disclosures, which should help, they feel, to monitor the outcomes of the DVDS in the West Midlands for the first time. The force also explained that it had now introduced an online application process for the DVDS (West Midlands Police, 2021).

Surveys by Forces of Disclosure Recipients' Perception of the DVDS

Northumbria Police and Nottinghamshire Police both replied to my April 2021 FOI request by supplying information about their own studies of disclosure applicants' and recipients' views on the DVDS process and outcomes. Of the two forces, Northumbria Police undertook the more limited study (Northumbria Police, 2018b). In December 2018, Northumbria Police surveyed 32 disclosure recipients, 18 of whom completed the survey. In total 15 out of these 18 Northumbrian respondents reported that they were satisfied with their experience of the DVDS. Reassuringly, and importantly, 9 of the 18 survey respondents reported that they felt they had taken some action which had reduced their risk, with 6 respondents reporting they had ended their relationship with the disclosure subject (Northumbria Police, 2018b). This self-evaluation by Northumbria did not appear to try and establish what the occurrence of victimisation amongst disclosure recipients had been, however.

In 2019, HMICFRS reported that Nottinghamshire Police have begun to undertake research with recipients of disclosures under Clare's Law, seeking "feedback on timeliness of completion from application to disclosure; the satisfaction level of the applicant; and an understanding of whether or not the disclosure made any difference to the applicant" (HMICFRS, 2019: 18). My April 2021 FOI request about self-evaluation of the DVDS secured me copies of the reports resulting from this introspective research by Nottinghamshire Police. I sent a follow-up FOI request to clarify a point about the methodology that the force had used to produce its own evaluations of the DVDS. Nottinghamshire reported that they surveyed 64 DVDS applicants and recipients in a period up to June 2019, contacting each person 10 to 12 weeks after disclosures were made;

although the force actually tried to contact 111 individuals in producing this group of survey participants. Of the 31 Right to Ask disclosure recipients surveyed, "nine (29%) participants stated that they already knew what the police had told them, with the remaining 22 (71%) stating the police told them things that they didn't know" (Nottinghamshire Police, 2019: 6). Significantly, Nottinghamshire Police found that 27 out of 31 Right to Ask disclosures-made participants reported that "the information disclosed to them has helped them, irrespective of whether they chose to continue or end the relationship with their partner" (Nottinghamshire Police, 2019: 7), while "18 out of 22 [Right to Know disclosure-made survey] participants felt that the information from Nottinghamshire Police helped them either a little or a lot; with only four stating that it made no difference to them" (Nottinghamshire Police, 2019: 9).

So it is clear that a strong majority of those disclosure recipients actually surveyed in Nottinghamshire felt that the DVDS disclosure made a positive difference to them. However, there is a methodological concern about how representative these participants were of the experience and process of the operation of the DVDS by the force, given that 42% of those individuals contacted (47 out of 111) did not complete the survey; and we must wonder what their motivations and feelings were in not doing so. Perhaps it is likely that by surveying people by telephone in 2019, Nottinghamshire Police were reaching those who wanted to speak to the police about the Scheme, and so not a random sample of possible victims of disclosure subjects. Most importantly, and in terms of the design of the telephone survey, there were also no questions, it would seem, in this survey of disclosure recipients, about their victimisation by the disclosure subject post-disclosure.

Nottinghamshire Police also re-ran this exercise in the 12 months up to February 2021, when they produced another internal report on their operation of the DVDS which they disclosed to me in their response to my FOI request in April 2021. In this instance, in order to produce a cohort of 60 telephone survey participants, the force contacted 108 individuals. This time, out of 27 participants in the survey who had been recipients of disclosures under Right to Ask processes, "[a]lmost 75% of [these] participants stated that the information disclosed to them had helped them, irrespective of whether they chose to continue or end the relationship with their partner, with only six participants stating the disclosure made no difference" (Nottinghamshire Police, 2021: 7), while in regard to Right to Know disclosure recipients in this 2021 survey, "19 out of 20 participants felt that the information from Nottinghamshire Police helped them either a little or a lot; with only one stating that it made the situation worse" (Nottinghamshire Police, 2021: 9). Again, this is a strong result, and one that may be used to underpin any initiative to 'push' the DVDS by the force in Nottinghamshire in the future. However, this would require the force setting aside the same methodological concerns about sampling and the lack of questions, again, about any victimisation by disclosure subjects.

The Cleveland Constabulary Case Study

Responses to a wave of freedom-of-information requests I sent to each force in England and Wales as part of my PhD research have shown that only one force in England and Wales, by the summer of 2018, had conducted a substantive review of the effect and operation of the DVDS, despite the DVDS being national policy since March 2014. This force was Cleveland Constabulary, who provided a statistical picture of the operation of the DVDS in their force area in 2017 only (Cleveland Constabulary, 2018). This FOI response data is reproduced without amendment in Table 5.1. To begin with, it should be noted that overall, in the Cleveland force area in 2017, and in relation to the 157 DVDS

Table 5.1 Cleveland Constabulary: results of disclosures across 2017

Results (Crime and incidents)	Total
Total number of disclosures	157
How many people who have been disclosed to under Clare's Law have become victims after?	54 (34%)
How many to the same perpetrator?	49 (31%)
How many to different perpetrators?	5
The number of perpetrators who have proceeded to offend against different victims?	19

Source: Cleveland Constabulary (2018)

disclosures by the end of 2017 alone, 54 people (34%) went on to be victimised by an offender and 49 (31%) by the disclosure subject. The rate of victimisation of disclosure recipients would logically be higher by now, to some degree, whether as a result of abuse by the disclosure subject or by another offender in turn. Given the Home Office impact assessment objective of at least a one-third avoidance rate following disclosures, this data from Cleveland Constabulary is promising with respect to the effectiveness of the DVDS. But it must be emphasised again that this is a case study over a very short timescale only—and from just one small force area—with only data concerning 2017 disclosures and 2017 harms as reported to the police.

When it comes to assessing the outcomes for applicants who did not receive disclosures, the key point is that there is evidence of 'false negatives' in Cleveland (again, in 2017 *alone*): 19 out of 148 non-recipients (12.8%) were offended against by the person they in theory could have been warned about, assuming there was information available to disclose, of course. These were 19 individuals who were not felt to be the object of a 'pressing need' for a disclosure (or again, where there was nothing about the subject of an application to actually disclose). Worryingly, in the light of studies that predict the greatest risk in a violent relationship may often come at the end of or after that relationship (Fleury et al., 2000), there is of course the view that in Cleveland in 2017, applicants who received disclosures under the DVDS were more than twice as likely (31% vs. 12.8%) to be victimised by those individuals they were warned about than those who were not warned for some reason. This is a crude correlation only, of course, but one cannot escape wondering if disclosures might, counterintuitively, actually increase the risk of harm in a relationship that ends as a result of the disclosure. Of course, there is also the issue that the police will be more likely to make a disclosure where there is a higher assessed risk, after all, to meet the requisite 'pressing need' standard for disclosure under the common law, and so we might, pragmatically, expect the rate of victimisation for disclosure recipients to be higher.

It should also be noted that at the time the data concerned were being compiled in Cleveland Constabulary, as outlined above, an inspection by HMICFRS found that in the force area across the middle of 2017, the "process for identifying domestic violence incidents as crimes and assessing the correct closure of such incidents within the force control room does not support accurate crime recording" (Her Majesty's Inspectorate of Constabulary and Fire & Rescue Services, 2018). Findings from the inspection report on Cleveland's data management problems show that crime recording issues could affect the reliability of the FOI data obtained from Cleveland, presented in Tables 5.1 and 5.2 (Her Majesty's Inspectorate of Constabulary and Fire & Rescue Services, 2018). So it should be noted that the one force, Cleveland, who appear to have put the most effort into evaluating the substantive effectiveness of the DVDS in their force area in 2017–18, also happen to be a force rated as 'inadequate' for their collection and management of crime reports data, which they likely would have used to compile their DVDS self-evaluation.

Cleveland Police have recently been criticised in a domestic homicide review report for failing to consider using a DVPN and DVPO against a perpetrator who was being processed (too slowly) as a DVDS disclosure subject at the time he murdered his partner, Natalie Saunders, in 2018 (Middlesbrough Community Safety Partnership, 2021). The processes around this domestic homicide review have seemingly had a considerable effect. In response to my FOI request of April 2021, Cleveland Constabulary provided me with a 'Clare's Law Position Statement', dated October 2020 (Cleveland Constabulary, 2021). This explained that disclosures and outstanding disclosures yet to be made are flagged for any officer in the force to see, so that officers attending incidents can be made aware of these. The force also noted in this statement that a dedicated

Table 5.2 Cleveland Constabulary: results of non-disclosures across 2017

Results (Crime and incidents)	Total
Total number of non-disclosures	148
How many people who have not been disclosed to under Clare's Law have become victims after?	23 (15.5%)
How many to the same perpetrator?	19 (12.8%)
How many to different perpetrators?	3
There has been one unknown perpetrator	1
The number of perpetrators who have proceeded to offend against different victims?	30

Source: Cleveland Constabulary (2018)

DVDS officer has been deployed to make disclosures using simplified language to aid recipients' understanding, and multi-agency panels are now convened to consider whether intelligence is held by any non-police agency when checks on Cleveland systems show there is nothing to disclose. This response to my FOI request in April 2021 also noted that DVDS applications for the first months of 2021 were up 51% during the same period in 2020 (Cleveland Constabulary, 2021).

The Metropolitan Police Case Study

As noted earlier in this book, in February 2020 the Metropolitan Police Service (MPS) briefed a *London Evening Standard* journalist on the use of the DVDS in Greater London. To follow up on the resulting news article, I submitted an FOI request to the MPS in order to establish what internal evaluation had taken place, if any, with regard to DVDS effectiveness. I received a response from the MPS on 7 April 2020. The MPS explained that in their self-evaluation work (Metropolitan Police Service, 2020), they had examined 59 DVDS disclosures at a point more than six months after disclosures had been made, searching their information systems for reports of victimisation of recipients by the subject of the disclosure.

Of 59 disclosures in the sample used by the MPS for their internal study (Metropolitan Police Service, 2020), where there had been offending in a relationship in the last six months prior to a disclosure, 29 relationships between victims and perpetrator saw no further recorded offending in six months after a disclosure, while 12 had not seen any recorded offending in the prior six months nor the following six months. So this makes 41 relationships with no offending for six months (69%) following a disclosure. However, of the 59 disclosures in the sample, there were 18 relationships where violence was known to continue post-disclosure. So there was a 31% minimum victimisation rate for the sample in six months based on data available to the Met (when there might have been abuse not reported to them, of course). Unfortunately, a significant limitation to this evaluation by the Met is the lack of a comparator group, where no disclosure was decided upon following an application to the DVDS—whereas the Cleveland self-evaluation did use this comparison.

5.4 The DVDS in a Domestic Homicide Review in Norfolk

A case study of the use of the DVDS in Norfolk can be made by highlighting the death of Karri McAuley. Killed by her boyfriend, Kerri McAuley was the victim of murder after the 'displacement' of the risk the perpetrator posed—from one woman, and on to Kerri. The domestic homicide review (DHR) report concerned with her death notes that: "A pro-active disclosure about the danger [her boyfriend] presented to potential partners had been given to a previous woman he was believed to be embarking upon a relationship with" (Graham, 2018: 8). Kerri McAuley's case is one of the few detailed examples in the public domain, perhaps the only one, of not just a hypothesis of the risk of 'displacement' of harm under Clare's Law but a fatality that occurred in one relationship because of a disclosure helping to end a different, earlier relationship.

In relation to the use of the DVDS in Norfolk, HMICFRS observed around the same time as the DHR about Kerri McAuley that (HMICFRS, 2018f: 13):

> the force is still taking a significant amount of time to give this information to individuals after it has decided to make the disclosure. This delay in providing the disclosure could have an effect on ensuring that vulnerable victims are appropriately safeguarded at the earliest opportunity.

Slow or delayed disclosures are a chronic problem with the DVDS in England and Wales. *The Observer* newspaper reported the results of its own FOI requests into the speed with which police forces made disclosures, asking about the proportion of disclosures that had been made within the seven weeks allowed by the DVDS guidance, as at the time of writing (Home Office, 2016b). *The Observer* found that 23% or 375 Right to Ask disclosures in 2020 were made outside of the timescale of seven weeks, from a sample of 1609 Right to Ask requests from across 14 police forces that replied in full (Lowe, 2021).

Norfolk Constabulary did not return a response to either the May 2018 or April 2021 FOI request that would indicate they had undertaken any detailed evaluation of how to improve the effectiveness of the

DVDS in their force area. As this section of this chapter explains, this is a concern, as Norfolk Constabulary had a considerable regulatory prompt in May 2018 to review their use of the DVDS. The statutory Domestic Homicide Review report on the failings of agencies in Norfolk concerning the January 2017 murder of Kerri McAuley makes the recommendation that "a national evaluation of Clare's Law [should be] commissioned to assess its use and effectiveness in protecting victims" (Graham, 2018: 68). Norfolk Constabulary could, arguably, have acted on their own initiative to better review their use of the DVDS; but their response to my April 2021 FOI request indicated that they held no relevant information about such a review in their force.

Admittedly, communicating with, and ultimately convincing, a potential victim who is reluctant to involve the police in their relationship space may be very difficult; and in Kerri McAuley's case "the police attempted to inform [her] of the full extent of the perpetrator's offending history but were unsuccessful" (Graham, 2018: 9). In relation to Kerri the DHR report notes (Graham, 2018: 34):

> In this case, Norfolk Constabulary decided, after [an attack against Kerri] that an application under Right to Know should be made. At the multi-agency panel meeting, it was agreed that a disclosure to [Kerri] would be lawful and proportionate and the application was approved. … The officer who was authorised to make the disclosure spoke to [Kerri] on the phone and explained about Clare's Law and why he needed to see her. It was agreed that she would come to the police station but did not attend. Following more phone calls, another appointment was made and again she did not attend. The officer then visited her at her home to make the disclosure, but she would not let the officer in. Of course, we cannot know for certain that the perpetrator was not in the flat at this point. The officer phoned [Kerri] on a number of times following this, but she did not answer the calls or respond to the messages left for her.

The case of Kerri McAuley also shows that there may well be 'fragmentation of knowledge' (Black, 2001: 107) issues, as in actual fact, a victim of domestic violence may already know all too well what a perpetrator is capable of. So too might their friends and family. In relation to Kerri/'April', the DHR report (Graham, 2018: 34) observes that:

> In November 2016, despite [a] restraining order, the perpetrator and April went to Rome. Whilst at their hotel he threatened and assaulted her again. She was so scared that she escaped the hotel running into street intent on escaping him. She was found by refuse collectors upset and scared. They flagged down, and paid for, a taxi who took her to the airport. When she got to the airport the airline staff realised that she needed help and got her on the next flight home. By this time the perpetrator was after her and had begun calling her mother asking where she was and was chasing her to the airport. The airline staff refused to let him board the same plane. Her family describe the panic and rush they had to get to the airport to collect her before the perpetrator arrived on the next plane. She told her family that it really was the end and that she had no intention of ever seeing him again. None of this was reported to the authorities.

Indeed, it is "known that at least one friend told April about the perpetrator's assaults on past girlfriends when learning of their relationship" (Graham, 2018: 8). Disclosures under a DADS, if they are effective because they carry the weight of official confirmation of risk, and when a potential victim already suspects they are at risk, may well be more effective if they are made earlier in a (potentially) abusive relationship. The DHR report (Graham, 2018: 36) argues that:

> an application under Clare's Law would have been appropriate in January 2016 when the police first knew that the perpetrator was in a relationship with April. We obviously cannot be sure what her reaction would have been if a disclosure had been attempted then, but it is possible that she may have been more open to this earlier in the relationship before his control on her became stronger.

However, police intelligence practices may well be too poor, at least in some forces, to allow this development of a routine practice of exploring opportunities to disclosure information early on in an abusive relationship. As the DHR report notes (Graham, 2018: 36):

> It is evident that the police were not routinely updating intelligence about the relationships involving repeat perpetrators of domestic abuse. … It is recommended that Norfolk Police reviews the way in which intelligence and information about the relationships of known repeat perpetrators is

analysed and acted upon. It is further recommended [that] when intelligence or information is received about a known perpetrator being in another relationship an application under the DVDS is always and automatically made.

Christine Graham, the DHR report author, is essentially urging Norfolk Constabulary to tackle the wider issue of their 'fragmentation of knowledge' (as Julia Black would put it (Black, 2001: 107)) about repeat perpetrators of domestic abuse. While this is a sound and salient recommendation, this is a great challenge for any police force during a time of resources pressure due to austerity; and so again we see that the under-prioritisation of funding the policing, investigation and punishment of domestic abuse is problematic.

5.5 An FOI Request About 'Early-wave' Recipients

In May 2018, I sent an FOI request to each of the 43 police forces in England and Wales. The request asked each force to identify how many of the first 20 recipients of their DVDS disclosures after 8 March 2014 had been victimised (i) by the person they were *at that time* in a relationship with, and thus the subject of the disclosure, and (ii) by any other person during that time—therefore over potentially more than four years for some of the victims concerned. In 2014, under Scheme guidance at the time, disclosures under the DVDS could only be made in respect of a potential perpetrator with whom an applicant was in an intimate relationship. This position was revised by the current (December 2016) Home Office guidance on the Scheme to include both current and former partners as a subject to an application/disclosure after the (then) Independent Police Complaints Commission (IPCC) made a recommendation to the Home Office in February 2016, following a death of a woman in Sussex at the hands of a former partner, and namely that the DVDS should apply to former partners as well as current partners as the possible subjects of valid disclosures (IOPC, 2018). These 'early wave' recipients therefore could be said to have had the greatest likelihood of being victimised by the subject of a disclosure, representing the group of recipients whose experience following disclosure is most crucial to understand or to picture.

I received responses concerning outcomes for the first 20 disclosure recipients, after 8 March 2014, for 26 forces in England and Wales, entailing the creation of a 'sample' of 520 individuals for the key question as to the likelihood that a recipient of a disclosure goes on to be victimised by the very person they were warned about. Many forces that replied to the request for information cited the 'costs exemption' under the Freedom of Information Act 2000—entailing that requests which would take more than 18 hours to process (at more than a notional cost of £450) can be rejected—resulting in 26 of the 43 forces in England and Wales making a response to the first half of my request. To explain the slightly smaller sample of 500 people in respect of the question on whether recipients had been victimised by someone other than their partner at the time a disclosure was made: Suffolk Constabulary were unable to retrieve information on whether the 20 individuals concerned were victimised by a person other than the subject of a disclosure within the necessary costs limits of £450 to deal with the FOI request—but Suffolk were still able to supply the information in relation to the number of individuals victimised by the subject of the disclosure concerned.

It can be assumed that in reality these FOI response figures are a *minimum* rate of victimisation for the 'early wave' cohort of recipients of disclosures across c.2014–15 due to potential issues of data quality/poor practices in crime recording by forces (Barr, 2019), as well as the obvious problem of under-reporting of domestic violence offences by victims themselves. Forces could also only likely report on the victimisation of the 20 identified individuals as reported on their own local IT systems and databases, and if relevant, having searched on relevant national systems and databases—but such information would be inaccessible in all likelihood if this was retained only on the local systems and databases of another force in England and Wales. And crucially, the under-reporting or non-reporting of victims of harms arising from domestic violence and abuse is staggering. The Office for National Statistics (2017) has observed that:

> Estimates based on those interviewed in the Crime Survey for England and Wales during the year ending March 2015 showed that around 4 in 5 victims (79%) of partner abuse did not report the abuse to the police. The data held by the police can, therefore, only provide a partial picture of the level of intimate violence experienced in England and Wales.

The year ending March 2015 is the period of time in which the sample of 520 disclosure recipients, described above, would have been receiving their DVDS disclosures—and so this ONS observation further supports the idea that the figure of a 45% victimisation rate in this sample, shown below, is in fact higher, in truth, due to under-reporting of victimisation to the police in the force areas concerned (Table 5.3).

The key point here is that 45% of disclosure recipients in my sample were recorded as victimised, post-disclosure, by their partners at the time of the disclosure, across a period of around four years since the disclosure concerned. This raises a number of quandaries even if it could be assumed to be accurate (which given the chronic issue of non-reporting of harms by victims it very likely is not). Plainly, for one thing, it calls to mind the possibility that victims—in a four-year period—might face a fluctuating level of risk in relation to a fluid relationship status and dynamic with a perpetrator—as staying in a relationship need not guarantee certain, immediate harm—and that ending a relationship does not entail an automatic cessation of risk (Table 5.4).

Table 5.3 FOI data on 20 disclosure recipients per force, 8 March 2014 onwards

	Number of recipients of disclosures who were victimised by the subject of the disclosure in c.4 years	Number of recipients of disclosures who were victimised by a perpetrator other than the subject of the disclosure in c.4 years
Total reports of victimisation:	234	139
From a sample of:	520	500
% victimisation	45.0%	27.8%

Source: Freedom-of-information request responses—see above table

Table 5.4 Freedom-of-information data on victimisation of first 20 recipients, 8 March 2014 onwards, from 26 forces in England and Wales

Force in England and Wales	Number of 20 recipients recorded as harmed by a disclosure subject, post-disclosure	Number of 20 recipients recorded as harmed by an offender other than a disclosure subject, post-disclosure
Bedfordshire	9	6
Cambridgeshire	8	4
Cheshire	8	7
Cleveland	13	10
Dorset	12	7
Essex	13	10
Gloucestershire	13	4
Gwent	4	10
Hampshire	8	3
Hertfordshire	7	7
Humberside	10	6
Kent	9	7
Lancashire	3	4
Leicestershire	8	2
Merseyside	10	4
Norfolk	11	1
North Wales	6	3
Northamptonshire	9	8
Northumbria	13	5
Staffordshire	3	0
Suffolk	7	Not supplied
Thames Valley	11	4
Warwickshire	7	3
West Mercia	10	4
West Midlands	9	7
West Yorkshire	10	9
Total reports	234	139
Total sample	520	500
Percentage victimisation by May 2018	45.00%	27.80%

Source: Freedom-of-information request responses—see above table

In terms of individual approaches by forces to handling the freedom-of-information request concerned, Essex Police returned a particularly interesting response, with added levels of detail I had not requested (Essex Police, 2018). In total 13 out of the first 20 individuals to receive disclosures under the DVDS in Essex were victimised by their partner at that time, in the period since c.2014. But more usefully, and troublingly, the Essex response illustrates very well different instances of *dual victimisation* (with 6 of 20 individuals perpetrated against by both their partner at the time of the disclosure *and* by a third party since the disclosure); *sole victimisation* (with 7 of 20 only victimised by their partner at the time of the disclosure); *displaced victimisation* (with 4 of 20 only victimised by a third party since the disclosure) and *no victimisation* (3 out of 20). We can only speculate, but it is perhaps this sort of troubling picture which means the lengthy pilot of a DVDS in New South Wales, discussed in Chap. 4, was unable give any real conclusion as to its effectiveness (Urbis, 2020).

5.6 Conclusions

There is mixed evidence available in the public domain as to the overall effectiveness of the DVDS at preventing domestic abuse arising through the bringing to an end of a risky relationship, or the empowerment of victims through the ability to increase their knowledge of their partners abusive past. Before my freedom of information-based research was conducted for this book, not a single study had been undertaken to quantify an estimate of the substantive *effectiveness* of this Scheme. Pilot evaluations backed by government regulators in England and Wales, and jurisdiction-wide police forces in Scotland and New South Wales have been, so far, procedural in their nature.

However, this chapter has presented the findings from two waves of FOI requests to police forces in England and Wales, first in mid-2018 and then in the spring of 2021, which show (i) that the rate of victimisation of individual recipients of disclosures under the DVDS, and by the very person they were warned against as the subject of a disclosure, could very well be at least 45%, and perhaps more than half over a four-year period, and (ii) that only a small minority of police forces in England and Wales had decided, at the time of writing, to undertake a review of the *substantive* effectiveness of the DVDS that they themselves have operated and promoted. This situation is clearly changing over time, and this self-regulation by forces is to be welcomed, even if it is on a disparate basis, from force to force.

All police forces in England and Wales should (be required to) undertake an exercise to establish whether the disclosures they have made under the DVDS in the last 12 months have had an effect, entailing checking to see if recipients have reported victimisation by the subjects of the disclosures concerned. This should be a requirement placed on the 43 forces in England and Wales by the relevant regulator(s), either the Home Office and/or the HMICFRS—and a similar evaluation should be carried out in relation to the DADS in Scotland and Northern Ireland by the forces in those regions. This programme of evaluations would partly remedy, when a composite was built of all the findings from these forces, the regulatory failing inherent in poor evaluation of the Scheme(s) to date. In this way, forces and regulators can begin to evaluate whether recent disclosures under the DVDS in England and Wales have been having a positive impact on the safety and empowerment of victims; or whether more needs to be done by the force to establish how 'Clare's Law' disclosures can be managed and made effectively in conjunction with other preventive measures aimed at tackling domestic abuse. Additionally, themes and factors affecting victimisation of disclosure recipients by disclosure subjects could be sought out in order to provide a better understanding as to how the public protection benefit of DADS might be maximised.

However, if public protection is properly secured by dangerous offenders being punished, and potentially imprisoned, then the biggest public protection failing in England and Wales, currently, is nothing to do with the effectiveness or otherwise of the DVDS but the backlog of pending prosecutions in the criminal courts (Cox & Lamont, 2020). Exacerbated by the impacts of the coronavirus pandemic on the courts, this backlog had reached more than 55,000 pending Crown Court trials by March 2021 (Baksi & Ames, 2021), and almost 60,000 cases for the Crown Court in England and Wales by late June 2021 (Dearden, 2021), with the number of sexual offences prosecutions waiting to begin increasing 67% in just one year (Dearden, 2021). It is of course very welcome that HM Government made available nearly £18 million of additional funding for support for victims of abuse and for perpetrator rehabilitation programmes for the winter of 2020–21 (GOV.UK, 2020); but this does not sit well alongside what can be seen to be plunging levels of prosecutions in overall numbers of domestic abuse cases from April 2017 to March 2020, including a huge fall in the number of domestic abuse-related rape cases that were prosecuted in that period (see Table 2.1, in Chap. 2). That the use of the DVDS can thrive in such a policy context despite the relative lack of evidence of its public protection effectiveness entails the need for an examination in the following chapter of the 'regulatory space' (Hancher & Moran, 1998) for the prevention of domestic violence in the jurisdiction of England and Wales.

References

Baksi, C., & Ames, J. (2021). Abuse trials pushed back to 2023 as backlog grows. [online] *Thetimes.co.uk*. Retrieved March 31, 2021, from https://www.thetimes.co.uk/article/abuse-trials-pushed-back-to-2023-as-backlog-grows-8766pk79g

Barr, C. (2019, September 19). Thousands of rape reports inaccurately recorded by police. *The Guardian*. Retrieved June 29, 2020, from https://www.theguardian.com/society/2019/sep/19/thousands-of-reports-inaccurately-recorded-by-police

Black, J. (2001). Decentring regulation: Understanding the role of regulation and self-regulation in a 'post-regulatory world'. *Current Legal Problems, 54*(1), 103.

Blackburn, K., & Graca, S. (2020). A critical reflection on the use and effectiveness of DVPNs and DVPOs. *Police Practice and Research, 22*, 1–17.

Bryson, R. (2020). This is how many people in Essex applied to find out if partner has history of violence. [online] *Echo*. Retrieved March 31, 2021, from https://www.echo-news.co.uk/news/19016343.figures-show-number-applications-clares-law-made-essex/

Bunyan, R. (2020). Girl who saw her mother shot dead calls for domestic abuse register. [online] *Mail Online*. Retrieved March 31, 2021, from https://www.dailymail.co.uk/news/article-9023273/Girl-watched-mother-shot-killed-stepfather-calls-domestic-abuse-register.html

Cleveland Constabulary. (2018). Response to a freedom-of-information request made by the author in April 2018.

Cleveland Constabulary. (2021). Response to a freedom-of-information request made by the author in April 2021.

Cox, P., & Lamont, R. (2020). Why the courts and police should be held responsible for failing victims of crime. [online] *The Conversation*. Retrieved March 31, 2021, from https://theconversation.com/why-the-courts-and-police-should-be-held-responsible-for-failing-victims-of-crime-151956

Dearden, L. (2020). Would-be partners of dangerous domestic abusers secretly warned by police. [online] *The Independent*. Retrieved March 31, 2021, from https://www.independent.co.uk/news/uk/crime/domestic-abuse-coronavirus-police-clares-law-b1765938.html

Dearden, L. (2021). Crown court backlog hits record high of 60,000 cases as victims wait years for justice. [online] *The Independent*. Retrieved June 24, 2021, from https://www.independent.co.uk/news/uk/home-news/crown-court-backlog-coronavirus-cuts-b1872051.html

Dorset Police. (2021, April). Adult Safeguarding Team response to a freedom-of-information request by the author.

Duggan, M., & Grace, J. (2018). Assessing vulnerabilities in the Domestic Violence Disclosure Scheme. *Child and Family Law Quarterly, 2*, 145.

Durham Constabulary. (2018, April). Clare's Law and Sarah's Law process improvement review—November 2015, author copy, obtained via freedom-of-information request.

Essex Police. (2018). Response to a freedom-of-information request made by the author in May 2018.

Fleury, R. E., Sullivan, C. M., & Bybee, D. I. (2000). When ending the relationship does not end the violence: Women's experiences of violence by former partners. *Violence Against Women, 6*(12), 1363.

GOV.UK. (2020). *Funding boost for rape and domestic abuse support*. [online]. Retrieved March 31, 2021, from https://www.gov.uk/government/news/funding-boost-for-rape-and-domestic-abuse-support

Graham, C. (2018, May). (Norfolk County Community Safety Partnership), *Domestic Homicide Review Report: Review into the death of April in January 2017*.

Hadjimatheou, K., & Grace, J. (2020). 'No black and white answer about how far we can go': Police decision making under the domestic violence disclosure scheme. *Policing and Society*. https://doi.org/10.1080/10439463.2020.1795169

Hancher, L., & Moran, M. (1998). Organizing regulatory space. In R. Baldwin, C. Scott, & C. Hood (Eds.), *A reader on regulation*. Oxford University Press.

Her Majesty's Inspectorate of Constabulary. (2017, March). *PEEL 2016: Police effectiveness 2016—A national overview*. Retrieved June 16, 2020, from https://www.justiceinspectorates.gov.uk/hmic/wp-content/uploads/peel-police-effectiveness-2016.pdf

Her Majesty's Inspectorate of Constabulary. (2018, March). *PEEL 2017: Police effectiveness 2017—A national overview*. Retrieved June 26, 2020, from https://www.justiceinspectorates.gov.uk/hmicfrs/wp-content/uploads/peel-police-effectiveness-2017-1.pdf

Her Majesty's Inspectorate of Constabulary and Fire & Rescue Services. (2018, August 7). Cleveland Police: Crime data integrity inspection 2018. Retrieved June 29, 2020, from https://www.justiceinspectorates.gov.uk/hmicfrs/publications/cleveland-police-crime-data-integrity-inspection-2018

Hertfordshire Constabulary. (2016). Domestic Abuse Action Plan 2016–19. Hertfordshire Constabulary and Police and Crime Commissioner for Hertfordshire, author copy, obtained via freedom-of-information request in April 2018.

HMICFRS. (2018a). *PEEL: Police effectiveness, efficiency and legitimacy 2017—An inspection of Avon and Somerset Police*. Retrieved June 26, 2020, from https://www.justiceinspectorates.gov.uk/hmicfrs/wp-content/uploads/peel-police-effectiveness-2017-avon-and-somerset.pdf

HMICFRS. (2018b). *PEEL: Police effectiveness, efficiency and legitimacy 2017—An inspection of Cheshire Police*. Retrieved June 26, 2020, from https://www.justiceinspectorates.gov.uk/hmicfrs/wp-content/uploads/peel-police-effectiveness-2017-cheshire.pdf

HMICFRS. (2018c). *PEEL: Police effectiveness, efficiency and legitimacy 2017—An inspection of Hertfordshire Police*. Retrieved June 26, 2020, from https://www.justiceinspectorates.gov.uk/hmicfrs/wp-content/uploads/peel-police-effectiveness-2017-hertfordshire.pdf

HMICFRS. (2018d). *PEEL: Police effectiveness, efficiency and legitimacy 2017—An inspection of Lancashire Constabulary*. Retrieved June 26, 2020, from https://www.justiceinspectorates.gov.uk/hmicfrs/wp-content/uploads/peel-police-effectiveness-2017-lancashire.pdf

HMICFRS. (2018e). *PEEL: Police effectiveness, efficiency and legitimacy 2017—An inspection of Lincolnshire Constabulary*. Retrieved June 26, 2020, from https://www.justiceinspectorates.gov.uk/hmicfrs/wp-content/uploads/peel-police-effectiveness-2017-lincolnshire.pdf

HMICFRS. (2018f). *PEEL: Police effectiveness, efficiency and legitimacy 2017—An inspection of Norfolk Constabulary*. Retrieved June 26, 2020, from https://

www.justiceinspectorates.gov.uk/hmicfrs/wp-content/uploads/peel-police-effectiveness-2017-norfolk.pdf

HMICFRS. (2018g). *PEEL: Police effectiveness, efficiency and legitimacy 2017—An inspection of North Yorkshire Police*. Retrieved June 26, 2020, from https://www.justiceinspectorates.gov.uk/hmicfrs/wp-content/uploads/peel-police-effectiveness-2017-north-yorkshire.pdf

HMICFRS. (2018h). *PEEL: Police effectiveness, efficiency and legitimacy 2017—An inspection of Northumbria Police*. Retrieved June 26, 2020, from https://www.justiceinspectorates.gov.uk/hmicfrs/wp-content/uploads/peel-police-effectiveness-2017-northumbria.pdf

HMICFRS. (2018i). *PEEL: Police effectiveness, efficiency and legitimacy 2017—An inspection of the Metropolitan Police*. Retrieved June 26, 2020, from https://www.justiceinspectorates.gov.uk/hmicfrs/wp-content/uploads/peel-police-effectiveness-2017-metropolitan.pdf

HMICFRS. (2018j). *PEEL: Police effectiveness, efficiency and legitimacy 2017—An inspection of South Yorkshire Police*. Retrieved June 26, 2020, from https://www.justiceinspectorates.gov.uk/hmicfrs/wp-content/uploads/peel-police-effectiveness-2017-south-yorkshire.pdf

HMICFRS. (2018k). *PEEL: Police effectiveness, efficiency and legitimacy 2017—An inspection of Suffolk Constabulary*. Retrieved June 26, 2020, from https://www.justiceinspectorates.gov.uk/hmicfrs/wp-content/uploads/peel-police-effectiveness-2017-suffolk.pdf

HMICFRS. (2018l). *PEEL: Police effectiveness, efficiency and legitimacy 2017—An inspection of Sussex Constabulary*. Retrieved June 26, 2020, from https://www.justiceinspectorates.gov.uk/hmicfrs/wp-content/uploads/peel-police-effectiveness-2017-sussex.pdf

HMICFRS. (2018m). *PEEL: Police effectiveness, efficiency and legitimacy 2017—An inspection of Wiltshire Police*. Retrieved June 26, 2020, from https://www.justiceinspectorates.gov.uk/hmicfrs/wp-content/uploads/peel-police-effectiveness-2017-wiltshire.pdf

HMICFRS. (2019). *PEEL: Police effectiveness, efficiency and legitimacy 2018–19—An inspection of Nottinghamshire Police*. Retrieved June 16, 2020, from https://www.justiceinspectorates.gov.uk/hmicfrs/wp-content/uploads/peel-assessment-2018-19-nottinghamshire.pdf

Home Office. (2013a). *Domestic Violence Disclosure Scheme (DVDS) pilot assessment*. London: Home Office.

Home Office. (2013b). Domestic Violence Disclosure Scheme impact assessment. Retrieved June 16, 2020, from https://www.gov.uk/government/uploads/system/uploads/attachment_data/file/260899/DVDS_IA.pdf

Home Office. (2016a). *Domestic Violence Disclosure Scheme (DVDS): One year on—Home Office assessment of national roll-out*. Home Office.

Home Office. (2016b). *Domestic Violence Disclosure Scheme (DVDS) guidance*. Retrieved June 16, 2020, from https://www.gov.uk/government/uploads/system/uploads/attachment_data/file/575361/DVDS_guidance_FINAL_v3.pdf

Independent Office for Police Conduct. (2018, January 7). National recommendation—The Home Office, February 2016. 2015/052671. Retrieved June 29, 2020, from https://policeconduct.gov.uk/recommendations/national-recommendation-home-office-february-2016

Kelly, L., Adler, J. R., Horvath, M. A., Lovett, J., Coulson, M., Kernohan, D., & Gray, M. (2016). *Domestic Violence Protection Orders (DVPO)—One year on: Home Office assessment of national roll-out*. Home Office Science. Home Office. https://assets.publishing.service.gov.uk/government/uploads/system/uploads/attachment_data/file/506148/2016-03-08_DVPO_report_for_publication.pdf

Lancashire Constabulary. (2021). Response to a freedom-of-information request by the author, made in April 2021.

Lowe, Y (2021). 'Women at risk' as police in England and Wales miss Clare's Law deadlines. *The Guardian* [online]. Retrieved May 10, 2021, from https://www.theguardian.com/society/2021/may/09/women-at-risk-as-police-in-england-and-wales-miss-clares-law-deadlines

Marshall, S. (Premier of South Australia). (2020). $600,000 boost to extend DV disclosure scheme and life-saving app. Retrieved June 23, 2020, from https://www.premier.sa.gov.au/news/media-releases/news/$600,000-boost-to-extend-dv-disclosure-scheme-and-life-saving-app

Metropolitan Police Service. (2020). Response to a freedom-of-information request submitted by the author in February 2020.

Middlesbrough Community Safety Partnership. (2021). *Domestic Homicide Review—Overview Report—'Jean'—Died October 2018*. [online]. Retrieved June 22, 2021, from https://www.middlesbrough.gov.uk/sites/default/files/DA-DHR4-report.pdf

Northumbria Police. (2018a). Domestic Violence Disclosure Scheme briefing note—January 2018, author copy, obtained by freedom-of-information request in April 2018.

Northumbria Police. (2018b, December). Evaluation Report—Domestic Violence Disclosure Scheme (Clare's Law), author copy, obtained by freedom-of-information request in April 2021.

Nottinghamshire Police. (2019). Clare's Law: Domestic Violence Disclosure Scheme—Twelve Month Review, author copy, obtained by freedom-of-information request in April 2021.

Nottinghamshire Police. (2021). Clare's Law: Domestic Violence Disclosure Scheme—Twelve Month Review, author copy, obtained by freedom-of-information request in April 2021.

Office for National Statistics. (2017, November 23). *Domestic abuse in England and Wales, year ending March 2017*. Retrieved June 29, 2020, from https://www.ons.gov.uk/peoplepopulationandcommunity/crimeandjustice/bulletins/domesticabuseinenglandandwales/yearendingmarch2017

Queensland Law Reform Commission. (2017, June). *Domestic Violence Disclosure Scheme* (Report No. 75). Retrieved June 23, 2020, from http://www.qlrc.qld.gov.au/__data/assets/pdf_file/0010/541189/qlrc-report-no-75.pdf

South Yorkshire Police. (2021). Extract from 'PVP Performance and Governance Overview Report', author copy, response to a freedom-of-information request made in April 2021.

Staffordshire Police. (2021). Response to a freedom-of-information request made by the author in April 2021.

Thomas, R. (2014, September 9). Administrative justice, better decisions, and organisational learning. *UK Const. L. Blog*. Retrieved June 26, 2020, from https://ukconstitutionallaw.org/2014/09/09/robert-thomas-administrative-justice-better-decisions-and-organisational-learning/

Urbis. (2020). NSW Domestic Violence Disclosure Scheme evaluation and crisis assistance service review pilots—Final Report. Retrieved June 23, 2020, from https://www.women.nsw.gov.au/__data/assets/pdf_file/0004/670009/Domestic-Violence-Disclosure-Scheme-Pilot-Evaluation-and-Crisis-Assistance-Scheme-Review-Final-Report.pdf

West Mercia Police and Warwickshire Police. (2018a). Extract from a report about 'Threat Assessment', author copy, obtained via a freedom-of-information request submitted in April 2018.

West Mercia Police and Warwickshire Police. (2018b). Extract—CSODS and DVDS, author copy, obtained via a freedom-of-information request submitted in April 2018.

West Midlands Police. (2021). Response to a freedom of information request made by the author in April 2021.

6

Domestic Abuse Disclosure Schemes in a Complex 'Regulatory Space'

6.1 Introduction

It is important to understand some of the regulatory and structural reasons why the policing of domestic abuse, and particularly for this book, why the operation of the DVDS and similar DADS may be made very difficult by contextual and institutional factors. By taking a step back to look at the regulation of the 'bigger picture' around DADS, this chapter uses regulatory theory in detail, and in order to attain new theoretical insights into the operation of the DADS and their place in the general public service architecture of the prevention of domestic violence in UK criminal justice governance today. A further aim of this chapter is to highlight that as much as DADS are concerned with the regulation of (and the prevention of) domestic violence in a particular manner, it is also about the regulation of potential *victims* of domestic violence. The nine regulatory problems that this chapter identifies play out across different granular tiers of regulation of DADS—at micro-level (amongst police forces); at meso-level (at a national level amongst police inspectorates and government departments) and at macro-level (dealing with

J. Grace, *Domestic Abuse Disclosure Schemes*,
https://doi.org/10.1007/978-3-030-89039-1_6

supra-national policy and legal frameworks). These divisions of the regulation of DADS are explored below.

The prevention of domestic violence in intimate relationships is, conceptually speaking, a prominent and highly complex 'regulatory space' (Hancher & Moran, 1998). The intimacy of a relationship does not preclude, however, given the 'politics of public protection' (Nash, 2010), the increasing interventionism by the state over time into this private sphere. This is because, in part, with the prevention of domestic violence, as with all questions of balancing public protection concerns with the perceived limits of state power, there are "no obvious limits of boundaries to regulation" (Hancher & Moran, 1998: 154). It is normally seen in the public law field that Parliament, as the UK 'super-regulator', will use its lawmaking sovereignty to set the overall macro-level regulatory framework for a public protection issue. Then there is meso-level regulation carried out by secretaries of state and their central government departments in issuing guidance underpinned by statute for local policy actors to follow, in turn, in dealing with public protection issues at the micro-regulatory, even case-by-case, level. Media, civil society and the electorate then play a systemic, interrelating role in shaping the priorities of all three tiers of regulatory actors outlined here.

This chapter takes, as its starting assumption, the idea that the DVDS is a policy intervention into a 'regulatory space'. That is, the policing of domestic violence—and in particular, responding to the risk posed to victims in potentially or currently abusive relationships, where there is some track record of abuse in the past of one partner. The DVDS is also a recent example of a newly made 'regulatory space', in and of itself. The DVDS inserts itself into the relationship/regulatory space between two individuals, who are in or who have been in an intimate relationship with each other, and hitherto unoccupied by the police as a (potential) actor in quite the same manner. Violent relationships have been subject to other forms of regulation under the law as it has developed for some time. These include legal remedies such as non-molestation orders, or the relatively new Domestic Violence Protection Notices and Orders (DVPNs and DVPOs), which came into national operation in March 2014, like the DVDS in England and Wales—although unlike the DVDS, DVPNs and DVPOs benefited from being originally founded in new statute law (the Crime and Security Act 2010), in terms of regulatory control, and their clarity of purpose in a public policy sense.

6.2 Disclosure Schemes as 'Regulatory Spaces'

The concept of 'regulatory space' comprises a number of key facets or dimensions. As Hancher and Moran (1998: 153) have outlined:

> The concept of regulatory space is an analytical construct. ... First, precisely because it is a space it is available for occupation. Secondly, because it is a space it can be divided unevenly between actors: there could, in other words, be major and minor participants in the regulatory process. Thirdly, just as we can identify a general concept of regulatory space in operation in a particular community we can also speak of specific concepts of regulatory space at work in individual sectors. ... Fourthly ... boundaries which demarcate regulatory space are defined in turn by a range of issues, so it is sensible to speak of regulatory space as encompassing a range of regulatory issues in a community.

When we come to measuring who are both the major and minor participants in the regulatory space that is a DADS, on a micro-level, it is plain that this varies according to whether one considers the Right to Ask or the Right to Know. In terms of the Right to Ask, the police and an applicant under the Scheme are the relevant principal actors. But in terms of the Right to Know, another public protection-oriented agency, such as a local authority, that itself makes an application to the police under the Scheme then suddenly becomes a key policy actor at that micro-level regulation of the relationship/regulatory space, with regard to one possibly abusive relationship. Furthermore, and again with the Right to Know strand of a DADS, the (possible) victim of domestic violence is then arguably relegated to the category, in a sense, of being a secondary actor in the regulatory space of the Scheme at a micro-level—and in a sense is only afforded the same share of the space *always* occupied by the *subject* of a potential disclosure. Thus sometimes, as with the subjects of disclosures, victims can be treated, regardless of whether we mean under the Right to Know or Right to Ask variant of the Scheme, as only a manageable risk of harm.

Different actors will see the regulatory space of the DVDS differently, depending on their policy priorities and regulatory roles. Police would approach a DADS application as an exercise in determining whether a disclosure should be made as an aid to crime prevention (i.e., the prevention of domestic violence). However, other professionals such as probation officers or social workers might see the disclosure of information by the police, responsible for the end of a violent relationship, as something which may, however, generate a different type of public protection work. In this example, the follow-on regulatory challenge is also with regard to the effects on the ongoing rehabilitation of an offender, since, for example, there is evidence to show that the breakdown of a relationship will precipitate offending on the part of a violent (ex-)partner, as noted by Duggan (2018a).

The operation of the DVDS is a micro-level *interventionary* regulatory space in and of itself. Disclosures are first considered and then possibly made by the police in an attempt to preclude domestic violence from arising in a relationship between two people. But the DVDS also operates in a wider, meso-level *directive* regulatory space—namely efforts by the police, the Home Office and other policy actors to attempt to prevent domestic violence through a number of other means, taken as a whole. Above those first two regulatory spaces sits a macro-level and *supervisory* regulatory space: of the courts and of Parliament, who ultimately delineate the interventionary and directive regulatory spaces that between them create, sustain and apply the Scheme as a creature of public protection policy. (There is a supra-national dimension to the macro-level regulation of a public protection or information disclosure issue, of course.) As Chap. 7 will address in detail, European human rights law and European Union data protection law have played a contextual role in shaping the ambit and operation of DADS in the UK, for example. Chapter 7 will make the case that European legal norms should be brought much more centrally into the detail of the guidance on the DVDS in England and Wales, with regard to the European Convention on Human Rights (ECHR) (1950) in particular.

However, there is an argument to be made that the Scheme can be viewed as an under-regulated space. On the micro-level, much discretion is afforded the police in interpreting the existence of the 'pressing need' that is a legal requisite for a disclosure under the Scheme. The Scheme could be said to be an under-regulated space on the meso-level, since little if any clear direction has been given to police forces, to date, by the Home Office or other policy actors, such as HMICFRS, as to how the Scheme should be aligned with the best interests of children (discussed in more detail in Chap. 7), or operated with a conscious regard to the human rights of victims of domestic violence (again, discussed in Chap. 7), or with a view to the experience of domestic violence when it comes to specific issues relating to the ethnicity or sexuality of victims, for example (as was highlighted in Chap. 2). Finally, at the macro-level, the Scheme could be said to be under-regulated since it remains a creature of policy and ultimately of the common law in terms of its doctrinal underpinnings (S.77 of the new Domestic Abuse Act 2021 does not alter the common law basis of the power to disclose under 'Clare's Law' in England and Wales—it simply requires police forces to have regard to Home Office guidance, which is now 'statutory' in nature). By contrast, many wider interventions in the realm of the prevention of domestic violence are statutory in nature, and newer interventions such as Domestic Abuse Protection Orders have been created on a statutory basis even at the time of writing in the new Domestic Abuse Act 2021. The courts have consistently afforded the police an ambit of discretion in local policy-making around disclosures of intelligence for public protection and crime reduction purposes (see Chap. 7 for details on common law powers of the police), but this chapter must consider whether the approach to the regulation of the Scheme, to date, represents an under-regulation of a policy space. This is part of a thorough analysis, in this chapter, of the regulatory responsibility shared across an array of policy actors for the operation of the Scheme.

As well as the issue of potential under-regulation of the DADS as regulatory spaces is the problem that arises from the very nature of the tiered system of regulation at micro-, meso- and macro-levels, when examined from the perspective of literature on 'multi-level governance'. As Bache and Flinders (2004: 37) explain:

> It is important to appreciate that not all relationships are channelled hierarchically in terms of passing through every tier of governance. In reality, it is increasingly common for sub-national actors and supra-national actors to communicate directly without working through the national level. This challenges the gatekeeping capacity of national executives.

The complexities of multi-level governance for Domestic Abuse Disclosure Schemes become a number of distinct regulatory problems. Before this chapter begins to sketch the nine regulatory problems that are a concern in relation to DADS and in particular the DVDS, it is first useful to consider the 'grammar' of the analytical construct that is regulatory space. Briefly, an initial overview must be given of the relationship between law and regulation as tools of the multi-level governance described here. Andrew Sanders (2008: 49; citing Crawford, 2006: 449) has noted that:

> Regulation has three elements: the goal (the rule or standard against which behaviour is to be compared and contrasted); monitoring (to monitor or evaluate what happens in pursuance of the goal); and realignment (a mechanism for enforcing rules where monitoring shows significant deviation from them).

The DVDS is a policy with a *goal* to regulate the prevention of domestic violence, in a particular manner, namely by regulating the behaviour of (potential) victims of domestic violence and by regulating the disclosure of information about offenders, as relevant. The DVDS is *monitored* in its operation by different bodies in a hierarchical manner, chiefly the Home Office and Her Majesty's Inspectorate of Constabulary, Fire and Rescue Services (HMICFRS). Both of these bodies have shown themselves, in terms of *realignment* and as discussed in Chaps. 2 and 3, to be 'realigning' the Scheme in a piecemeal fashion, where disparate approaches to police practice and hard-to-define legal tests for disclosure are concerned. The DVDS can be readily said to be an example of structural regulation of policing behaviour itself, too. For Andrew Sanders (2008: 49), in the policing context, structural regulation stresses "the broader social structures which shape police behaviour"; and the DVDS, as we have seen, is starting to become more and more deeply embedded in the landscape of policing of domestic abuse in the UK and elsewhere.

So this chapter posits that the DVDS is an item of structural regulation of the prevention of domestic violence; and while there might not be 'huge numbers' of applications and disclosures under the Scheme, per capita, the Scheme gives the police the regulatory mandate to enlist victims in the regulation of the prevention of domestic violence, and so aid them in their mission to maintain order. Such 'regulatory pluralism' has the involvement of third parties (here, victims themselves) as commonplace (Sanders, 2008: 50). In reality the prominence, use and interconnected nature of the Scheme as a policy innovation in the area of offender management, as well as public protection or victim safeguarding, is something that impacts the work of other agencies and regulatory bodies aside from police organisational structures. This raises considerable questions over the extent to which the operation of the Scheme aligns with notions of 'regulatory formalism'.

The notion that the state should have overall responsibility to strategise, to create policy and to *regulate* in order to prevent and reduce levels of domestic violence, or to regulate to affect any societal behaviour, is characteristic of what Braithwaite would model as an aspect of 'regulatory formalism' (Braithwaite, 2002). In general, and in the context of this book, state actors are more senior actors in a hierarchical formalist regulatory structure. State actors have a greater ability to influence and direct other agencies or actors in a regulatory system. State actors are also senior in the particular context of the operation of the Domestic Violence Disclosure Scheme (with the Scheme as only one potential means of preventing domestic violence). State actors rely on the *hierarchical* nature of relevant regulatory systems to exert their influence. As Garland (1996: 448) has highlighted, in the context of UK policing:

> The notion that a single sovereign power could govern all social life was enhanced in the mid-nineteenth century by the creation of a strong state apparatus, and in particular, by the development of a public police force which came to be regarded, however inaccurately, as having a professional monopoly over the function of crime control.

While on a superficial level the 'professional monopoly' over the operation of the Scheme is possessed by the 43 different police forces in England and Wales today, in reality the control and regulation of the Scheme is a more nuanced issue—not least because, as we will see in more detail, (potential) victims of domestic violence are involved in the operation and regulation of the Scheme. But in the sense of an alternative theoretical model of regulation to that of measuring the degree of regulatory *formalism* present as a quality of the Scheme, there is another scale upon which the Scheme also clearly falls: *responsive regulation*. As an alternative theoretical model to regulatory formalism, and with respect to the nature of what is termed *responsive* regulation, Braithwaite (2014: 432) has explained that responsive regulation "is about the idea that regulation is more likely to be just and effective when it is contextually responsive to environments, social and physical, particularly to how regulated actors are responding to attempts to regulate them".

Thus 'responsive regulation' is regulation which is attuned and recognisant to the need to involve an actor in their own self-regulation (Braithwaite, 2002). The DVDS is a form of 'responsive regulation' and is one manner of preventing domestic violence, at the level of an individual, potential victim of domestic violence to whom a disclosure about a 'risky' partner may be made. The recipient of that information is thereby encouraged to manage their own relationship with that 'risky' person; perhaps to leave them or end the relationship in some manner, or to otherwise attempt to reduce their own vulnerability or likelihood of victimisation somehow. In this way the Scheme might be thought of as 'responsibilising' victims in a manner that is a gamble with their vulnerabilities. If this 'responsive regulation' of the prevention of the domestic violence through the responsibilisation of potential victims as an aspect of the Scheme seems somewhat inappropriate, it is perhaps because the prevention of crime or the deterrence of offenders is most commonly seen as the purview of the state.

6.3 The Regulation of the DVDS in England and Wales

The operation of the Domestic Violence Disclosure Scheme is conducted chiefly by the police in England and Wales, but it is situated within the purview of a number of regulatory agencies with the 'polycentric' regulation of the criminal justice system. Bodies responsible for the oversight of the broader policy aim of the prevention of domestic violence (which the Scheme aligns with) include HMICFRS, the National Police Chiefs' Council (NPCC), the College of Policing, Police and Crime Commissioners and their Police and Crime Panels, as well as, most importantly, the Home Office and Ministry of Justice as key central government departments. These bodies are very much oriented in their work towards particular national strategies such as preventing violence against women and girls (VAWG).

The operation of the Scheme cuts across the different regulatory capacities of a number of regulatory actors in the criminal justice system, and their regulatory functions in pursuing stated policy objectives, such as the reduction of violence against women and girls (e.g., in the case of the Home Office). This occurs in a way that requires in certain instances the application of policy in terms of the management of police information and intelligence, for example (HMIC, 2015). This is an example of 'decentred' or 'polycentric' regulation of policy and practice (in the use of information and intelligence sharing towards the prevention of domestic violence) in effect. 'Polycentric regulation' and 'decentred regulation' are drawn upon here as concepts from work by Black (2007: 58). These concepts support the idea that the Domestic Violence Disclosure Scheme, particularly through the Right to Know strand, is best understood as something that potentially engages large swathes of the criminal justice system. The Scheme may also involve even broader portions of the public protection 'landscape' in its impacts, also involving health and social care agencies and actors. For example, as McCarthy, Hunt and Milne-Skillman (2017: 279) have observed in relation to the potential protection of women with learning disabilities from domestic violence:

> Healthcare and social care professionals have a role in making women with learning disabilities aware of relevant laws and how to invoke them … knowledge of the Domestic Violence Disclosure Scheme … could be very useful to women with learning disabilities entering new relationships and who are worried about their partners behaviour. However, they are likely to need help to understand the process of applying for disclosure, as well as the rights and responsibilities attached to it.

Given the observations of McCarthy, Hunt and Milne-Skillman here, we can see that the creation of the Scheme has presented both an opportunity and a challenge for professionals working outside of the criminal justice system but still connected with the 'politics of public protection' (Nash, 2010). Just from this one example alone we can see that the Scheme is operated on a 'decentred' basis on the 'frontline' of safeguarding work.

As Black (2007) might explain it, the DVDS is a 'decentred' regulatory approach, rather than an example of *true* regulatory 'polycentrism', because there is no 'de-apexing' of the Domestic Violence Disclosure Scheme. This is because there is still a sole 'apex' (or chief) regulatory actor, as the Home Office clearly write and publish the Scheme guidance. The Home Office are also the chief strategy owners of government work within the criminal justice system to prevent 'violence against women and girls' and other forms of domestic abuse. On the other hand, 'public protection', a broader policy concept than the prevention of domestic violence, is a much more complex 'polycentric' area of regulation—since 'public protection' includes issues such as the management and supervision of all offenders in the community (and not just serial domestic violence perpetrators), or the protection of children in schools, or the safeguarding of vulnerable adults in hospitals, for example—the domains of the Ministry of Justice, the Department of Education and the Department of Health, at the least.

The business of public protection is played out in this way not just between different police organisations but probation agencies, prison authorities, local authorities, educational establishments (in primary, secondary, further and higher education sectors), as well as National Health Service bodies, central government departments, and so on. These sorts of bodies and agencies all have a distinct political and professional interest in crime prevention through the most accurate, effective and prompt sharing of 'criminality information' (Grace, 2013) or public protection risk information. The crimes to be prevented are chiefly viewed, as a more pressing priority, as those potential sexual or violent crimes against the person (Robbins et al., 2014; Home Office, 2014). In the 'public protection routine' this crime prevention is typically the result of the minimisation or the outright avoidance of vulnerable children and adults coming into inappropriate contact with 'risky' individuals. This process of information sharing-driven efforts to prevent sexual or violent crimes is commonly known as child or adult 'safeguarding' (Stevens, 2015). There are thus, given the wider array of settings where criminality information sharing can facilitate better-informed decision-making in relation to such 'safeguarding' issues, a very considerable number of different contexts and purposes within which that criminality information sharing becomes crucial (Robbins et al., 2014; Home Office, 2014).

Criminality information sharing can take the form of disclosures by the police and other public protection agencies to members of the public who are at risk of harm themselves, or to parents of children at risk of harm, or to employers, whose places of business might be the potential site of criminal offences by particular 'risky' individuals. This mixture of different strategies for crime prevention based on the disclosure of criminality information includes the Domestic Violence Disclosure Scheme.

The careful balance between, on the one hand, public protection, and the protection of the rights and wellbeing of the vulnerable and the at-risk and, on the other hand, the protection of the rights and proportionate privacy protection for 'risky' individuals requires a careful and complex 'polycentric' regulatory arrangement for each and every one of the methods or avenues of using criminality information to guide decision-making in the policing of domestic abuse. An HMICFRS update report from 2019, on the policing of domestic abuse, explained that police forces in England and Wales "need monitoring processes, supported by accurate data, to ensure that they are taking positive action such as arrest, and are making effective use of powers, for example domestic violence protection orders and the Domestic Violence Disclosure Scheme" (HMICFRS, 2019: 64).

Reports of investigations by the Independent Office for Police Conduct (IOPC) show, however, that the use of a power like that to make disclosures under the DVDS can be error-prone for a wide range of reasons. The IOPC reported in June 2020 that a member of Wiltshire Police staff had been investigated and disciplined for misconduct after it transpired that they had badly handled a 'Right to Ask' request. The officer checked the date of birth of a man whose partner enquired about him under the DVDS using the date of birth as she had supplied it to Wiltshire police. This date of birth was incorrect, and the man had in fact a considerable history of perpetrating domestic abuse against previous partners. The woman was then seriously assaulted by the partner she had enquired about. The IOPC review of the matter determined that all 'Right to Ask' applicants should be met with in person so that further questions can be asked about the potential subject of a disclosure (IOPC, 2020a). In December 2020, the IOPC released their findings in relation to an investigation of a Derbyshire case where a woman had been stabbed by a man with a history of violence against her and other victims in the past. The IOPC found that as well as failings in relation to the non-recording of reports of violence by Aaron Booth towards his victim, there should have been consideration for making a DVDS disclosure to that victim about Booth's offending history before he stabbed her with a knife (IOPC, 2020b). The IOPC also reported "a failure to take appropriate steps following an application for disclosure under the Domestic Violence Disclosure Scheme" in relation to a harassment case that eventually led to the death by suicide of a woman and the conviction of her ex-partner for (presumably constructive act) manslaughter in 2017 (IOPC, 2019). However, an IOPC report from 2018 shows that the DVDS process can muddle the proper police response to a report of domestic violence, as, in relation to a Northamptonshire case in 2017, instead of attending a property and interviewing and potentially arresting an offender and deploying a DVPN, following a report of domestic abuse from a victim over the phone, the process for a DVDS disclosure was followed because these were the victim's wishes. After the victim had been graded as being a low risk, and while officers were waiting for a window of opportunity to visit the victim when her partner was not around in order to progress her DVDS application, her abusive partner abducted and assaulted her (IOPC, 2018).

6.4 The Regulation of Victim Self-regulation

To summarise the key points made by this chapter so far, while the DVDS itself is a form of decentred regulation in the prevention of domestic violence, the involvement of other regulatory structures in the wider criminal justice system entails that public protection is a polycentric regulatory exercise. For example, the hierarchical, capacity of the Ministry of Justice (MoJ), and the regulatory functions of MoJ-subordinate bodies in the probation field (such as the National Offender Management Service, or NOMS), entail that the management of serial domestic violence perpetrators in the community is a multi-agency, and polycentric, regulatory exercise. This is because the police (subordinate to the Home Office) are also responsible for managing individual interventions to prevent offending under statutory multi-agency public protection arrangements (MAPPAs) created under the Criminal Justice Act 2003.

The 'responsive' regulatory nature of the Scheme, that is, the manner in which the regulation of the prevention of domestic violence via the Scheme, is undertaken through the regulatory 'enrolment' of a chief protagonist; namely, the (potential) victim of that domestic violence. According to the model and theory of the *responsive* 'regulatory pyramid' (Braithwaite, 2002), the uptake and use of the Domestic Violence Disclosure Scheme should be, at least in theory, one of the most common, if not the most common, triggers for state actor involvement in the context of preventing domestic violence, at least that committed by serial domestic violence perpetrators. This is because the Scheme is always at least partly about 'responsive' regulation and the involvement of (potential) victims in their own self-regulation. As Braithwaite (2014: 432) has noted:

> The regulatory pyramid is an aspect of responsive regulation that designs a mix of regulatory options by arraying them hierarchically, with the least

interventionist options intended to be the most common at the base of the pyramid.

By placing the onus on victims and potential victims of domestic violence to regulate themselves (i.e., to minimise the risk of coming to harm through domestic violence themselves, through exercising more informed choice over their personal relationships once a relevant disclosure by the police is made to them), the Scheme is clearly an exercise in 'self-regulation' for those victims or potential victims. In this way the Scheme is an example of what Black has referred to as the 'new challenge' of 'regulation of self-regulation' (Black, 2001: 104), as well as, more plainly and controversially, what can be referred to as questionable victim responsibilisation (Duggan, 2012). Less controversial in this sense than the operation of the DVDS, and to be welcomed, are the results of the three-year piloting of the 'Drive' programme, which focused on issues of *offender* self-regulation, but which focused on intensive interventions to assist serial domestic violence perpetrators change their offending behaviour (Bows, 2016; Shaw, 2020).

'Self-regulation' of course also has a certain meaning in an emotional or psychological sense, as reflected in a distinct body of academic literature; it can be seen in that sense as an explicably emotional or rational failure to manage one's own risk more carefully following a disclosure by the police; and can as such also be termed self-'underregulation' (Baumeister & Heatherton, 1996). The self-under-regulation by potential victims of domestic violence, who do not themselves act upon police disclosures to preclude any risk to them from escalating, in turn, present a regulatory challenge for the police and other agencies in public protection 'networks' to resolve.

The 'responsive regulatory conversation' of the Scheme is understandably something which might be seen as evidence of empowerment for the potential victims of domestic violence, and disclosures of information by the police certainly make victims as self-regulators better aware of potential risks posed to them. But there is a difficulty in seeing the Scheme as enhancing 'informed choices' for potential victims. This could be if, for example, through deciding upon *non-action* ('not leaving him', stereotypically) as the response to a disclosure by the police under the Scheme, a mother (typically) is automatically subject to more intense scrutiny or investigation by the social services department of a local authority because of a perceived increased risk to her children. In Chap. 2, I highlighted traces of this by-product of operating the DVDS in England and Wales when presenting two case studies on 'Clare's Law' from reported care order cases. And as Nicole Westmarland (2015: 27) has observed, "In multi-agency meetings I have attended, there seems an almost automatic referral to Children's Services if women with children decide not to leave their partner after being told about his violent past".

It is possible to give a theoretical account of the means by which a policy idea, even one with its criticisms and which has never been rigorously evaluated, may spread; perhaps because of the political capital to be won by a 'director' agency like a central government department (like the Home Office) keen to be seen throwing the proverbial kitchen sink at a blight on society such as domestic violence. A department of justice in one jurisdiction will face many of the same public protection challenges and associated political problems and pressures faced by any other, and so the 'mimetic isomorphism' (Halliday, 2013: 319) entailed in adopting an unevaluated but attractive-looking policy initiative from another jurisdiction may be hard to resist. And the junior partners in any arrangement within that jurisdiction (including mid-level regulators such as an Inspectorate of Constabulary, or any number of regional police forces themselves) will struggle to resist evolving national policy in any hierarchical regulatory arrangement; thus producing 'coercive isomorphism' in relation to the 'regulatory space' that defines a quickly spreading policy notion such as Domestic Abuse Disclosure Schemes. However, overly hasty 'coercive isomorphism' could produce what Paul Carney would describe as 'uninformed' policy transfer: "when the borrowing country has incomplete information about the crucial elements that made the policy a success in the lending country" (Cairney, 2012: 259). If the policy concerned was in fact not a success in its original jurisdiction, however, this can result in Cairney's 'inappropriate transfer' (Cairney, 2012: 259): "when not enough attention is paid to adaptation or the differences in policy conditions, structures and aims of the lending country".

It may well be that any difficulties with officer engagement with the DVDS in England and Wales may well stem from a lack of 'normative isomorphism' (Halliday, 2013: 319) in relation to the Scheme, with perhaps some frontline officers unable to accept the mantra of disclosures under 'Clare's Law' as something that can empower a potential victim of domestic violence to make 'informed choices' about their own safeguarding. It must be difficult to be optimistic about this purported aspect of the DVDS when one has professional experience of the struggles that victims of an abusive or controlling relationship may often face to re-acquire a sense of autonomy and empowerment.

At this juncture it is appropriate to catalogue a thorough set of the regulatory problems existing across different tiers of the multi-level governance of the DADS in the UK, as have come to light through the application of the regulatory tools explored up to this point in this chapter, as well as the policy analyses of previous chapters.

6.5 Nine Regulatory Problems Concerning the Operation of DADS in the UK

There are nine regulatory problems which amount, between them, as to why Domestic Abuse Disclosure Schemes in the UK today may be a poor series of criminal justice policy developments, in the 'regulatory spaces' of domestic violence prevention, whether at 'micro-levels', 'meso-levels' or 'macro-levels' of that public protection regulatory space. In this section, a 'regulatory problem' is taken to mean a breach of the standards of sound and appropriate regulation in a judgement informed by the regulatory literature surveyed by the earlier sections of this chapter. Overall, the argument is built in this section that there has been a failure of *regulatory responsibility* on the part of national government when it comes to DADS in the UK today.

The nine regulatory problems highlighted in this chapter can be characterised in many ways as problems stemming from under-regulation, and are broken down into three groups, each with three problems. The three groupings of problems each focus on regulation at a particular level of the 'regulatory space' that is a Disclosure Scheme.

Regulatory Problems at the Micro-Level of the DADS

Firstly, there is a considerable problem, at the micro-level of the regulation of the DADS, and the micro-regulation of abusive relationships that is a Disclosure Scheme, when it comes to the issues of 'fragmentation of knowledge' (Black, 2001: 107). Police organisations may not know of all the risk-related information it is possible to know about an individual, potential offender and domestic violence perpetrator. As Fitz-Gibbon and Walklate (2017: 291) have observed:

> A key impediment to the effectiveness of Clare's Law lies in the hidden nature of domestic violence. Both elements of the Scheme [rely] on the accuracy of information contained in the Police National Computer (PNC), available to all police forces carrying details of convictions, bail conditions, custodial history, pending prosecutions, cautions, driving records, reprimands formal warnings among other details.

As Duggan (2018b: 213) has put it:

> The DVDS is predicated on preventing future victimisation (the abuse of the new partner) through a reliance on the commission of a previous crime and existing victim, thus in order for future criminality to be prevented it must have been committed (and recorded) for the necessary information to exist.

This gives rise to the regulatory problem of the 'false negative' from a public protection perspective—where the police wrongly but rationally conclude an individual situation does not warrant a disclosure under the rules of the DADS concerned, given the information that is known at that time. The capacity and ability of the police to disclose only what they know, as Duggan and Grace (2018: 165–166) have concluded, entails that the framework for DADS in the UK today "fundamentally overlooks the abuser who has hitherto escaped detection". 'False negatives' put the rights and wellbeing of victims at risk. For example, the Queensland Law Reform Commission, in concluding that a DVDS for Queensland was not to be recommended, noted that a key theme of their consultation were the “safety concerns arising from inaccurate disclosure or non-disclosure, which might give rise to a false sense of safety” on the part of potential or future victims (QLRC, 2017: iii). At the same time, albeit as less of a public protection concern, there is the issue of ‘false positives’, where the police rationally, but unhelpfully, make a disclosure about a risky individual under the Scheme to their partner, when in truth that individual does not then go on to offend against that partner, or any other partner. It should be noted that these ‘false positives’ put the privacy rights of reformed or reforming offenders at risk.

The second problem at the micro-regulatory level of DADS is the disparity in the outcome of applications under the two strands of each DADS in operation in the UK today, expressed as a rate of disclosures versus applications for disclosures; and the rate of applications and disclosures per capita by police force area. Disparities in the operation of DADS in the UK have rendered the application of ‘Clare’s Law’ by police forces a ‘postcode lottery’ (Grace, 2018) and a serious regulatory concern, therefore. There is no obvious benchmark to be sought for the rate of applications per capita, and no obvious standard by which the rate of disclosures versus potential disclosures should be judged.

In November 2018, however, the BBC revealed, following a series of their own freedom-of-information requests, that there are issues with forces not recording disclosure decision-making in a standardised way. BBC journalist Francesca Williams specifically cited Cumbria police, with their high disclosure rates as reported by the ONS, as a force acknowledging their own exclusion of ‘mischief-making’ applications, and applications for which there was nothing to disclose about a subject, from the data returned to the Home Office and the ONS about the DVDS (Williams, 2018). Other forces would presumably not take this approach, resulting in lower disclosure rates overall in that case. However, it should also be noted that ONS data on the DVDS in the year to March 2019 and the year to March 2020 still saw some outlier forces reporting much higher than average disclosure rates—so perhaps little has been done by the Home Office, HMICFRS or the ONS regulators to check this poor consistency in data reporting, if indeed this is an issue.

The third problem at the micro-regulatory level of DADS in the UK today is the qualitatively different practices that occur with regard to the operation of DADS at force level, as revealed by inspection reports and policy overviews from police monitoring bodies, and as explored in earlier work in this book. As Duggan and Grace (2018) have highlighted, the police inspectorate have been urging individual police forces to review their use of the Scheme but little evidence is in the public domain to suggest this practice of evaluation in detail of the force-level use of DADS has begun to take off. Research for this book (see Chap. 5) has started to uncover the force-level self-regulation that has taken place in England and Wales to date, at least.

Regulatory Problems at the Meso-Level of the DADS

At the meso-regulatory level, DADS in the UK to date have suffered from the following three regulatory problems: the first of these is a lack of an offender management and rehabilitation emphasis in policy development terms. Richard Ericson and Kevin Haggerty would not have been surprised by an under-emphasis on the rehabilitation rights of serial domestic violence perpetrators in relation to the lack of a complete bar on the disclosure of spent convictions and cautions under the DVDS, for example. As the authors of *Policing the Risk Society* explained, in 1997, one "may possibly escape one's past, but never institutional futures" (Ericson & Haggerty, 1997: 119). Official guidance on DADS in the UK is published for a police audience only, and places an emphasis on police roles in public protection and the prevention of domestic violence—no official guidance exists for probation officers or social workers as to how DADS should be approached, even though DADS in the UK today are each to some extent based around multi-agency decision-making, which would include non-police agencies as part of the disclosure-making processes concerned. No substantial evidence is yet available that shows how social workers or probation officers may feel about the operation of DADS with regard to an offender rehabilitation perspective, for example, and the Home Office have hardly sought this out, beyond involving some non-police agency participants in the DVDS pilot evaluation focus groups (Home Office, 2013). This Home Office failure arguably has serious repercussions in the longer term for a subset of reformed and reforming perpetrators. Writing about the practice of disclosures of non-conviction information and other items of police intelligence with lower levels of provenance in Enhanced Criminal Record Certificates, Joe Purshouse (2018: 684) has noted that while "it may seem counterintuitive, selective protection against non-conviction disclosure may also serve the public's interest in crime prevention and public safety", since, in the employment context: "such disclosure may … diminish the individual's social bonds to the community, increasing the likelihood that the individual will engage in offending behaviour".

Secondly, there have been a series of uncritical steps and policy moves with regard to the roll-out of DADS in the UK. As the Queensland Law Reform Commission have observed (QLRC, 2017: 143–144), Home Office reviews of the pilot of Clare's Law and of the roll-out of the DVDS 'one year on' were problematic, as these "reviews were limited to assessments of how the Scheme process was working in practice; they did not consider the impact of the scheme on the incidence of domestic and family violence, or analyse its 'value for money'."

Thirdly, there are problems arising, in a regulatory sense, from a minimal, non-transparent process of evaluation in relation to DADS in the UK. For example, before it was rolled out across the whole of Scotland, the DSDAS had a pilot phase in Ayrshire and Aberdeen, which was evaluated by academics from the University of Glasgow. This study (University of Glasgow, 2015) was not published (I obtained a copy of it through an FOI request as part of the research for this book), and the DSDAS was ultimately rolled out across Scotland without any public reference to or discussion of the study, even though the Glasgow study's authors also found that the focus groups of police officers from Aberdeen and Ayrshire, where the DSDAS had been piloted, raised a number of concerns about the Scheme, since although the "potential to act as a deterrent in the long run was acknowledged, it was felt that disclosures might escalate and indeed precipitate [domestic abuse] incidents in the short term" (University of Glasgow, 2015: 10).

The three meso-level or national-scope regulatory problems I have focused on here have been the lack of focus on offender rehabilitation on drawing up the scope and system of the UK DADS; a lack of proper assessment of disclosures (under the DVDS, as the original UK DADS);

and a lack of transparency in evaluating the DSDAS before it was adopted for the whole of Scotland, despite some misgivings from officers involved in the pilot. However, these problems are not insurmountable, and could readily be addressed by policymakers across the UK, if they could summon the political will.

Regulatory Problems at the Macro-Level of the DADS

At the macro-regulatory level, DADS in the UK continue to be faced by three key regulatory problems—and these have a kind of near-permanency, in the current status quo, compared to the manner in which the three meso-level regulatory problems, as outlined above, could be addressed in actions and programmes of regulatory reform.

Firstly, the continuing legal basis of the three DADS in operation in the UK today varies between the three jurisdictions of England and Wales, Scotland and Northern Ireland. The DVDS in England and Wales is based upon police common law powers to disclose information for public protection purposes where there is a 'pressing need' to do so in a proportionate and reasonable way. In Scotland, the DSDAS draws, according to its 'standard operating procedures' (Police Scotland, 2015), on the language of an additional, very broad 'policing principle' found in S.32 of the Police and Fire Reform (Scotland) Act 2012, 'to improve the safety and well-being of persons' in Scotland. In Northern Ireland, the legal basis of the DVADS, and the common law power to disclose, is enhanced by a statutory duty under S.32 of the Police (Northern Ireland) Act 2000 to protect life and property and prevent the commission of offences. This variety of legal bases across these three DADS ultimately has a knock-on effect as to how they are evaluated, in connection with a meso-level regulatory concern, and how they are operated at the micro-regulatory level of decision-making in a particular case. Disclosure tests, and processes, vary between the three jurisdictions in the UK today. The guidance regulating the DVADS in Northern Ireland, and the DSDAS in Scotland, both refer explicitly to the positive obligation to protect the human rights of potential domestic violence victims as part of the disclosure decision-making tests and processes concerned, while the DVDS guidance does not.

Secondly, at the macro-level of regulation of DADS in the UK today, there is also the issue and problem of disparities in the treatment of the categories of what police intelligence can be disclosed under each of the DADS in the UK today caused by approaches that differ in policy on DADS set by devolved government versus central government. Spent convictions and other arguably problematic-to-disclosure 'intelligence' will be treated differently by the three Schemes concerned, stemming at least in part from their different legal bases but also the issue that three different government departments, across the three jurisdictions in the UK, are involved in setting guidance on the Scheme. This devolved approach to precise DADS policy in the UK today is again near-permanent as a problem, given the current devolved political settlement between the three jurisdictions in the UK today.

Thirdly and finally (and as the last of the nine separate regulatory problems with UK DADS given an overview here), each of the separate DADS will need to take steps in their operational guidance, produced by three different bodies or sets of bodies, in order to keep abreast of changes to supra-national legal changes or shifts in the way that the law in the UK evolves to take into account its changing relationship with bodies of supra-national law and regulation. The approach taken will differ on whether an issue is reserved to the policy-making ambit of the Westminster government, or not. For example, the Scottish Parliament and government recently created a specific criminal offence of 'domestic abuse' that, in the UK, existed only in Scotland for a time (under Part 1 of the Domestic Abuse (Scotland) Act 2018 asp 5), until the enactment in March 2021 of section 1 of the Domestic Abuse and Civil Proceedings Act (Northern Ireland) 2021. Even more recently, the Westminster government, in control of the legislative programme and the creation of the Domestic Abuse Act 2021, did not see fit to include a new specific statutory offence of domestic abuse in England and Wales under the 2021 Act, only defining the broad meaning of domestic abuse in statute law for the first time; so that existing offences against the person, and so forth, will continue to provide the basis for the charging of domestic abuses perpetrators.

6.6 Conclusions

Under the Domestic Abuse Act 2021, at the time of writing, the extent of the statutory basis of the DVDS in England and Wales, at least, is simply that police forces would have a legal duty to have regard to Scheme guidance published by the Home Office, as an attempt, purportedly, to increase police usage of the Scheme. This does not mean that this guidance would go entirely un-reformed, per se, and no doubt HMICFRS will continue to detail police use of the Scheme in their inspections of forces, but this is only a limited reform. Statutory duties to review DADS in the UK on a regular basis to set minimum standards about police processes, support for victims making applications under DADS and regulating disclosure tests to standardise them across the UK jurisdictions as well as to clarify them, therefore, have been overlooked in putting the 2021 Act on the statute book.

Mark Taylor (2012: 15) has observed that a good regulatory framework would result in 'clarity', 'generality', 'certainty' and 'relative constancy'. Additionally, Christina Lienen (2018: 665) has argued that a legal system "should strive for coherence; the adjudicative process should produce results the underlying reasoning of which is intelligible and, to some extent, predictable". As well as seeking to foster these values, any attempt to codify the DADS in the UK today should also attempt to manage risks of domestic violence in such a way that they are a positive contribution to the public protection landscape. But the regulation of risk in the domestic violence prevention context presents considerable challenges that any reform of the DADS must be cognisant of, since, as Julia Black (2005: 522) has argued, "in setting out what are considered to be acceptable and unacceptable risks, risk-based regulation implicitly or explicitly defines what risks the regulator should be expected to prevent, and those which it should not".

In the context of DADS, of course, a considerable (and politically sensitive) risk in a regulatory sense is that disclosures under DADS will in some cases precipitate an escalation or risk to a victim (as they might be harmed in the process of a relationship coming to an end)—or by contrast that a failure or inability to disclose information might do so, as a kind of false reassurance, as has been noted at several points above. Better, politically, to ignore that these risks exist, where policymakers are concerned. Aside from these issues, which this research has already explored to a greater extent, there is the problem of a regulatory risk occurring from the effects, or damage, that disclosures under the DADS may have on the rehabilitation, in practice, of domestic violence perpetrators. There is also the impact on their legal right to rehabilitation to consider. Black's point, above, is that part of the task of risk-based regulation is determining what it is that regulators should be accountable for. There is an issue here for the DADS under discussion in this book: they are all framed in policy terms as a policing exercise, and the guidance published or produced which regulates their operation is aimed at a police audience and police actors; and yet literally a sizeable proportion of the individual parties affected by the ongoing operation of DADS are, of course, offenders. And yet there is no real attention paid in the Home Office guidance on the DVDS for police, for example, on how to work with probation services in managing the after-effects of a disclosure on a (possibly former) domestic violence perpetrator. Perhaps this will be forthcoming under the next revision of the Home Office guidance.

Specific guidance on the DVDS for prison professionals and probation professionals concerning potential disclosures was written in 2020, which stipulated that "disclosure of previous abusive behaviour must be considered when an individual with a history of domestic abuse enters a new relationship; or where a risk of domestic abuse to a current or ex-partner is identified" (Ministry of Justice, 2020: 26). In this way, probation and prison professionals are guided to make Right to Know referrals through the DVDS, or to use emergency disclosures where the DVDS process would not be timely enough in a high-risk situation. It might be very welcome, at least in the policing side of the public protection landscape in England and Wales, for probation services to pick up some of the burden of operating DADS, since some Chief Constables already feel that the police are not the best suited service to deal with very high volumes of lower-risk domestic abuse offences. Sir David Thompson, Chief Constable of West Midlands Police, observed that the police were increasingly responsible for policing relationships, but that it was debatable whether this is a function that is "actually something best discharged by the police in all cases" (Hamilton, 2020).

In an attempt to be fair to Home Office policymakers, perhaps it is still too early to be the case that secondary policy actors or groups of actors have begun to shape the nature of the DVDS as a creature of policy. In terms of the DADS in the UK, these secondary policy actors are the local and regional police forces themselves who operate the Scheme, and the media which they have relied upon to promote the Scheme amongst members of the public. And these secondary actors are being pushed the line that the DVDS is, from the perspective of the Home Office and Her Majesty's Inspectorate in particular, an unqualified success in term of its substantive efficacy—with merely more of a procedural push needed to secure more usage of the DVDS and the other DADS over time. Having used a variety of regulatory tools of analysis to present findings around a theme of regulatory responsibility, it is now an appropriate juncture to present the group of findings from this research that cluster thematically around the detailed legalities of the DVDS and other DADS, according to several different jurisprudential and doctrinal measures. It is the task of the next chapter to explore and justify these findings from a wider legal analysis of the DADS in the UK.

References

Bache, I., & Flinders, M. (2004). Multi-level governance and the study of the British state. *Public Policy and Administration, 19*(1), 31.

Baumeister, R. F., & Heatherton, T. F. (1996). Self-regulation failure: An overview. *Psychological Inquiry, 7*(1), 1–15.

Black, J. (2001). Decentring regulation: Understanding the role of regulation and self-regulation in a 'post-regulatory world'. *Current Legal Problems, 54*(1), 103.

Black, J. (2005). The emergence of risk-based regulation and the new public risk management in the United Kingdom. *Public Law, 512*.

Black, J. (2007). Tensions in the regulatory state. *Public Law, 58*.

Bows, H. (2016). Will changing the focus from victim to perpetrator end domestic violence? *The Conversation*, 1 March. Retrieved March 1, 2016,

from http://theconversation.com/will-changing-the-focus-from-victim-to-perpetrator-end-domestic-violence-55206
Braithwaite, J. (2002). *Restorative justice and responsive regulation*. Oxford University Press.
Braithwaite, J. (2014). Limits on violence; Limits on responsive regulatory theory. *Law & Policy, 36*(4), 432.
Cairney, P. (2012). *Understanding public policy: Theories and issues*. Palgrave Macmillan.
Crawford, A. (2006). Networked governance and the post-regulatory state? Steering, rowing and anchoring the provision of policing and security. *Theoretical Criminology, 10*(4), 449.
Duggan, M. (2012). 'Using victims' voices to prevent violence against women: A critique. *British Journal of Community Justice, 10*(2), 25.
Duggan, M. (2018a). 'Idealising' domestic violence victims. In M. Duggan (Ed.), *Revisiting the ideal victim: Developments in critical victimology*. Policy Press.
Duggan, M. (2018b). Victim hierarchies in the Domestic Violence Disclosure Scheme. *International Review of Victimology, 24*(2), 199.
Duggan, M., & Grace, J. (2018). Assessing vulnerabilities in the Domestic Violence Disclosure Scheme. *Child and Family Law Quarterly, 2*, 145.
Ericson, R. V., & Haggerty, K. D. (1997). *Policing the risk society*. Clarendon Press.
Fitz-Gibbon, K., & Walklate, S. (2017). The efficacy of Clare's Law in domestic violence law reform in England and Wales. *Criminology & Criminal Justice, 17*(3), 284.
Garland, D. (1996). The limits of the Sovereign state strategies of crime control in contemporary society. *British Journal of Criminology, 36*(4), 445.
Grace, J. (2013). Privacy, stigma and public protection: A socio-legal analysis of criminality information practices in the UK. *International Journal of Law, Crime and Justice, 41*, 303.
Grace, J. (2018). Four years on: The postcode lottery of Clare's Law. *SIPS blog*, 8 March. Retrieved April 14, 2018, from https://sheffieldinstituteforpolicystudies.com/2018/03/08/four-years-on-the-postcode-lottery-of-clares-law/
Halliday, S. (2013). The governance of compliance with public law. *Public Law, 312*.
Hamilton, F. (2020). David Thompson: Free police from handling some domestic cases, suggests chief. *The Times*, October 29.

Hancher, L., & Moran, M. (1998). Organizing regulatory space. In R. Baldwin, C. Scott, & C. Hood (Eds.), *A reader on regulation*. Oxford University Press.

HMIC. (2015). *Building the picture*. Her Majesty's Inspectorate of Constabulary, July.

HMICFRS. (2019). *The police response to domestic abuse: An update report*. [online]. Retrieved March 31, 2021, from https://www.justiceinspectorates.gov.uk/hmicfrs/wp-content/uploads/the-police-response-to-domestic-abuse-an-update-report.pdf

Home Office. (2013). *Domestic Violence Disclosure Scheme (DVDS) pilot assessment*. Home Office.

Home Office. (2014). *Multi-agency working and information sharing project: Final report*. Home Office.

Independent Office for Police Conduct. (2018, January 7). *Investigation into the handling of a domestic violence case – Northamptonshire Police*. March 2017. Retrieved July 14, 2021, from https://www.policeconduct.gov.uk/recommendations/investigation-handling-domestic-violence-case-northamptonshire-police-march-2017

Independent Office for Police Conduct. (2019). *Complaints regarding police actions and decisions before a woman is found dead – Staffordshire Police*. February 2017. Retrieved March 31, 2021, from https://www.policeconduct.gov.uk/recommendations/complaints-regarding-police-actions-and-decisions-woman-found-dead-staffordshire

Independent Office for Police Conduct. (2020a, June 3). *Response to request for a domestic violence disclosure check – Wiltshire Police*. April 2019. Retrieved June 30, 2020, from https://policeconduct.gov.uk/recommendations/response-request-domestic-violence-disclosure-check-wiltshire-police-april-2019

Independent Office for Police Conduct. (2020b). *Force accepts learning after investigation into contact with Derbyshire woman stabbed by her ex-partner*. Retrieved March 31, 2021, from https://www.policeconduct.gov.uk/news/force-accepts-learning-after-investigation-contact-derbyshire-woman-stabbed-her-ex-partner

Lienen, C. (2018). Common law constitutional rights: Public law at a crossroads? *Public Law, 649*.

McCarthy, M., Hunt, S., & Milne-Skillman, K. (2017). 'I know it was every week, but I can't be sure if it was every day: Domestic violence and women with learning disabilities. *Journal of Applied Research in Intellectual Disabilities, 30*(2), 269.

Ministry of Justice. (2020). *Domestic abuse policy framework*, April.

Nash, M. (2010). The politics of public protection. In M. Nash & A. Williams (Eds.), *Handbook of public protection*. Willan.

Police Scotland. (2015). Disclosure Scheme for Domestic Abuse Scotland (DSDAS) – Standard operating procedure. Author copy, obtained via a freedom-of-information request in 2017.

Purshouse, J. (2018). Non-conviction disclosure as part of an enhanced criminal record certificate: Assessing the legal framework from a fundamental human rights perspective. *Public Law, 668*.

Queensland Law Reform Commission. (2017). *Domestic Violence Disclosure Scheme*, Report No. 75, June. Retrieved June 23, 2020, from http://www.qlrc.qld.gov.au/__data/assets/pdf_file/0010/541189/qlrc-report-no-75.pdf

Robbins, R., McLaughlin, H., Banks, C., Bellamy, C., & Thackray, D. (2014). Domestic violence and multi-agency risk assessment conferences (MARACs): A scoping review. *The Journal of Adult Protection, 16*(6), 389.

Sanders, A. (2008). Can coercive powers be effectively controlled or regulated?: The case for anchored pluralism. In E. Cape & R. Young (Eds.), *Regulating policing: The police and criminal evidence act 1984 – Past, present and future*. Hart.

Shaw, D. (2020). Domestic violence prevention work 'should focus on offenders'. *BBC News*, 21 January. Retrieved July 18, 2020, from https://www.bbc.co.uk/news/uk-51177628

Stevens, E. (2015). Safeguarding vulnerable adults: Exploring the challenges to best practice across multi-agency settings. *The Journal of Adult Protection, 15*(2), 85.

Taylor, M. (2012). *Genetic data and the law: A critical perspective on privacy protection*. Cambridge University Press.

University of Glasgow. (2015). *Audit of the disclosure scheme for domestic abuse (Scotland)*, September. Author's copy obtained via freedom-of-information request.

Westmarland, N. (2015). *Violence against women: Criminological perspectives on men's violences*. Routledge.

Williams, F. (2018). Clare's Law: The women who risk their lives by refusing information. *BBC News*, 29 November. Retrieved June 19, 2020, from https://www.bbc.co.uk/news/uk-england-42920020

7

The Governance and Legalities of Domestic Abuse Disclosure Schemes

7.1 Introduction

The period 2010–2021 has not seen much consistency in the way of policy from HM Government on dealing with the prevention of domestic violence. Newer legal powers and processes to tackle domestic violence, such as Domestic Abuse Disclosure Schemes (DADS) and Domestic Violence Protection Notices and Orders, have been undermined by reductions in funding to wider public services that support victims of violence and abuse. For example, according to Women's Aid, there is a shortfall of 30% in terms of the number of refuge places required in the UK (Women's Aid, 2020: 20), which should be space for one family per 10,000 residents in a population (Council of Europe, 2008: 51). At the time of introducing the DVDS on a national scale in England and Wales, the Home Office, in their policy impact assessment (Home Office, 2013), undertook estimates of the costs of introducing and operating the DVDS in its current form (with a 'Right to Ask' strand allied to a 'Right to Know' strand). Total operating costs per annum in England and Wales were put at £3.18 million, but this modest costs commitment to operating a DVDS is at odds with the evidence of reduced funding for domestic

J. Grace, *Domestic Abuse Disclosure Schemes*,
https://doi.org/10.1007/978-3-030-89039-1_7

violence prevention services and support in an era of austerity (Women's Aid, 2020; Trust for London, 2012).

Austerity policies have sometimes had a harmful, if lawful, effect on the rights of women who are the victims of domestic violence. For example, in the case of *R (DA and others) v Secretary of State for Work and Pensions* [2019] UKSC 21, two of the four ultimately unsuccessful claimants had been victims of domestic violence. In *DA*, the courts had to examine the issue of whether a 'benefits cap' unlawfully and disproportionately impacts upon single mothers, and whether this was a breach of the principle of non-discrimination under Article 14 ECHR taken with Article 8 ECHR. This was because a disproportionate number of lone parents with children under two are women, and who are more likely to struggle to find employment that pays well enough to cover costs of childcare and housing, but when working less than 16 hours per week are caught by the benefits cap (reduced in November 2016 to £20,000 per annum for lone parents outside of London, and £23,000 per annum inside London). Austerity policies, such as the benefits cap, are highly problematic when we consider that there are links between poverty and domestic violence prevalence (Child Poverty Action Group, 2019). This example of (lawful) austerity policy undermining anything else done *prima facie* to better promote the welfare of victims of domestic abuse is given to show that the UK DADS are far from the only contentious piece of policy that are designed, ostensibly, to deal with a social 'problem' (e.g., parents in unemployment), but which actually have unavoidable impacts on (the disproportionately female) victims of domestic violence.

Ultimately, however, the courts require government policy as expressed in guidance to follow not moral standards but to reflect the law, and legal standards, and with a solid degree of certainty. But public authorities need not, in the words of Lord Sales and Lord Burnett in *R (A) v Home Secretary* [2021] UKSC 37 at 40, "invest large sums on legal advice to produce textbook standard statements of the law which are not in fact required to achieve the practical objectives the authority might have in view". Albeit, public authorities are subject to the rule of law and the judicial review of much of their decision-making, and must surely strive to avoid unlawfulness, since if "policy directs them to act in a way which contradicts the law it is unlawful" (*R (A) v Home Secretary* [2021] UKSC

37 at 41). As such, in its next series of sections, this chapter explores the finer detail of how the UK DADS are constructed as procedures in policy for different police forces to follow—and the way that these procedures do, and do not, sit well with legal standards relating to the protection of the rights of both victims and disclosure subjects.

7.2 The Common Law Basis of the Domestic Violence Disclosure Scheme

In *Michael v Chief Constable of South Wales Police* [2015] UKSC 2 the majority of the UK Supreme Court found that the police do not owe a duty under the tort of negligence to a victim of murder. But this concerns private law duties on the police—in terms of public law duties, public protection values in the common law are somewhat more tangible. In *Michael*, at 195, Lady Hale explained there was a common law position on the public law duty on the police: "There is no doubt that the police owe a positive duty in public law to protect members of the public from harm caused by third parties". This section focuses on the relevant common law position of police powers to share information as part of their role in public protection and crime prevention. Current DVDS guidance can probably be criticised for its glossing over, and to a degree its over-simplification, of the relevant common law powers and duties of the police. This guidance highlights the nature of the Scheme as a lens to focus the common law power of the police to disclose information when it is 'necessary to prevent crime', explaining that (Home Office, 2016: 4):

> The Domestic Violence Disclosure Scheme did not introduce any new legislation. The scheme is based on the police's common law power to disclose information where it is necessary to prevent crime. The scheme provides structure and processes for the exercise of the powers. It does not, in itself, provide the power to disclose or to prevent disclosures being made in situations which fall outside this scheme.

The Home Office guidance also explains that in relation to considering a disclosure to a potential victim of domestic violence (A), under the

DVDS, and concerning a past offender (B), then: "The police have the common law power to disclose information about an individual where it is necessary to do so to protect another individual from harm" (Home Office, 2016: 18). Is the common law power of the police to disclose information under the DVDS only bounded by 'necessity to prevent crime', or 'necessity to prevent harm', however? This is, to a degree, a shifting and context-dependent parameter to apply in the common law. As Lord Nolan explained in *Marcel v Commissioner of Police of the Metropolis* [1992] Ch. 225 at 261:

> The statutory powers given to the police are plainly coupled with a public law duty. The precise extent of the duty is, I think, difficult to define in general terms beyond saying that the powers must be exercised only in the public interest and with due regard to the rights of individuals.

Mr Justice Laws (as he then was) highlighted in his judgement in *Hellewell v Chief Constable of Derbyshire* [1995] 1 W.L.R. 804 that the sharing of information by the police with possible victims of crime had to be for reasonable crime prevention purposes. The current Home Office guidance on the DVDS states that: "it may not be necessary to tell the applicant the precise details of the offence for the applicant to take steps to protect A" (Home Office, 2016: 19). This emphasis in the DVDS guidance on disclosing only a necessary amount of information accords well with the decision of Laws J in *Hellewell* and the emphasis placed in that judgement upon the nature of a lawful disclosure of police-held information as one made reasonably, with the information disclosed to be used in good faith and to be disclosed to those with a 'reasonable concern' to know (*Hellewell v Chief Constable of Derbyshire* [1995] 1 W.L.R. 804, 810–811).

Hellewell concerns the Long Eaton Shop Watch Scheme, begun in 1992, with the dissemination of posters to shopkeeper-members in the town, with the posters featuring 'mugshots' of local thieves. In *Hellewell*, Mr Justice Laws concluded (at 810) that, in relation to the sharing of a photograph of a convicted shoplifter, the police:

> may make reasonable use of it for the purpose of the prevention and detection of crime, the investigation of alleged offences and the apprehension of suspects or persons unlawfully at large. They may do so whether or not the photograph is of any person they seek to arrest or of a suspected accomplice or of anyone else. The key is that they must have these and only these purposes in mind and must, as I have said, make no more than reasonable use of the picture in seeking to accomplish them ... the term 'reasonable', as in so many areas of the law, is fluid and its application will depend on the circumstances of a particular case. I recognise also that it is as impossible as it is undesirable to lay down anything like a lexicon of the kinds of facts that will amount to reasonable use of such a picture by the police. However, where the use in question is decided upon by the honest judgment of professional police officers, that will, of itself, go a long way to establish its reasonableness. Provided these bounds of principle are not transgressed, there will be an obvious and vital public interest in the use made of such photographs which the courts will uphold.

So the common law looks to a fluid concept of reasonable purposes to shape the lawful use of information in the prevention of crime. The common law certainly does not justify an aggressive and uniform policy as treating all convicted persons as a disclosure subject outright and without careful thought. Lord Bingham took the view in the Divisional Court in *R v Chief Constable of North Wales ex p Thorpe* [1997] 3 W.L.R. 724 at 733 that: "It would plainly be objectionable if a police force were to adopt a blanket policy of disseminating information about previous offenders regardless of the facts of the individual case or the nature of the previous offending or the risk of further offending". Furthermore, Lord Bingham also highlighted in the Divisional Court in *Thorpe*, in reviewing a body of case law, that:

> When, in the course of performing its public duties, a public body (such as a police force) comes into possession of information relating to a member of the public, being information not generally available and potentially damaging to that member of the public if disclosed, the body ought not to disclose such information save for the purpose of and to the extent necessary for performance of its public duty or enabling some other public body to perform its public duty. (*R v Chief Constable of North Wales ex p Thorpe* [1997] 3 W.L.R. 724, 732)

There is an important qualification to be made, of course, about the role of the police in managing risks to the public. As Lord Bingham further concluded in the Divisional Court in *Thorpe*:

> if the police, having obtained information about an individual which it would be damaging to that individual to disclose, and which should not be disclosed without some public justification, consider in the exercise of a careful and bona fide judgment that it is desirable or necessary in the public interest to make disclosure, whether for the purpose of preventing crime or alerting members of the public to an apprehended danger, it is proper for them to make such limited disclosure as is judged necessary to achieve that purpose. (*R v Chief Constable of North Wales ex p Thorpe* [1997] 3 W.L.R. 724, 733)

Furthermore, in *Thorpe* in the Court of Appeal, Lord Woolf determined that "as a matter of English administrative law, the police are entitled to use information when they reasonably conclude this is what is required (after taking into account the interests of the applicants), in order to protect the public and in particular children" (*R v Chief Constable of North Wales ex p Thorpe* [1999] Q.B. 396 at 409–410, 429). Finally, in *Thorpe* in the Court of Appeal, Lord Woolf also addressed not just the *parameters* of the common law power of the police to disclose information to protect the public through preventing an apprehended danger, or public protection risk, but also the *threshold* for that risk to warrant disclosure: "Disclosure should only be made when there is a pressing need for that disclosure" (*R v Chief Constable of North Wales ex p Thorpe* [1999] Q.B. 396 at 409–410, 428).

As a result, then, it does appear that in the key case law concerned, the common law power of the police to disclose information is indeed broadly founded, and on the power to share information where necessary to prevent crime. However, the DVDS guidance and the overall common law test for disclosure should in truth be phrased more comprehensively, *per* Mr Justice Laws (as he then was) in *Hellewell*, *per* Lord Bingham in *Thorpe* in the Divisional Court and *per* Lord Woolf in *Thorpe* in the Court of Appeal. The current DVDS guidance (Home Office, 2016) could be amended to state that:

Disclosure of limited information under the DVDS is permissible where necessary in the public interest, as is reasonable to achieve the purpose of preventing crime or alerting members of the public to an apprehended danger, in good faith and where there is a pressing need for that disclosure.

In *Thorpe*, however, Lord Woolf created the 'pressing need' standard without explicit reference to any pre-existing case law however, and as noted above did not elaborate any further other than to state that: "Disclosure should only be made when there is a pressing need for that disclosure". The 'pressing need' for disclosure test has, however, been cited on a number of occasions in the relevant case law post-*Thorpe*. However, such elaborations (often *obiter*) as there are in this body of case law on the 'pressing need' rule from *Thorpe* do not create much elucidation or precision on the nature of what can be said to be a 'pressing need'; there is as much repetition if anything of the point made by Lord Woolf in *R v Chief Constable for North Wales ex parte Thorpe* [1998] EWCA Civ 486 at 15 that: "Each case must be judged on its own facts".

However, in trying to find those elements of judicial commentary that do exist in relation to a better attempt to define the 'pressing need' standard for disclosure, we can begin with the words of Stuart-Smith J in *R (L) v Chief Constable of Cumbria Constabulary* [2013] EWHC 869 at 89, who observed that the 'pressing need' threshold for a lawful disclosure would not be reached if there were "limited circumstances in which a possible risk of repetition [of the criminality concerned] might arise", or if there were a "relative lack of gravity of the alleged conduct", information about which would form the basis of the disclosure. More broadly however, and from a contrastingly public protection-oriented perspective, Beatson LJ in *R (A) v Chief Constable of Kent Constabulary* [2013] EWCA Civ 1706 at 94 suggested that a 'pressing need' for disclosure would exist "where [disclosure] is necessary to do so to protect the vulnerable group from the risks to them".

In an interesting case in the context of disclosure of details of a criminal history, and in finding no unlawfulness in the disclosure of past allegations of child abuse to a new, different partner with children, Weatherup J, in the case of *In the Matter of an Application by James Martin for Judicial Review* [2002] NIQB 67 at para. 33, noted that:

> The respondent [public body] had reasonable cause to suspect that the applicant's new partner's children would be likely to suffer significant harm and had grounds to conclude that action was required to safeguard the childrens' [sic] welfare. An assessment was made based on the facts and circumstances of the particular case. A pressing need for disclosure was established. A balance of the considerations affecting the applicant's interests and the public interest was carried out.

As a result of this further case law that develops our understanding of the 'pressing need' test for disclosure, a further new formulation of the guidance on the 'pressing need' test for disclosures under the DVDS could be phrased as requiring *(i) reasonable cause to suspect a person would be likely to suffer significant harm and (ii) grounds to conclude a disclosure is required to safeguard their welfare.*

This results in an overall exposition of the common law test for disclosure under the DVDS, for example, that could read as follows:

> *Disclosure of limited information under the DVDS is permissible where necessary in the public interest, as is reasonable to achieve the purpose of preventing crime or alerting members of the public to an apprehended danger, in good faith and where there is a pressing need for that disclosure, entailing (i) a reasonable cause to suspect a person is likely to suffer significant harm and (ii) grounds to conclude a disclosure is required to safeguard their welfare.*

7.3 Disclosure Standards in the Three UK Domestic Abuse Disclosure Schemes

A recent study (Hadjimatheou & Grace, 2020) of the force-level disclosure policies around the DVDS, as used by a number of police forces in England and Wales, uncovered a great deal of inconsistency in the manner of operation of the Scheme from force to force, in terms of the management and degree of supply of data to victims or people at risk of domestic abuse. Hadjimatheou and Grace (2020) used interviews with police officers, and an analysis of FOI-obtained internal policy documents from 12 different forces, and found that forces "diverge on whether they disclose spent convictions, convictions, charges, or other information indicating risk, such as reported crimes that resulted in 'no further action'" (Hadjimatheou & Grace, 2020: 6). Forces "also diverge on whether they make disclosures only to victims assessed as high-risk or also to those assessed as medium or standard risk", while the "level of detail included in a disclosure also varies greatly between forces, with some merely copying and pasting court records and others providing detailed descriptions of the ways in which perpetrators have harmed and attacked ex-partners" (Hadjimatheou & Grace, 2020: 6). Any future refresh of the current DVDS guidance (Home Office, 2016), now to be statutory guidance following the enactment of S.77 of the Domestic Abuse Act 2021, is an opportunity to reform the operation of the DVDS by drawing on wider legal standards, which are layered on top of the common law rules discussed in the last section.

Human Rights Standards in Protecting the Rights of Victims of Domestic Violence

As mentioned earlier in this chapter, in the *Michael* case, the Supreme Court baulked at imposing a private law duty of care in negligence on the police in relation to victims of domestic violence, noting public policy arguments about the financial burden that would arise on the police, and with little practical effect on reducing domestic violence, in all likelihood. Additionally, the common law duty on the police to protect the public from serious harm, identified by Lady Hale in *Michael*, is broad in application, and so this section focuses on the human rights standards and duties that apply more concretely in the context of the police protecting (potential) victims of domestic violence in the UK. The Articles of the ECHR considered in turn here, and in some detail, are Article 2 ECHR covering the right to life, Article 3 ECHR providing the right to freedom from torture and inhuman or degrading treatment and Article 8 ECHR—in the sense of it encompassing the right to respect for private and family life. Article 14 ECHR, and its prohibition of any discrimination in the enjoyment of these rights that is without a 'manifestly reasonable foundation', is of course 'parasitical' in nature, and as a result will be discussed where relevant in relation to other rights in this section, and in the conclusion to this chapter.

Article 2 ECHR and the Right to Life

Article 2 ECHR describes the right to life. It has both a substantive and a procedural strand to prevent the loss of life and to investigate the loss of life, respectively. The DVDS may well be a piece of public policy that contributes towards evidencing the commitment of the Home Office and police forces to meeting their duty in relation to potential victims of domestic violence under the substantive strand of Article 2 of preserving life. Assuming that the DVDS does indeed prove effective, in an individual case, and the assumption that a disclosure might lead to the end of a potentially lethal relationship is correct in an individual case, then we can readily say that a disclosure under the Scheme is a way of meeting the duty under Article 2 ECHR that the HRA 1998 places upon the police in this context.

However, is a disclosure that does *not* lead to the end of an abusive relationship sufficient to meet the duty to preserve life under Article 2, namely where the subject of the disclosure goes on to kill the recipient who had drawn upon their Right to Ask? And, for that matter, is a non-disclosure in an instance where the violent partner then does go on to kill the applicant concerned also a decision that meets the duty to preserve life under Article 2? This would depend upon the precise circumstances of the facts of the case, in essence, and whether the substantive duty to preserve life in that case was engaged, and whether a disclosure of information about a subject under the Scheme guidance was sufficient for an intervention or operational measure to meet that duty. Of course, to best meet the requirements of Article 2 ECHR post-disclosure, the police would need to have kept an individual case of risk of domestic violence under review. However the Scheme guidance makes it plain that the police have a *discretion* as to what advice should accompany a disclosure, including signposting recipients to local support services (Home Office, 2016: 21); while the guidance also recommends the consideration of whether a disclosure subject needs to be referred to a local Multi-Agency Public Protection Arrangements (MAPPA) panel, or the local Integrated Offender Management (IOM) programme (Home Office, 2016: 22). The Scheme guidance does *not* make this increase in rigour, in terms of offender management, a mandatory outcome from a decision to disclose.

But the legal position of a police force as to whether it has met its Article 2 ECHR duty to preserve life is very much dictated by the standards laid down in the touchstone case of *Osman v UK* (1998). Stemming from this case, to paraphrase, there are duties on the police in the UK, under the positive obligation to protect life under Article 2 ECHR, to take sufficient steps to intervene where there is a known, real and immediate risk to life. As the Strasbourg Court noted in the case of *Osman* itself:

> where there is an allegation that the authorities have violated their positive obligation to protect the right to life in the context of their [duty] to prevent and suppress offences against the person … it must be established … that the authorities knew or ought to have known at the time of the existence of a real and immediate risk to the life of an identified individual or individuals from the criminal acts of a third party and that they failed to take measures within the scope of their powers which, judged reasonably, might have been expected to avoid that risk. (*Osman v UK* (1998) *(87/1997/871/1083)*, 116)

One way of achieving compliance with this duty is for the police to issue '*Osman* warnings' to those individuals facing credible threats to their lives on the assessment of police intelligence (BBC News, 2015). The DVDS fits into a fairly similar mould, it could be argued. A disclosure under the Scheme could be said to be 'sufficient' as a response to a known, real and immediate risk to life; and surely more confidently so, in the eyes of the courts, if it were part of a package of interventions against a subject of that disclosure, such as arrest, charge and bail with conditions, if after an investigation these are warranted, and/or the use of a Domestic Violence Protection Notice or Order (DVPN or DVPO)—soon to be Domestic Abuse Protection Notices and Orders, with a wider ambit, following the creation of the Domestic Abuse Act 2021.

Article 3 ECHR and Article 8 ECHR

Articles 3 and 8 of the ECHR are set out in the following way:

Article 3
No one shall be subjected to torture or to inhuman or degrading treatment or punishment.
…

Article 8

1. Everyone has the right to respect for his private and family life, his home and his correspondence.
2. There shall be no interference by a public authority with the exercise of this right except such as is in accordance with the law and is necessary in a democratic society in the interests of national security, public safety or the economic well-being of the country, for the prevention of disorder or crime, for the protection of health or morals, or for the protection of the rights and freedoms of others.

Under Article 3 ECHR, if the harm complained of is sufficiently serious, then "the [Strasbourg] Court must next determine whether the national authorities have taken all reasonable measures to prevent the recurrence of violent attacks against the applicant's physical integrity" (*Opuz v Turkey* (2009) *33401/02*, 161–162). Under Article 8 ECHR, however, the Strasbourg Court noted in *A v Croatia* (2010) *55164/08* at 60 that "States have a duty to protect the physical and moral integrity of an individual from other persons … [and] they are to maintain and apply in practice an adequate legal framework affording protection against acts of violence by private individuals". So the Domestic Violence Disclosure Scheme could be seen as part of the fulfilment of the requirement to adopt 'measures in the sphere of the relations between individuals', as part of an 'adequate legal framework affording protection against acts of violence by private individuals'. However, particular decisions to disclose information (or not) under the Scheme, and whether these are complemented by any other preventive measures, are clearly subject to the discretion afforded by the margin of appreciation, which works in favour of the state agents or public bodies concerned under Article 8 ECHR.

Human rights compliance for DADS in the UK then turns on the extent to which the police do, or do not, use the process of a disclosure scheme as the only support for a likely victim of domestic violence, or whether such a disclosure is augmented by one of their preventive powers, such as DVPNs or the DVPOs the police can apply for. However, it is important to note that the Centre for Women's Justice produced a report in March 2019, on which they grounded a police 'super-complaint', which identified that police forces were routinely under-using DVPNs and DVPOs, as well as not sufficiently pursuing offenders for breaches of non-molestation orders, failing to apply pre-charge bail conditions on suspected domestic abuse perpetrators, and failing to apply for restraining orders when an investigation has been completed (Centre for Women's Justice, 2019). Additionally, as discussed below, the DVDS guidance as currently published by the Home Office for England and Wales, and unlike the guidance on the DSDAS for Scotland and the DVADS for Northern Ireland, does not explicitly refer to positive obligations to protect the human rights of potential victims of domestic violence as one of the criteria for determining whether a disclosure should be made/another intervention undertaken.

Right to Know disclosures, because of their inherently more proactive context in being triggered often by inter-agency intelligence sharing, would be more likely to be an appropriate response to at least consider on the part of the police, when Article 3 or Article 8 is deemed to be engaged, and in using a risk assessment process. This is also, however, a position that happens to be supported by Marian Duggan's empirical finding; that in the operation of the DVDS by one English police force, the RtK disclosure recipients receive a higher spot in a hierarchy of treatment compared to RtA recipients (Duggan, 2018). This is presumably, but of course need not always be, that the offenders whose probation officers pass information to the police under the Right to Know might be known to pose a (higher) risk, or that social work teams are flagging the arrival of a seemingly 'risky' new partner in the life of a family with vulnerabilities or a history of victimisation already.

The Subject's Right to be Consulted

With regard to criminality information sharing as part of the 'politics of public protection' (Nash, 2010), the retention and disclosure of criminal records to prevent or forestall offending exploits the gap between due process, on the one hand, and 'preventive justice' (Ashworth & Zedner,

2014), on the other. For example, in relation to the retention, and therefore the possible disclosure in England and Wales of information about acquittals, His Honour Judge Jarman QC wrote in *R (YZ) v Chief Constable of South Wales Police* [2021] EWHC 1060 (admin) at 48–49 that that there are "two different regimes in play", meaning the institutions of criminal process which pay due to regard to the presumption of innocence, for example, versus the "issue of law enforcement and the safeguarding of individuals", which does not readily accord with the presumption of innocence at all. This of course comes about because of the clash between the rights of (potential) victims and the procedural rights of subjects of disclosures.

Early on in the lifespan of the DVDS, as the original DADS, there was little or no evidence as to how subjects' procedural rights to be consulted prior to disclosures being made were being treated by police forces in England and Wales, despite the strong legal arguments concerning duties to take into account the views of possible disclosure subjects where this is practicable (Grace, 2015). However, given the common law duties on the police to prevent harm to the public, and positive obligations under Articles 2, 3 and 8 ECHR towards victims of abuse, namely to protect them from repeated and/or foreseeable imminent harm, there is little wonder that the 2016 Home Office guidance on the operation of the DVDS is open to but very cautious on the idea of pre-disclosure consultation with the subject. The Home Office guidance is worded to include a strong consideration of non-consultation with 'B' (the subject of the potential disclosure to a victim, 'A'), since "[d]ue consideration must be given on whether the disclosure to B would have potential to escalate the risk of harm to A", and that if "this were to be the case, no disclosure must be given to B" (Home Office, 2016: 19). This is likely lawful, in taking the more public protection-oriented position, and despite the (admittedly fluid) right to a fair hearing possessed by a (potential) disclosure subject under Article 6 ECHR, and under common law principles of natural justice, requiring a fair and impartial process, classically outlined by the House of Lords in *Ridge v Baldwin* [1964 AC 40].

In shedding some light on the issue in practice, DCI Barry Byford of Suffolk Constabulary has indicated that his force would never tell a disclosure subject that a disclosure has been made, and therefore, at least in

Suffolk, and despite the Home Office guidance on the issue, a potential disclosure subject would very likely never be consulted with by that force (Potter, 2020). It is very much conceivable that consultation prior to disclosures is relatively, even extremely rare, given the need to take into account potential harm to disclosure recipients from disclosure subjects who are provoked by a DVDS application.

Updating the Disclosure Standards in the Current UK DADS Guidance

Partly as a result of their different legal bases, highlighted below, the three sets of guidance for the DADS in operation across the UK present the relevant legal tests for a lawful disclosure of information somewhat differently. For the DVDS in England and Wales, the Home Office guidance from 2016 explains that a lawful disclosure can be made if (Home Office, 2016: 18):

a. it is reasonable to conclude that such disclosure is necessary to protect A from being the victim of a crime;
b. there is a pressing need for such disclosure; and
c. interfering with the rights of **B**, including **B**'s rights under Article 8 of the European Convention of Human Rights, to have information about his/her previous convictions kept confidential is necessary and proportionate for the prevention of crime. This involves balancing the consequences for B if his/her details are disclosed against the nature and extent of the risks that B poses to A.

In Scotland, the Standard Operating Protocol (SOP) for the DSDAS outlines instead that (Police Scotland, 2015: 8):

> there is the power to disclose the information (in terms of Section 32, Police and Fire Reform (Scotland) Act 2012 [and in applying] Articles 2,3 and 8 of the European Convention on Human Rights ... and [the] Data Protection Act 1998 [sic].

In greater detail, the SOP goes on to explain that (Police Scotland, 2015: 9):

Accordingly, when considering whether to recommend a disclosure of information, the local DMF [Decision Making Forum] ought to follow this 3 stage test

5.18.1 That the local DMF has the ability to recommend a disclosure of information by Police Scotland in terms of the Police and Fire Reform (Scotland) Act 2012. Such a disclosure would be lawful if it accorded with one of the general policing duties in terms of the 2012 Act.
5.18.2 Police Scotland must be able to show that it is reasonable to conclude that such disclosure is necessary to protect the public (or particular sections of the public) from crime …
5.18.3 In the context of this scheme, Police Scotland would have to conclude that disclosure to the applicant is necessary to protect 'A' from being a victim of a crime or abusive behaviours: and
5.18.4 Any disclosure is an interference with the rights of 'B' (under Article 8 of the European Convention of Human Rights) and it must be proportionate.

The guidance regulating the operation of the DVADS in Northern Ireland is also built around three key disclosure tests, as follows (Department of Justice (Northern Ireland), 2018: 22):

i. As PSNI is relying on its common law and statutory power to disclose, it must be shown that it is reasonable to conclude that disclosure is necessary to protect the public, or particular sections of the public, from crime. This would make the disclosure lawful;
ii. PSNI will be required to conclude that disclosure is necessary to protect 'A' from harm or being a victim of crime; and
iii. any disclosure that interferes with 'B's rights—under Article 6 [the right to a fair hearing] and Article 8 of the European Convention on Human Rights (ECHR), the Data Protection Act 1998 and the forthcoming General Data Protection Regulation [sic]—must be proportionate.

Additionally, the DVADS guidance from the Department of Justice in Northern Ireland also makes specific reference to the positive obligations to protect victims from imminent risks of harm under Articles 2 and 3 ECHR (Department of Justice (Northern Ireland), 2018: 21). It is also a positive aspect of the DSDAS guidance (or SOP) that it explicitly recognises the issues of positive obligations to protect victims of (potential) domestic violence arising under certain Articles of the ECHR. The DVDS guidance published by the Home Office in December 2016 makes specific mention of the Article 8 ECHR rights of *subjects* of (potential) disclosures in two sections of the document (Home Office, 2016: 18 and 45), but the DSDAS guidance is more oriented towards the rights of victims than the DVDS guidance from 2016. The positive obligation to preserve life under Article 2 ECHR is acknowledged by the DSDAS guidance or SOP, which at least mentions "relevant case law including Osman v United Kingdom" (Department of Justice (Northern Ireland), 2018: 5). Mention is also made of the need to apply Articles 2, 3 and 8 of the ECHR in the decision-making forum when considering a possible disclosure decision under the DSDAS (Police Scotland, 2015: 8).

The right to respect for private life (in the relevant sense of 'physical and moral integrity') as a component part of the right in Article 8 ECHR is outlined in case law from the European Court of Human Rights in the context of the duties on contracting states to prevent, deter and prosecute domestic violence. For example, in the key case of *A v Croatia* (2010) *55164/08* at 60 the Strasbourg Court observed that: "Under Article 8 States have a duty to protect the physical and moral integrity of an individual from other persons. To that end they are to maintain and apply in practice an adequate legal framework affording protection against acts of violence by private individuals." However, Article 8 ECHR is also engaged by and protects to a degree the interests in rehabilitation for former domestic abusers and other offenders (see Sect. 7.4), and this must be a key factor in lawful considerations over possible disclosures.

However, none of the guidance published in relation to any of the UK DADS *explicitly* highlights positive obligations under Article 2 ECHR in such a way as to make them a *practical* aid to public protection decision-making by officers. As noted above, the application of the right to life as a positive obligation under Article 2 ECHR is classically outlined in

Osman v UK (1998). Since none of the UK DADS guidance documents actually point to a test to apply with regard to this positive obligation under Article 2 ECHR, this potential addition to all UK DADS guidance documents could be framed in the following way:

> *Given what you know about any real and immediate risk to the life of the applicant, is a disclosure under the Scheme a reasonable part of the measures you must take to safeguard against the risk to life of that person? Do you need to conduct immediate inquiries to determine whether intelligence exists as to the risk to the life of the person?*

Likewise, none of the three UK DADS in their guidance documents stipulate a particular test in applying the positive obligation under Article 3 ECHR. The right to freedom from inhuman or degrading treatment (as protected by Article 3 ECHR) is defined in the influential Strasbourg judgement of *Opuz v Turkey* (2009) *33401/02*, where the European Court of Human Rights observed (at 161–162) that under Article 3 ECHR, if the harm suffered by a victim was sufficiently serious "the Court must next determine whether the national authorities have taken all reasonable measures to prevent the recurrence of violent attacks against the applicant's physical integrity". As a result, in the future, one might expect to see an element of the disclosure tests framed in DADS guidance for all jurisdictions of the UK underpinned with reference to this standard developed from Article 3 ECHR, and along the lines of the following statement or instruction:

> *Should there be a risk of serious harm to an applicant, then you must consider whether a disclosure under the DADS would be a reasonable measure to prevent violence or other serious harm against the applicant.*

7.4 Disclosing Older Convictions

The three main DADS in the UK are the creation of the Home Office (in England and Wales) as well as the Department of Justice for Northern Ireland and the Justice Directorate of the Scottish Government. An example of the disparities this can create concerns the way the

Rehabilitation of Offenders Act 1974 is applied by each of the three main DADS in the UK at the time of writing (as noted in Duggan & Grace, 2018). A different approach is taken by the regulation and guidance on the DSDAS, which prohibits the disclosure of spent convictions, as opposed to the regulation and guidance on the DVDS and the DVADS, which allow disclosure of spent convictions and cautions (see Table 7.1). There is in many contexts a presumption that spent convictions cannot be disclosed, other than in the case of Enhanced Criminal Records Certificates in a special category of background checks in sensitive employment contexts, for safeguarding purposes. But the case of *N*, discussed below, shows that there is a ready human rights law argument for

Table 7.1 UK Ministry of Justice spent convictions guidance

	Buffer period for adults (18 and over at the time of conviction or the time the disposal is administered). This applies from the end date of the sentence (including the licence period)	Buffer period for young people (under 18 at the time of conviction or the time the disposal is administered). This applies from the end date of the sentence (including the licence period)
Custodial sentence of over 4 years, or a public protection sentence	Never spent	Never spent
Custodial sentence of over 30 months (2½ years) and up to and including 48 months (4 years)	7 years	3½ years
Custodial sentence of over 6 months and up to and including 30 months (2½ years)	4 years	2 years
Custodial sentence of 6 months or less	2 years	18 months
Community order or youth rehabilitation order	1 year	6 months

Source: Ministry of Justice (2020: 5)

allowing the disclosure of spent convictions where necessary and proportionate under DADS, despite the provisions of the 1974 Act.

At the moment, there is a disparity between jurisdictions on this issue within the UK. Home Office guidance for England and Wales, and Department of Justice guidance in Northern Ireland, make it clear that in circumstances where it is both necessary and proportionate, and where the spent conditions is of sufficient relevance to the 'pressing need' in question, such information can be disclosed under the DVDS or DVADS. However, the standard operating procedure for the DSDAS operated by Police Scotland makes it plain that spent convictions should not be disclosed under the common law basis of the 'right to ask' and the 'power to tell' strands of the DSDAS (see Table 7.2).

Table 7.2 Regulation of the (non)-disclosure of spent convictions in DADS guidance

	DVDS: "Where police officers have the power in the course of their duties to disclose spent convictions under the Domestic Violence Disclosure Scheme it is important that disclosure still needs to be reasonable and proportionate. The police will want to take into account the age of the spent conviction during the decision-making process."	**DVADS**: "Where police consider the disclosure of relevant spent convictions to be applicable under the scheme, it is important that disclosure is reasonable and proportionate ... [taking] account of the age of the spent conviction during the decision making process."	**DSDAS**: "Police Scotland may consider the impact of a spent conviction when conducting a risk assessment on 'A', regardless of the fact that the spent conviction cannot then be disclosed to the DMF or to 'A' (or 'C')."
Sources:	(Home Office, 2016: 16–17)	(Department of Justice (Northern Ireland), 2018: 19)	(Police Scotland, 2015: 19)

The European Court of Human Rights has explained in *Catt v United Kingdom* (2019) (Application no. 43514/15) para. 94 that in relation to the protection of the right to respect for private life of those subject to criminal records disclosure, under Article 8 ECHR, domestic law, including policy as 'soft law', must be:

> foreseeable as to its effects ... [affording] adequate legal protection against arbitrariness and accordingly indicate with sufficient clarity the scope and discretion conferred on the competent authorities and the manner of its exercise.

The issue then is whether the DVDS, with its guidance with considerable room for interpretation, offers the requisite 'sufficient clarity' so as to afford the correct degree of 'protection against arbitrariness' in relation to the disclosure of older and possibly spent convictions. The view of the Strasbourg Court is very much that the disclosure of older criminal convictions would be an interference with Article 8 ECHR rights, but not necessarily an unlawful one; albeit the 'staleness' of the convictions considered for disclosure is a relevant factor. The Strasbourg Court explained in *MM v United Kingdom* (2012) (Application no. 24029/07) at para. 188 that:

> although data contained in the criminal record are, in one sense, public information, their systematic storing in central records means that they are available for disclosure long after the event when everyone other than the person concerned is likely to have forgotten about it, and all the more so where, as in the present case, the caution has occurred in private. Thus as the conviction or caution itself recedes into the past, it becomes a part of the person's private life which must be respected.

On spent convictions, in addition to the required threshold for disclosure of a 'pressing need', allowing the police to use their common law power of disclosure in pursuit of public protection aims, the Home Office (2016: 16–17) guidance on the DVDS explains in some detail that:

> Where police officers have the power in the course of their duties to disclose spent convictions [or cautions etc.] under the Domestic Violence

> Disclosure Scheme it is important that disclosure still needs to be **reasonable and proportionate.** The police will work to take into account the age of the spent conviction during the decision-making process. Legal advice should be sought where necessary. Where such disclosure is lawful the Rehabilitation of Offenders Act 1974 provides an exemption under the Act from prosecution for the disclosure. [Bold emphasis in the original]

An issue with the DVDS and the other two main UK DADS, from the perspective of whether it interferes unlawfully with the Article 8 ECHR rights of disclosure subjects, is that they do not contain a truly clear time bar or 'currency rule' as part of its governing policy guidance, and which would preclude disclosures of police intelligence of criminal convictions after a certain point in time, and this is perhaps a missed opportunity in the guidance for all UK DADS. The European Court of Human Rights has recently determined in *MC v United Kingdom* (2021) (Application no. 51220/13) at para. 55 that a currency rule or disclosure time bar which separates disclosable and non-disclosable information based on the severity of the relevant offence is "not a blunt instrument but is intended to distinguish between ex-offenders on grounds which are in themselves relevant to whether disclosure should be made".

The issue of the degree to which spent convictions are disclosable for public protection purposes was explored by Whitford J in the High Court case of *X v Commissioner of Police of the Metropolis* [1985] 1 W.L.R. 420. Whitford J found that there was no offence committed under Section 9 of the 1974 Act when a Metropolitan police officer disclosed the spent convictions of X to Interpol. Interestingly, in *X* at 421 Whitford J also noted that it could be accepted that Section 4 of the 1974 Act creates no positive duty for the police to refrain from disclosing spent convictions information in the course of their duties. Following *Thorpe*, as discussed above, there is now a duty to disclose only according to the presence of a suitable 'pressing need' for disclosure, however, and taking into account the balance of human rights duties under the auspices of the Human Rights Act 1998, between the Article 8 ECHR rights of the offender and the (weightier) positive obligations to uphold Articles 2, 3 and 8 ECHR rights of their potential victim(s).

Notably, the construction and effect of Section 4 of the 1974 Act came into consideration in the case of *N v Governor of HMP Dartmoor* [2001] EWHC Admin 93. This was a case concerned with the proposed disclosure of spent convictions by a prison governor to social services. This related to a prisoner, N, who had spent convictions for indecency with a child and who was serving a long sentence for unrelated offences. The social services professionals concerned wished to know about these spent convictions in the event that N was either visited in prison by a child, or that when he was released he might go on to live with a partner and their children. In *N* the High Court determined that the protection afforded under the 1974 Act to spent convictions 'for all purposes in law' should be taken to mean the protection of spent convictions 'for all legal purposes', which we should take to mean in the sense of creating legal (and particularly contractual) relationships in the employer-employee setting of the workplace. Thus, with this narrower statutory interpretation, there was a more purposive, 'public protection'-type approach taken by the High Court in *N*, focusing on the perceived purpose of Parliament in preventing a mischief; that is, *unfairly* stigmatising rehabilitated offenders, and to refrain from following a literal approach to interpreting the language of Section 4 of the 1974 Act to prevent the working of an important feature of the public protection system. To inform this more purposive approach, specific reference was made by the High Court in *N* to the need to read the language of Section 4 of the 1974 Act with an eye to the public protection balance, again, between the Article 8 ECHR rights of the offender and the positive obligations to uphold Articles 2, 3 and 8 ECHR rights of their potential victim(s).

As noted earlier in this chapter, Hadjimatheou and Grace (2020) found that the police forces of England and Wales are divided in practice as to whether spent convictions should be disclosed under the DVDS. The Home Office guidance on the DVDS, when it is re-written, needs to take into account the need to specify exactly what criteria need to be met (and which Articles of the ECHR should be balanced) in making reasonable and proportionate disclosures of spent convictions, which is legally possible, as noted above, under the current legal framework—and the guidance must reflect this better. Police forces in England and Wales have lacked sufficient guidance on the matter to date. As noted above, there is as yet no direct case law arising from any of the UK DADS—and the legality of any aspect of the precise operation of the Schemes has never been challenged by way of judicial review—let alone a challenge to the guidance of the DVDS specifically in relation to the potential disclosures of spent convictions. It is good to think, from a public protection perspective, that the scope of the Scheme is not fixed and rigid with regard to the potential disclosure of spent convictions. However, a question remains as to whether the purposive, public protection-minded approach by the High Court in both *X* and *N* would be favoured in a judicial review of the language of DADS guidance concerning spent convictions. This is not least because the cases of *X* and *N* deal with the inter-agency sharing of spent convictions information (police officer to Interpol, and prison governor to social services, respectively), and the UK DADS are archetypically concerned with disclosures by the police, as a criminal justice agency, to members of the public individually in relation to their personal and private life.

7.5 International Legal Standards and Victims of Domestic Violence and Their Children

This section examines the relevant standards from two different international law instruments that apply to the operation of DADS and considers their ramifications for the UK legal system in the context of the DVDS in particular in England and Wales. These two sets of applicable standards are found in the Istanbul Convention (2011) and the United Nations Convention on the Rights of the Child (1989) in turn.

The Istanbul Convention

The *Council of Europe Convention on preventing and combating violence against women and domestic violence* (2011) is often known as the Istanbul Convention for ease of reference. The Istanbul Convention is more an 'aspiration' for the criminal justice system of England and Wales to adhere to in protecting the rights of victims of domestic violence, as HM Government recently failed to bring the Istanbul Convention into legal effect in the UK through ratification and further legislative provision as part of the Domestic Abuse Act 2021 (UK in a Changing Europe, 2021). But bringing the Istanbul Convention into effect in the UK in the future would mark an important policy position on the prevention of violence against women and girls, and at a time when some states under the Council of Europe banner are rowing back on their commitments to justice for female victims of violence: in March 2021, it was reported that Turkey is to withdraw from the Istanbul Convention (Eski, 2021).

In his book *Domestic Abuse and Human Rights*, Herring (2020: 158) notes that in his view, Domestic Abuse Disclosure Schemes would "play an important part in meeting the general duty to protect women from violence" under the Istanbul Convention. Grans has concluded that the Istanbul Convention represented a positive step in terms of building pressure on European states to commit resources to preventive measure combatting domestic violence. The ECHR and the Istanbul Convention take a different approach in their levels of specificity, and Grans (2018: 154) has observed that: "[t]he preventive obligations in the Istanbul Convention are more detailed, but … their content also needs to be spelled out".

Under the Istanbul Convention itself, then, there are layered duties which cumulatively would make measures including the DVDS more of a necessity, it could be argued, in relation to the regulation of domestic violence prevention, should the Convention become binding in the UK. Article 5(2) of the Istanbul Convention ('State obligations and due diligence') states that: "Parties shall take the necessary legislative and other measures to exercise due diligence to prevent, investigate, punish and provide reparation for acts of violence covered by the scope of this Convention that are perpetrated by non-State actors". This is tantamount to the systemic standard laid down by Articles 3 and 8 of the ECHR that requires states, as noted above, to adopt 'measures in the sphere of the relations between individuals' and 'to maintain and apply in practice an adequate legal framework affording protection against acts of violence by private individuals' under Article 8 ECHR (per *Irene Wilson v UK* (10601/09), 37); and under Article 3 ECHR, to take "all reasonable measures to prevent the recurrence of violent attacks" against individuals (*Opuz v Turkey* (2009) *33401/02*, 161–162).

In addition to this, under Article 7 of the Istanbul Convention (concerned with 'Comprehensive and co-ordinated policies'), we see that requirements for coherent regulation of measures and interventions designed to prevent domestic violence are stipulated in some detail, as follows:

1. Parties shall take the necessary legislative and other measures to adopt and implement state-wide effective, comprehensive and co-ordinated policies encompassing all relevant measures to prevent and combat all forms of violence covered by the scope of this Convention and offer a holistic response to violence against women.
2. Parties shall ensure that policies referred to in paragraph 1 place the rights of the victim at the centre of all measures and are implemented by way of effective co-operation among all relevant agencies, institutions and organisations.

Prima facie then, the UK DADS in operation would help HM Government demonstrate their meeting these standards as set by the Istanbul Convention. However, the current lack of a body of satisfactory evidence that the DVDS, for one, actually works to prevent domestic violence, as opposed to displacing it (as discussed in previous Chapters), would suggest that DADS are not necessarily measures yet mandatory under the requirements for 'effective, comprehensive and co-ordinated policies' demanded in Article 7(2). Indeed, any evidence that DADS might heighten the vulnerability for some victims could put the operation of a particular DADS policy at odds with the 'victim-centred' rationale found in Article 7(2). Research conducted for this book has found an estimated rate of abuse by disclosure subjects, post-disclosure, in relation to at least 45% of disclosure recipients, for example (see Chap. 5).

In Chapter III of the Istanbul Convention (concerned with 'Prevention'), we see that Article 12(2) requires that Parties shall take the necessary legislative and other measures to prevent all forms of violence covered by the scope of this Convention by any natural or legal person", while Article 12(3) demands that "Any measures taken pursuant to this chapter shall take into account and address the specific needs of persons made vulnerable by particular circumstances and shall place the human rights of all victims at their centre". In addition to this, Article 18(1) creates a general duty: "Parties shall take the necessary legislative or other measures to protect all victims from any further acts of violence". Much more specifically, the multi-agency decision to consider a disclosure under the Scheme, or the possibility of a more interventionist or offender-oriented measure separate to the potential disclosure under the Scheme, would be regulated by Article 51(1) of the Istanbul, which states that:

> Parties shall take the necessary legislative or other measures to ensure that an assessment of the lethality risk, the seriousness of the situation and the risk of repeated violence is carried out by all relevant authorities in order to manage the risk and if necessary to provide co-ordinated safety and support.

The DVDS guidance, in its current version, would at least play its own part in ensuring compliance with this multi-agency standard, as in the Scheme guidance it is emphasised that (Home Office, 2016: 57):

> Once the police have determined whether the initial trigger can be categorised as a 'concern' or 'no concern', the final decision to disclose must be referred to the local multi-agency forum for consideration at their next meeting. **While it will be for the police to make the final decision on whether the trigger is a 'concern' or 'no concern' and, consequently, whether a disclosure should be made, this should be done with the input of the multi-agency forum**. [Emphasis in the original]

It remains to be seen if the Istanbul Convention will be ratified and brought into effect in the UK by way of statute should the UK government correct the flaw in the Domestic Abuse Act 2021 which precludes much support for migrant domestic abuse victims with 'no recourse to public funds' (UK in a Changing Europe, 2021). However, the Istanbul Convention is not the only possible, or unincorporated, international law standard which sets potential guiding principles on the prevention of domestic violence in the UK. The United Nations Convention on the Rights of the Child is something that at least features in a considerable amount of judicial deliberation in the UK already, and is considered in relation to the operation of DADS in the section below.

The 'Best Interests of the Child'

The United Nations Convention on the Rights of the Child (UNCRC) addresses the notion of the interests of children in legal processes, and the DVDS guidance from the Home Office for England and Wales is, surprisingly, largely silent on the operation of the Scheme in the parent-child/family sphere. Current Scheme guidance simply suggests that the police, in making a disclosure, should put the onus on an individual receiving a disclosure to use that information to help them keep their child(ren) safe (Home Office, 2016); and that the police should carry out checks to see if support has been sought by an individual in order to keep their child(ren) safe (Home Office, 2016: 51–52). The current DVDS guidance (Home Office, 2016) does not, however, put the 'best interests' of children sufficiently into the mix in terms of consideration and decision-making as to whether a disclosure should actually be made.

Domestic violence victims receiving disclosures under any of the three main UK DADS may well be parents or carers for children. As Westmarland has noted, mothers may have a difficulty in acting on information supplied to them under the DVDS (Westmarland, 2015: 27). For victims who are parents, and for child victims of domestic abuse in general, and aside from the operation of just the DVDS, the United Nations Convention on the Rights of the Child (UNCRC) is a relevant international law set of standards that arguably apply in this context—although there is some judicial disagreement as to the extent to which the UNCRC is actually in effect in the UK 'dualist' constitution (as discussed in *R (DA and others) v Secretary of State for Work and Pensions* [2018] EWCA Civ 504). The UK dualist constitution is such that international law protections must be 'incorporated' for them to take legal effect, normally through statute law, even when HM Government has already signed the relevant treaty. There is no doubt though that if provisions of the UNCRC did apply directly in the UK then there would be an effect on the procedural operation of the DVDS where children were concerned.

The UNCRC contains as a 'headline' duty the principle, in Article 3(1) UNCRC, that: "In all actions concerning children, whether undertaken by public or private social welfare institutions, courts of law, administrative authorities or legislative bodies, the best interests of the child shall be a primary consideration". If this applied directly to UK police forces, and thus to the operation of the Scheme, then this would mean that the needs of children affected by (potential) domestic violence in a relationship would need to be taken into account, according to the 'best interests' of the children concerned. Hypothetically this could give weight to an argument in favour of withholding information from a potential victim under the Scheme as well as giving weight to the argument to provide information to them, depending on the exact circumstances of the known risks, the stability of the family and the exact nature of the information concerned.

Currently, the 'best interests of the child' as a principle of 'primary consideration' likely applies only in terms of interpreting the extent and application of Articles of the ECHR in a possible disclosure scenario under one of the UK DADS. The recent deliberations of the Supreme Court has, however, make it plain that if the Article 3 UNCRC 'best interests' of children standard was not a principle that could be 'engaged' on the facts of a case, and so could not apply directly as a 'standalone' ground of review (*R (SC and others v Secretary of State for Work and Pensions)* [2021] UKSC 26), it could be used in a more broadly interpretive fashion in order to augment discussion of ECHR grounds themselves (see also *R (DA and others) v Secretary of State for Work and Pensions* [2018] EWCA Civ 504).

As things stand the most useful thing using the provisions of Article 3(1) UNCRC to inform police officers, in applying Article 3 ECHR or Article 8 ECHR to a disclosure decision-making process, would be to put the 'best interests' of children explicitly into the consideration as part of the process for deciding on a disclosure according to a 'pressing need'. The 'best interest of children' test should be as much at the heart of decision-making under the Scheme as the securing of safety from harm for potential adult victims of domestic violence (although these will often be common issues). The guidance on disclosure processes for the UK DADS should be refined accordingly.

It might, thankfully, be an inevitability that statutory DVDS guidance will, at least for the use of a disclosure scheme in England and Wales, come to explicitly consider the vulnerability and the wellbeing of children in the context of any possible disclosure. The Domestic Abuse Act

2021 has now been enacted by Parliament, and S.77(1) of the Act stipulates that: “The Secretary of State must issue guidance to chief officers of police about the disclosure of police information by police forces for the purposes of preventing domestic abuse”. In terms of the new statutory definition of domestic abuse in England and Wales, S.1 of the 2021 Act indicates that behaviour between two people who are ‘personally connected’ can qualify as ‘domestic abuse’ in one or more of a variety of ways (namely physical, sexual, psychological, emotional or economic abuse; or coercive, controlling or threatening behaviour; and whether as a single incident or course of conduct). Importantly, S.3(2) of the 2021 Act then entails that children are to be defined as the victims of any of these types of abuse directed at their parents, family or any person who has parental responsibility for them.

It is difficult to determine, however, how a directly applicable procedural duty to consider the ‘best interests’ of a child in deciding whether to make a DVDS disclosure, or in the manner in which such a disclosure is made, would actually work in practice. Of course, this issue would need considerable research in the field, or consultation with child protection experts, before a definitive answer could be given, but it could not, *prima facie*, be a bad thing to have a more holistic set of factors in DVDS decision-making processes, especially concerning the issue of the interests of children in a disclosure being made, or not made.

7.6 Part 3 of the Data Protection Act 2018 and the UK Domestic Abuse Disclosure Schemes

At the time of writing, none of the guidance documents that govern the operation of the three main UK Domestic Abuse Disclosure Schemes make reference to the Data Protection Act 2018 and the details of the statutory framework it creates for the management and disclosures of criminal histories information, which are discussed below. Suffice to say that these three guidance documents should all be updated in due course with regard to this need for revision; and this is, of course, a recommendation of this research. The practical changes to the operation of the UK Domestic Abuse Disclosure Schemes that the relevant provisions of the DPA 2018 may require, and which would need to be reflected in those revisions to the guidance documents, are discussed below.

Disclosures of personal data of subjects of the Domestic Abuse Disclosure Schemes undertaken by police forces in the UK are done for 'law enforcement purposes'. These are defined by Section 31 of the DPA 2018 as "the purposes of the prevention, investigation, detection or prosecution of criminal offences or the execution of criminal penalties, including the safeguarding against and the prevention of threats to public security". Disclosures under the UK Domestic Abuse Disclosure Schemes are of course considered and then made with the aim of preventing criminal offences connected with possible domestic abuse in the future. Section 35 of the DPA 2018 requires that processing for a law enforcement process is 'lawful and fair', in the context of the operation of the UK Domestic Abuse Disclosure Schemes, if it is 'based on law' (S.35(2)), which would include the common law bases of the UK Domestic Abuse Disclosure Schemes, and 'necessary' for the purpose of preventing criminal offences (S.35(2)(b)); or, where the disclosure involves sharing sensitive personal data concerning, for example, the ethnicity or health data of an individual, then the disclosure must be 'strictly necessary' for the purpose of preventing criminal offences where a person is at risk of harm, and on the basis of any published Scheme guidance as an 'appropriate policy document in place' (S.35(5)(a)(b)(c) and Schedule 8 of the 2018 Act).

Section 37 of the DPA 2018 requires that "personal data processed for any of the law enforcement purposes must be adequate, relevant and not excessive in relation to the purpose for which it is processed". These principles of 'adequacy', relevance and non-excessiveness (or a certain interpretation of 'proportionality', therefore, it could be suggested) require that disclosures under the DVDS must be carefully balanced between the need to impress upon a recipient that the disclosure is in response to the 'pressing need' required for the disclosure, from a risk assessment-perspective, but also the need to make only the most limited disclosure to achieve that intended effect. This limited degree of disclosure will always be difficult to judge in practice, however, as police practitioners will struggle to predict how a disclosure recipient might react.

The provisions of Section 38 of the DPA 2018 would be important in the context of a possible challenge from a subject of a disclosure. Section 38(2) of the 2018 Act entails that disclosures under the UK Domestic Abuse Disclosure Schemes must be made in such a way that the factual information being disclosed (say the details of arrests, or convictions, of a subject) must be conveyed in such a way as to make it plain that it is different in quality from the finding of any risk assessment (a 'personal assessment', in the language of Section 38(2)); that is, the subjective determination that an applicant or recipient of a disclosure is in 'pressing need' of a disclosure to protect them from the subject concerned. The latter is of course a 'personal assessment' of the police decision-making panel or forum concerned. In terms of how this might affect victims' vulnerability, it could be argued that any perceived disparity between the convictions information relayed, for example, and the risk assessment made by officers might cloud any feeling the victim had in their own mind as to the dangerousness of the disclosure subject, with potentially dangerous consequences indeed. Furthermore, police labelling of a risky subject needs to be couched in terms of whether a subject was a convicted abuser or a suspected abuser only. Section 38(3) of the 2018 Act entails that if the police only have information of an arrest of a subject ("persons arrested"), they may not be able to most clearly label him, despite their own suspicions, as a domestic violence perpetrator, if there are no convictions on the criminal record of a subject for such offences ('persons convicted').

Some provisions of Part 3 of the 2018 Act focus on the procedural protections to be afforded to the subjects of disclosures. Taken together, the provisions in Sections 38(4) and 38(5) would seem to suggest that if it were reasonable in the circumstances, a subject should be approached to clarify the vaguer details in a police intelligence report that might be disclosed under the Domestic Abuse Disclosure Schemes in question, absent any 'hard' evidence of the perpetration of domestic abuse on the part of a subject, such as a conviction.

Lady Hale has set out the rationale behind the presumption in common law that the criminal records and police intelligence of perpetrators of domestic violence would be, as a matter of public policy, required to be maintained, perhaps rectified or clarified, but not deleted. Lady Hale wrote in *Catt R (Catt and T) v ACPO* [2015] UKSC 9 (at para. 54) that:

> It is well known that, for a variety of reasons, complaints of domestic violence are often not followed through to prosecution and conviction. But it is vital for the police, when responding to any new complaint, to know whether there have been similar complaints in the past. Domestic violence often escalates in seriousness with each new incident, and the police have to be aware of this when considering how to respond. It is not too dramatic to say that lives have been saved as a result.

In relation to this, under the provisions of Section 46 of the 2018 Act, there is a recodification of the common law position on the ability of an individual to have their criminal record accurately represented in its retention and disclosure. However, Section 37(4) of the 2018 Act suggests that the police are under a statutory duty to *proactively* consider whether criminal records information and intelligence is accurate and complete before they disclose it—again perhaps strengthening the argument that an individual should be consulted, as a potential subject of a disclosure, and before a disclosure is made. However, as discussed above, this would raise concerns about the vulnerability of victims of domestic violence as applicants and recipients of information under the UK Domestic Abuse Disclosure Schemes. Aside from the issue of the procedural rights of disclosure subjects, section 33(6) of the Data Protection Act 2018 now explains that "*Restriction of processing* means the marking of stored personal data with the aim of limiting its processing for the future". So if a UK police force felt that it could not render information accurate because of sufficient doubt, on the balance of probabilities, over the event it recorded (e.g., where we are talking about 'intelligence' on an offence, rather than a record of an arrest), that information should be internally barred from disclosure as a result.

7.7 Conclusions

This chapter has addressed a rationale for more comprehensively setting out the parameters of disclosures under DADS in the UK, which despite an evolving statutory framework in England and Wales, as well as in Scotland and Northern Ireland, are still common law based at their heart.

Additionally, in the future the operation of parts of both the Istanbul Convention and the UNCRC might be written into the DVDS guidance in a fourth or later iteration; whereas we can assume the Data Protection Act 2018 would be more automatically included in an update. With regard to the UNCRC and Istanbul Convention principles explored in this chapter, this might make more standardised a requirement of bringing more perspectives from non-police agencies to bear on DVDS decision-making, and would arguably make decision-making around disclosures more oriented towards the 'best interests' of children. In terms of the Home Office DVDS guidance specifically, greater emphasis on protecting vulnerable victims, including children, and making disclosure decisions with due regard to their needs and best interests, and protections under human rights standards, are the aim of a number of recommendations included in the next and final chapter of this book.

References

Ashworth, A., & Zedner, L. (2014). *Preventive justice*. Oxford University Press.

BBC News. (2015, October 28). Police letters warn 1,900 people of 'threat to life'. *BBC News*. Retrieved June 30, 2020, from http://www.bbc.co.uk/news/uk-34651682

Centre for Women's Justice. (2019, March 19). *Centre for Women's Justice Supercomplaint: Police failure to use protective measures in cases involving violence against women and girls*. Retrieved June 20, 2020, from https://www.centreforwomensjustice.org.uk/news/2019/3/20/cwj-launch-super-complaint-police-failure-to-use-protective-measures-in-cases-involving-violence-against-women-and-girls

Child Poverty Action Group. (2019, December 6). Domestic abuse is an economic issue—For its victims and for society. Retrieved July 19, 2021, from https://cpag.org.uk/news-blogs/news-listings/domestic-abuse-economic-issue-%E2%80%93-its-victims-and-society

Council of Europe (CoE). (2008). *The Final Activity Report of the Council of Europe Task Force to Combat Violence against Women, including Domestic Violence (EG-TFV)*. Strasbourg: Gender Equality & Anti-Trafficking Division Directorate General of Human Rights & Legal Affairs, Council of Europe.

Department of Justice (Northern Ireland). (2018). *Domestic Violence and Abuse Disclosure Scheme guidance.*

Duggan, M. (2018). Victim hierarchies in the domestic violence disclosure scheme. *International Review of Victimology, 24*(2), 199.

Duggan, M., & Grace, J. (2018). Assessing vulnerabilities in the Domestic Violence Disclosure Scheme. *Child and Family Law Quarterly, 2*, 145.

Eski, B. (2021). Protests as Turkey pulls out of treaty to protect women. [online] *The Guardian*. Retrieved March 31, 2021, from https://www.theguardian.com/world/2021/mar/20/turkey-pulls-out-of-international-accord-designed-to-protect-women

Grace, J. (2015). Clare's Law, or the national Domestic Violence Disclosure Scheme: The contested legalities of criminality information sharing. *The Journal of Criminal Law, 79*(1), 36–45.

Grans, L. (2018). The Istanbul convention and the positive obligation to prevent violence. *Human Rights Law Review, 18*(1), 133.

Hadjimatheou, K., & Grace, J. (2020). 'No black and white answer about how far we can go': Police decision making under the domestic violence disclosure scheme. *Policing and Society*. https://doi.org/10.1080/10439463.2020.1795169

Herring, J. (2020). *Domestic abuse and human rights*. Intersentia.

Home Office. (2013). Domestic Violence Disclosure Scheme impact assessment. Retrieved June 16, 2020, from https://www.gov.uk/government/uploads/system/uploads/attachment_data/file/260899/DVDS_IA.pdf

Home Office. (2016). *Domestic Violence Disclosure Scheme (DVDS) guidance*. Retrieved June 16, 2020, from https://www.gov.uk/government/uploads/system/uploads/attachment_data/file/575361/DVDS_guidance_FINAL_v3.pdf

Ministry of Justice. (2020). *Guidance on the Rehabilitation of Offenders Act 1974 and the exceptions order 1975*. [online]. Retrieved June 24, 2021, from https://assets.publishing.service.gov.uk/government/uploads/system/uploads/attachment_data/file/945449/rehabilitation-of-offenders-guidance.pdf

Nash, M. (2010). The politics of public protection. In M. Nash & A. Williams (Eds.), *Handbook of public protection*. Willan.

Police Scotland. (2015, October). Disclosure Scheme for Domestic Abuse Scotland—Standard operating procedure, author copy, obtained from a freedom-of-information request in 2017.

Potter, T. (2020). More people using right to find out if partner has history of violence. [online] *East Anglian Daily Times*. Retrieved March 31, 2021, from https://www.eadt.co.uk/news/clare-s-law-applications-rise-in-suffolk-6636536

Trust for London. (2012). Measuring the impact of cuts in public expenditure on the provision of services to prevent violence against women and girls. Retrieved June 30, 2020, from https://www.trustforlondon.org.uk/publications/measuring-impact-cuts-public-expenditure-provision-services-prevent-violence-against-women-and-girls/

UK in a Changing Europe. (2021). Istanbul convention: 10 years on, still not ratified. Retrieved July 19, 2021, from https://ukandeu.ac.uk/istanbul-convention-10-years-on-still-not-ratified/

Westmarland, N. (2015). *Violence against women: Criminological perspectives on men's violences*. Routledge.

Women's Aid. (2020). *The Domestic Abuse Report 2020: The Annual Audit*. Bristol: Women's Aid.

8

Reflections, Conclusions and Recommendations

8.1 Introduction

This book has already highlighted that in England and Wales, the main focus as a jurisdiction for this research, there is a paucity of good news or improving performance in the way that the criminal justice systems tackles domestic abuse, with falling prosecutions and court backlogs. Despite the recent policymaking shake-up represented by the Domestic Abuse Act 2021, there remain many troubling shortcomings in terms of the prevention of violence against women and girls and the degree of support for victims of domestic violence in particular. In 2020, for example, there were only 66% of the estimated required minimum number of independent domestic violence advisers (IDVAs) in England and Wales due, in part, to a 37% increase in the number of cases heard by multi-agency risk assessment conferences (MARACs) between 2016 and 2020 (Safelives, 2021). Charles Thomson (2020) has reported that in the Metropolitan Police Service (MPS), between 2015–2016 and 2019–2020, 'positive outcomes' (such as an arrest) in domestic abuse cases fell by two-thirds, from 36% of domestic abuse cases to just 14% of such cases; and that while this was partly down to more victims of domestic abuse supporting

J. Grace, *Domestic Abuse Disclosure Schemes*,
https://doi.org/10.1007/978-3-030-89039-1_8

alternatives to arrest and prosecution, it was also due to officer levels in the MPS decreasing slightly, at a time when yearly numbers of domestic abuse reports to the force rose significantly, and by more than 20% in the same period. As reported by Barr and Topping (2021), the officer leading on rape crimes for the National Police Chief's Council, Sarah Crew, is of the view that one factor in rape prosecutions falling to a five-year low in the year to March 2020 was the impact on specialist units of rape investigators caused by 'austerity', that is, government funding cuts. Amidst this uncertainty, and lack of support in real terms for progress on the prevention of domestic abuse as a public protection issue, comes a distinct increase in the use and promotion of the Domestic Violence Disclosure Scheme (in a way that is being replicated in the 'policy spiral' highlighted in earlier chapters).

The recent Parliamentary process of creating the Domestic Abuse Act 2021 featured a distinct move to augment with, or to operate in parallel to, the DVDS, a register of perpetrators of domestic abuse a proposal that became, in the end, a statutory widening of the scope of Multi-Agency Public Protection Arrangements. At the last stages of the passage of what would become the Domestic Abuse Act 2021, in the House of Commons in the Westminster Parliament, a number of MPs hotly debated whether the police service of England and Wales needed to have greater statutory regulation of their work with convicted domestic abusers. Members of Parliament were debating an amendment to the Domestic Abuse Bill (2020) that would see a broadening of the range of offenders to be placed on the scheme of Multi-Agency Public Protection Arrangements and subject to routine monitoring by law enforcement and rehabilitation agencies. Victoria Atkins MP, refuting the need for what was commonly labelled a domestic abuse perpetrators' register, explained that the proposed system was not necessary, given the new offenders strategy, that was forthcoming; new inter-agency information sharing requirements to follow in the Police, Crime, Sentencing and Courts Bill (2021); and a commitment to more funding for perpetrator programmes (HC Deb, 2021, vol 693, col 118). However, Stella Creasy, a Labour MP, was unimpressed, asking (HC Deb, 2021, vol 693, col 125): "What does the Minister think will stop the cycle of violence, if not to clarify who these men are and monitor them—not to ask, as Clare's Law does, for victims to come forward, looking after their own safety, but for us to take collective responsibility?"

In early 2021, it emerged that part of the arrest and crime report records relating to around 115,000 people with profiles on the Police National Computer had been accidentally deleted; and while none of these records were conviction details, the Local Government Association was reported as being concerned about the safeguarding details that might have been lost (Proctor, 2021). But a more serious intelligence failing in the context of policing domestic abuse is the lack of proper legal drivers to create linkages and comprehensive records to help forces manage serial domestic abusers. In explaining the notion of a register of domestic abusers to match that of sexual offenders, and to help remedy this issue in part, Lord Hunt of Kings Heath said in a debate on the Domestic Abuse Bill that (*Hansard*, 10 February 2021 col 360):

> There is no legal framework or national process in England and Wales by which serial [domestic abuse] perpetrators are routinely identified, monitored and managed. … Without MAPPA-plus, Clare's law will never work effectively, because there is no duty on the police to add any information or intelligence about a perpetrator's previous offending to a local or national system. If information is put on a local system, it lacks the detail required. The burden is placed on the victim, and too often the perpetrator's narrative is believed rather than the victim's.

In the debate on the second reading in the House of Commons for the Domestic Abuse Bill (2020), Liz Saville Roberts MP observed that (HC Deb 28 April 2020 vol 675, col 293):

> The final point I would like to raise is about the domestic violence disclosure scheme, which is also known as Clare's law. Although in and of itself it is beneficial, it continues to place responsibility on the potential victim to act and to take the initiative: to request information from the police when that person has concerns about a partner's past as a domestic abuse perpetrator. I would continue to ask the Government to consider again the value of a domestic abuse register for repeat perpetrators as a way to shift the responsibility to where it belongs—away from the potential victims and on to the authorities and the offender themselves.

Following this, in the debate following the report stage of the Bill in the House of Commons, Yvette Cooper MP argued that (HC Deb 6 July 2020, vol 678 col 715):

> We need to make sure that when the call comes in about domestic abuse by someone who has been convicted before for abuse against someone else, it is not just treated as a new or one-off offence. We need to ensure that there are systems in place to join up the dots to link police, probation and support services together and to monitor people who have a series of previous domestic abuse or stalking convictions so that if they start a new relationship, the police and local services know that a new family are at risk and can take action. Too often, that does not happen. Clare's law does not solve the problem because it relies on an individual asking about an offender's history. What if they do not know to ask? What if they are too scared? Why is it still left to victims to ask for help, rather than having a proper system in place to monitor serial abusers and offenders?

However, the relevant cross-party amendment aiming to add a domestic abusers and stalkers register, entailing notification requirements and strict monitoring processes, was not added to the final framework of the Act. Instead ministers promised that new statutory guidance on domestic abusers and stalkers would be created under the Multi-Agency Public Protection Arrangements (MAPPA) in place under the Criminal Justice Act 2003. Charlotte Kneer, the chief executive of Reigate and Banstead Women's Aid refuge in Surrey, has highlighted that (Oppenheim, 2021):

> There is currently no monitoring of serial perpetrators. This is a common sense amendment to the domestic abuse bill that could save lives. … It is devastating that with a landslide vote in the Lords, it was voted against. I genuinely don't understand why they are voting against it. If the government is saying they are prioritising violence against women and girls, today's vote shows their words don't ring true.

A forthcoming system of new Domestic Abuse Protection Notices and Orders might also have had a boost from a new statutory duty to create better access to criminal histories data for police officers considering using the new notices. Baron Hunt of Kings Heath spoke during a reading of the Domestic Abuse Bill and explained that on police data sharing and linkage (Hansard HL 27 January 2021 col 1640):

> we know that police forces do not share data systematically, apart from via the national police computer, which records only charges. This calls into question the full effectiveness of Clare's law and police forces' ability to give full information to potential victims about known abusers and, in the process, to prevent future abuse. The system can clearly be improved. Enshrining in legislation the ability for the police to use previous criminal records to determine whether to hand out a notice could be an important prompt to improve data sharing and, in doing so, save lives.

Perhaps most notoriously, in passing the Domestic Abuse Act 2021, the government, in controlling Parliament, did not see fit to level the playing field for victims of domestic abuse who had an insecure immigration status and who are labelled with the phrase 'No Recourse to Public Funds' (NRPF). The charity Women's Aid have highlighted that currently just 4% of refuges in England can accept women with NRPF status (Topping, 2021), for example.

8.2 Recent Policy Options on the DVDS

The Home Office impact assessment on the 2020 Domestic Abuse Bill, as it then was, had mooted the following policy options on possible reform to the basis for the DVDS in England and Wales (HM Government, 2020a: 11):

> (a) Option 1: Do Nothing. This will maintain the current situation where the scheme is not consistently applied across forces. This likely results in missed opportunities for the scheme to be used and potentially reduces the sharing of information with potential victims of domestic abuse. (b) Option 2: Place the guidance underpinning Domestic Violence Disclosure Scheme on a statutory footing: This will require the police to have regard to the guidance and so improve consistency in the application of the scheme. … Option 2 is the Government's preferred option because it will raise awareness of the DVDS and drive better consistency in its application.

There was no consideration of placing the exact workings of the DVDS on a statutory basis in detail, however. The Home Office Impact Assessment also noted that, based on estimates averaged over the costs for disclosures for six Anglo-Welsh forces, police costs for disclosures were or are: "£1,006 for each disclosure from the 'right to ask' (where the police disclose information via a request from a member of the public) [and] £789 for each disclosure from the 'right to know' (where a proactive decision is made to consider disclosing information in order to protect a potential victim)" (HM Government, 2020a: 32). This would mean a total cost of the operation of the DVDS in England and Wales, alone, of more than £5.75 million in the year to March 2019: equivalent to the annual salaries of 178 therapeutic support workers assisting victims of domestic violence and their families based on a benchmark annual salary for a therapeutic victim-support professional of £32,181 (Women's Aid, 2019: 28).

But what also of the social cost of 'displacement' from one victim to another, if an offender is not rehabilitated, potentially resulting in even more violence? And what of the increased risk and harm to a victim themselves in leaving a relationship? More use of the Scheme would result logically in more of these sorts of wider 'costs'. The Home Office impact assessment explained "it is assumed that the policy leads to an increase in volumes [of disclosures] between 5 and 10 per cent" (HM Government, 2020a: 32). But the use of the DVDS has been increasing at much greater rate than this for the last six years, while the wider social costs of the DVDS in terms of actual harms to victims receiving disclosures, or otherwise, have not been mapped, as we know.

The human rights impact assessment published concerning the 2020 Bill noted that (HM Government, 2020b: 23–24): "Clause 64 puts the guidance issued by the Secretary of State supporting the domestic violence disclosure scheme on a statutory footing. This is with a view to encouraging greater, consistent and transparent use of the scheme by police chief officers." But transparency surely requires a duty to evaluate and review the use of the Scheme by each force and/or the Home Office, and to be publicly accountable for this. A key issue for police forces to be re-regulated over the DVDS would be the issue of children and their 'best interests' in terms of how they would be affected by possible disclosures due to the effect of Article 3 UNCRC. Another such key issue would be a more concrete basis and series of tests for disclosures to satisfy the foreseeability requirements of positive obligations to offenders under a qualified right like Article 8 ECHR, and a statutory duty to consider victim safety planning in the event of a disclosure in order to satisfy the requirements of Article 3 ECHR to take reasonable steps to prevent repeated victimisation at the hands of an offender. As well as these substantive elements of disclosure decision-making, the provisions of this clause in the Bill could have put procedural duties on chief constables and the Home Secretary to review the true effectiveness and impact of the operation of the DVDS.

The Explanatory Notes to the Domestic Abuse Bill put before Parliament in early March 2020 did commit the government to some greater scrutiny and a degree of reform as to the operation of the DVDS, explaining that the guidance on the DVDS produced by the Home Office, a new statutory basis, would cover:

> Recommended minimum levels of knowledge and experience required by practitioners to discharge their functions under the DVDS effectively. … Suggested step-by-step processes and timescales for the two disclosure routes under the scheme (the 'right to ask' and the 'right to know'), including example scenarios for each route. … Minimum standards of information to be obtained from the applicant … [and] Minimum standards of intelligence checks to be completed. (HM Government, 2020c: 46)

This list of areas of re-focus promised by the explanatory notes to the Bill, as outlined by HM Government as the Bill was discussed by Parliament, did look to satisfy some of the concerns that this research has raised about the operation and regulation of the DVDS, particularly in relation to the need for clearer guidance, as follows (HM Government, 2020c: 46):

> Guidance on robust risk assessment and safety planning in order to safeguard the individual or individuals potentially at risk of domestic abuse. … Suggested types of information which may be disclosed under the scheme, such as details of allegations, charges, prosecutions and convictions for

relevant offences … [and] Guidance on what constitutes a 'reasonable and proportionate' disclosure in line with relevant human rights and data protection legislation and the [Rehabilitation of Offenders Act 1974].

Jess Phillips MP argued at the relevant Public Bill Committee for an amendment to the provisions of the Bill concerning a statutory basis for the DVDS. I had written to the Parliamentary office of Jess Phillips, with a summary of the conclusions of my research on the DVDS, and provided her office with some suggested amendments. Jess Phillips MP then (unsuccessfully) moved and argued for the text of the amendments I had suggested (Domestic Abuse Bill (2020a) Public Bill Committee Proceedings, 2020: 15) using the following proposed amendments to Clause 64 of the Bill, as it was then:

(1A) Before issuing guidance under this section, the Secretary of State must undertake a comprehensive assessment of the contribution of the disclosure of police information to the prevention of domestic abuse, drawing on disclosures made by chief officers of police prior to this section coming into force. (1B) Disclosures of police information for the purposes of the prevention of domestic abuse may only be made—(a) where reasonable, necessary, and proportionate, (b) with regard to the best interests of children likely to be affected by the disclosure, and (c) after ensuring there is an operational plan to support the recipients of such disclosures. … (2B) Each chief officer of police of a police force must annually review—(a) the compliance of their own force with any guidance issued under this section, and (b) the overall contribution of the disclosures under that guidance to the prevention of domestic abuse in their force area.

Victoria Atkins MP, government minister for safeguarding, responded to the moved amendment (Domestic Abuse Bill (2020b) Public Bill Committee, 2020), explaining that the government

share the ambition that local forces should be aware of how they are operating Clare's law, including whether that is in accordance with the published statutory guidance and with a full understanding of the impact and outcomes of the scheme on victims. Again, I maintain that that is a matter for the new statutory guidance, but our discussions on that will be taken forward as part of our review. I hope the hon. Lady will be content with those representations.

Jess Phillips MP then withdrew the relevant amendment I had written for her to move. So it remains to be seen how much work HM Government will do in 2021–2022 on these reforms to DVDS guidance for police forces in England and Wales. At the time of the completion of this book, there is doubt over how the operation of the DVDS can be better demonstrated, procedurally or substantively, to better incorporate or comply with Article 3 UNCRC, Article 3 ECHR and Article 8 ECHR (see the discussion in Chap. 7).

8.3 A Summary of the Findings in This Book

This book has sought to address three key research questions:

1. To what extent do Domestic Abuse Disclosure Schemes show a lack of regulatory responsibility for preventing domestic violence?
2. To what extent do the Domestic Abuse Disclosure Schemes adequately address issues of victim vulnerability?
3. To what extent do the Domestic Abuse Disclosure Schemes pose issues of coherence in terms of their legality, and in relation to the context of disclosures?

An overview can now be given in this concluding chapter as to the findings of this book on these three points.

Regulatory Responsibility

This research has shown that elements of strong regulatory responsibility have been missing from the governance of Domestic Abuse Disclosure Schemes. This is true particularly in England and Wales, where there is less of an excuse for this shortfall in the degree of regulatory responsibility shown, since there has been more time for the DVDS to have been thoroughly reviewed and reformed as to its effectiveness, and the consistency of its operation. The general trend for the last several years has been for greater volumes of applications to both the Right to Ask and Right to Know strands (see Table 1.1 in Chap. 1). New statutory guidance on the operation of the DVDS is forthcoming now that the Domestic Abuse Act 2021 has been passed by Parliament. However, under section 77 of the 2021 Act this process will only update the current DVDS guidance (and not those for the other two main UK DADS), and will simply put a duty on chief officers to 'have regard' to it; although as reprised below in this chapter, there might be some issues where the current DVDS guidance is not entirely fit for purpose. But a main concern about the operation of the DVDS in England and Wales is the great variation in disclosure rates geographically, that is, between police forces (see Table 1.2 in Chap. 1). Police data recording needs to be standardised in how forces report applications and disclosures, and basic reasons for refusals of applications. At the moment, not only do we not know why there are these great differences in disclosure rates between police force areas, we do not know if they are truly to be believed.

Victim Vulnerability

In terms of the research question explored in this book concerning victims' vulnerability, a key concern is the ongoing doubt over the efficacy of actual disclosures under any DADS. This is the core concern in this research around issues of DADS failing to tackle, and to take into account, victims' vulnerability. At least 45% of recipients of DVDS disclosures in a period in 2014–2015 in England and Wales went on to be the victims of abuse by the very subject of that disclosure by mid-2018, as shown by police force responses to my FOI requests, as received from 26 forces over the summer of 2018 (see Tables 5.1 and 5.2 in Chap. 5). Furthermore, the details of the Domestic Homicide Review report in relation to the tragic death of Kerri McAuley (Graham, 2018) shows that the risk of 'displacement' of offending (where a perpetrator of abuse moves on to another and potentially more vulnerable victim following a disclosure to an initial partner) is very real.

Coherent Legality

As for the third research question addressed by this research, on the issue of a coherent legality, and as between the UK DADS: There is a need to update and to standardise elements of the DVDS guidance for England and Wales to match the best-practice features of the guidance on both the Domestic Violence and Abuse Disclosure Scheme (DVADS) in Northern Ireland and the Disclosure Scheme for Domestic Abuse (Scotland) (the DSDAS). These ongoing issues in terms of legal (in)consistencies, both doctrinal and constitutional, and in ways that mean the UK DADS will all operate differently, meaning that an opportunity for a statutory basis for more coherent legality across the UK DADS has probably just been lost, with the provisions in the Domestic Abuse Act 2021 only governing the DVDS in England and Wales. It can be hoped that ongoing revisions of DADS guidance in different parts of the UK, even if a staggered process, can reach commensurate incorporation of points of reference and applicable standards from the UNCRC, the Istanbul Convention, Part 3 of the Data Protection Act 2018, and, crucially, explicit priorities and factors in decision-making stemming from Articles 2, 3 and 8 ECHR.

8.4 A Summary of Regulatory Problems Contributing to the 'Policy Spiral' of DADS

There is an innate tension in the nature and operation of the Domestic Abuse Disclosure Schemes which this research has surveyed; namely that their policy formulation and implementation has more of an underlying trade-off; that is, between values of offender rehabilitation as a strand of respect for the private life of individuals and values of public protection as a strand of the positive obligation to prevent degrading treatment of the vulnerable and of victims of domestic violence. However, this tension between public protection and rehabilitation, and the complexities of 'forgetting' criminal histories due to concerns over 'safeguarding' is to an extent also true of the practices surrounding 'criminality information' management in other arenas—not least with regard to employment vetting and safeguarding in a range of institutional and commercial settings, across bodies and organisations in both the public and private sector, and in terms of recruitment practices. The Domestic Abuse Disclosure Schemes under consideration in this research extend this regulatory complexity, and policy balancing act, to the domestic domain of intimate relationships. In a connected issue, and as discussed in earlier chapters, there is ready criticism to be found, and rightly so, when it comes to the notion that Domestic Abuse Disclosure Schemes are victim-responsibilising regulatory tools: though this research is hardly the first piece of academic work to lay this particular charge at the door of a policing policy tool such as the Domestic Violence Disclosure Scheme.

This research is also not the first piece of scholarship to reach the conclusion, offered in earlier chapters, that the spread of Domestic Abuse Disclosure Schemes has been hurried and too uncritical on the part of policymakers in relevant government units and on the part of decision-makers and leaders in police organisations and inspectorates. However, this is the first piece of academic research to evaluate those self-same DADS as potential 'policy spirals'; indeed, at this juncture, with the findings laid out in the chapters above, we can confidently conclude that Clive Walker's definition of 'policy spirals' would apply to DADS, as Walker (2018) found it would to UK counter-terrorism policy in recent years. The rapid spread of DADS in a common law global 'policy spiral' is in spite of some considerable regulatory problems, which this research has gathered together and presented holistically for the first time. I briefly reprise these regulatory problems here.

Regulatory Problems at the Micro-Level of the DADS

1. A 'fragmentation of knowledge' (Black, 2001): the police can potentially arrive at non-disclosures as 'false negatives' that put victims at risk from perpetrators of violence who are unknown to the police; and the latter cannot know as much of the potential violence in a relationship as they might in theory due to this 'fragmentation of knowledge'.

2. The 'postcode lottery': We have seen that there are great variations between forces' disclosure rates in different force areas in England and Wales.
3. Inconsistent resources, processes and timelines at force-level for the operation of the DVDS, and presumably the DSDAS and DVADS by way of comparison.

Regulatory Problems at the Meso-Level of the DADS

1. There can be seen to be a lack of coherent national DADS-related offender/victim policy in an era of austerity.
2. While procedural reviews of the operation of the DVDS in England and Wales have been conducted by the Home Office, no rigorous (published) review of effectiveness has been conducted by any policy actor in the field.
3. There has been a lack of transparency in the roll-out from the DVDS to the DSDAS to the DVADS, allowing for discrepancies to emerge in terms of policy/decision-making emphases in differing guidance for the three Schemes across the UK

Regulatory Problems at the Macro-Level of the DADS

1. There are (principally due to a broader context of devolution) differing legal bases for each of the three UK DADS: the DVDS, the DSDAS and the DVADS—albeit with the relatively vague (and common law) 'pressing need' test a problem in all three to a varying extent.
2. There is scope for a great breadth and inconsistency of the disclosure of non-conviction 'intelligence' due to the lack of firm policy barriers on the disclosure of non-conviction information as well as some inconsistencies in the (non)inclusion of spent convictions and cautions.
3. Across the three DADS in operation in the UK today, their guidance shares a lack of emphasis on emerging international law standards, for example, the UNCRC test as to the welfare of children, and up-to-date data protection law requirements.

Not only is the Domestic Violence Disclosure Scheme being operated in a 'postcode lottery' fashion with regard to how applications and disclosures come about at different rates in relation to different forces in England and Wales, but according to responses to my freedom-of-information requests to police forces in England and Wales (see Table 7) it may not be as effective as the rapid spread of similar Schemes across a number of other jurisdiction would imply. I found that 45% or more of disclosure recipients are still harmed by those offenders they are warned about via the operation of the DVDS.

The DVDS and other DADS will always entail, from a legal perspective, the balancing and ordering of competing and contrasting rights claims between the rights to privacy, due process and rehabilitation of (former or potential) perpetrators of domestic violence on the one hand, and the right to safety and freedom from harm and to personal autonomy for (potential and possible) victims of their violence. As John Braithwaite (1989: 185) has written, "[t]he good society, in short, is both strong on duties and strong on rights, and especially strong on duties that protect rights".

There can be no doubt that an emphasis on policing policy evaluation and evolution rooted in respect for and prioritisation of the human rights of victims of crime would be of great societal value. The same was true, on a much wider scale, when Peter Neyroud and Alan Beckley assessed the early impact of the Human Rights Act 1998 as a potentially transformative tool for the police service as a whole (Neyroud & Beckley, 2001). Indeed, although the impact of the HRA presented a policy management 'challenge' for the police service as a whole, the development of a more niche policy concern such as the opportunity to operate DADS still offers a policy management 'challenge' connected to human rights (Neyroud & Beckley, 2001: 211) that, if realised in an effective way, could bring about greater benefits.

In evaluating the draft Domestic Abuse Bill, and the intention through the Bill to put DVDS guidance on a statutory footing, the Parliamentary joint committee that gave pre-legislative scrutiny of the Home Office proposals concerned gave an endorsement of the move to put the DVDS guidance on a statutory footing. The Joint Committee noted that putting DVDS guidance on a statutory footing might raise more awareness of the

Scheme, and noted criticisms from some quarters of the *under-use* of the Right to Know, currently, judging that use of the Right to Know "would increase with improved multi-agency working and we recommend further work is done in this area" (Joint Committee on the Draft Domestic Abuse Bill, 2019: 38). The effectiveness of doing so may well continue to remain unclear.

8.5 Recommendations for Re-drafting the (Now Statutory) DVDS Guidance

The new statutory guidance for the DVDS should put new emphases in the duties on police forces in England and Wales in operating the Scheme, as summarised below. I hope that these recommendations are as applicable as possible to other jurisdictions, given the similarities in many DADS globally, with their 'Right to Ask' and Right to Know' strand equivalents, the general problem of only being able to disclose what is recorded in information systems, and the difficulty of avoiding the responsibilisation of victims taking receipt of disclosures, and so forth. My recommendations are arranged in eight areas, as follows:

1. *Force-level reviews of disclosure schemes*
   Put a duty on all police forces in England and Wales (or in the relevant jurisdiction) to undertake internal reviews of the effectiveness of DVDS (or equivalent) disclosures by way of auditing the extent of victimisation for recipients after an appropriate length of time (one or two years) following each disclosure.
2. *Force-level analysis of the results of disclosures*
   Put a responsibility on police forces to identify commonalities in cases where the recipients of disclosures in that force both do and do not go on to become victims of the subject of the disclosure, and take steps to address/reinforce practices in the light of these reviews.
3. *Attempts to mandate joined-up public protection work*
   Put a policy duty on police forces to consider using a Domestic Abuse Protection Notice, and then applying for a Domestic Abuse Protection

Order with offender notification or registration requirements (however these could be utilised) when a DVDS disclosure is made, according to the relevant statute (or statutory guidance) in place, and where the risk level to the victim makes this practicable and appropriate. Regular police contact with an offender resulting from this notification/registration requirement might be one way of mitigating the risks of 'displacement' of abuse onto even more vulnerable victims.

4. *Clarification of disclosure thresholds and legal considerations*
   A new formulation of the guidance on the 'pressing need' test for disclosures under the DVDS could be phrased with the 'pressing need' standard requiring: '(i) reasonable cause to suspect a person would be likely to suffer significant harm and (ii) grounds to conclude a disclosure is required to safeguard their welfare'. Another useful step would be re-drafting the DVDS guidance to make sure it explains, in relation to the decision-making around a disclosure, the positive obligations in human rights law to prevent victimisation, under Articles 2, 3 and 8 ECHR (where each is relevant), and to add guidance on the balancing of these obligations with the obligation to protect the (qualified) Article 8 ECHR rights on the part of a subject of a potential disclosure. Currently, both the DSDAS and DVADS guidance do this more clearly than in the DVDS guidance.
5. *Decision-making on disclosures to more explicitly prioritise child protection*
   It would be appropriate to re-draft the DVDS guidance to put more emphasis on the rights of children to be protected from harm in the context of a possible disclosure. Again, the DVDS guidance is shorter on detail in relation to this consideration in disclosure decision-making compared to the guidance on similar Schemes elsewhere in the UK.
6. *Greater regulatory clarity through better data collection*
   Ensure that the reporting of statistical data on the operation of the DVDS to the Home Office and the ONS, undertaken annually by the range of police forces in England and Wales, is standardised to a much higher degree, and made to include basic categories of reasons as to why a disclosure is made or refused following either a Right to Ask application or a Right to Know application.
7. *Greater procedural fairness in making disclosures*

A new formulation of the guidance on disclosures under the DVDS should make it clear that the factual information being disclosed (say the details of arrests, or convictions, of a subject) must be conveyed in such a way as to make it plain that it is different in quality from the finding of any risk assessment; that is, the subjective determination that an applicant or recipient of a disclosure is in 'pressing need' of a disclosure to protect them from the subject concerned. So for example, the police description of a disclosure subject would need to be couched in terms of whether a subject was a convicted abuser or a suspected abuser only. Furthermore, disclosures under the DVDS must be carefully balanced between the need to impress upon a recipient that the disclosure is in response to the 'pressing need' required for the disclosure, from a risk assessment perspective, but also the need to make only the most limited disclosure to achieve that intended effect. If a force felt that it could not deem information accurate because of doubt over the event it recorded (e.g., where we are talking about 'intelligence' on an offence, rather than a record of an arrest), and where a disclosure subject cannot be contacted for their view of the information because this would increase the risk to a potential victim or victims, the information should be considered for internal barring from disclosure as a result. These approaches to making the new DVDS guidance adhere more to procedural fairness principles would also allow police forces to more confidently comply with the provisions of Part 3 of the Data Protection Act 2018, as discussed in Chap. 7.

8. *Making plain the equality issues surrounding disclosure schemes*
   As discussed in Chap. 2, victims of domestic abuse from a range of minority and/or intersectional groups may have greater barriers, in a range of ways, in terms of their drawing on the DVDS. The DVDS guidance to police officers needs to be reconfigured to highlight the difficulties that individuals from disabled, ethnic minority, migrant and/or LGBTQ communities will have in drawing on the 'Right to Ask' strand of the DVDS, or in acting on disclosures under the 'Right to Know' strand or the 'Right to Ask' strand.

These eight recommendations for the soon-to-be statutory guidance would *augment* the list of issues that HM Government have listed, in the most recent Explanatory Notes to the Domestic Abuse Bill, as the features of the DVDS that policymakers plan to be addressed in forthcoming statutory guidance—and which would improve the operation of the Scheme in a range of similar ways (HM Government, 2020c: 66–67).

8.6 Concluding Comments

The Domestic Homicide Review of the failings of agencies in Norfolk concerning the January 2017 murder of Kerri McAuley made the recommendation that "a national evaluation of Clare's Law [should be] commissioned to assess its use and effectiveness in protecting victims" (Graham, 2018: 68). This research has shown that estimating the overall efficacy of the DVDS and other DADS is possible using the records the police themselves hold about outcomes for disclosure recipients. But without impetus for further research coming from government (the Home Office) or a range of national police organisations (chief amongst them HMICFRS), we may never see the UK Domestic Abuse Disclosure Schemes evaluated as to their effectiveness in detail. In the absence of policymakers asking tough questions about the effectiveness of the UK DADS, such disclosure schemes may remain questionably or misleadingly part of the public protection and domestic violence prevention agenda or strategy in the UK. It is vital that policymakers and police professionals gain a better understanding of the circumstances in which a disclosure under a DADS will truly help a potential victim; and not instead increase or fail to reduce the risk posed to them by an abusive partner or former partner.

Jo Miles (2011: 513) has written that "it is essential to understand the dynamics of abuse and the diverse help-seeking behaviours of victims. … Getting it wrong in any legal context, whether concerning access to housing, access to justice or otherwise, potentially threatens the lives of vulnerable adults and children." The continued *unmeasured* use of disclosures to the vulnerable partner in a violent relationship may well, too, be 'getting it wrong'. It is important that the ongoing, unmeasured use of disclosures to vulnerable partners in violent relationships does not continue immoral victim responsibilisation. It is also important that the (in)effectiveness of disclosure schemes is explored, and separately but more importantly, that the necessary political momentum is reached for the prioritisation and the proper funding of two equally important problems: a shortfall in domestic violence refuge spaces for victims and their children, and more intensive policing and *rehabilitation* of serial domestic abusers.

References

Barr, C., & Topping, A. (2021). Radical change needed in handling of rape cases, says England and Wales police lead. [Online]. *The Guardian*. Retrieved March 30, 2021, from https://www.theguardian.com/society/2021/feb/14/radical-change-needed-in-handling-of-cases-says-england-and-wales-police-lead

Black, J. (2001). Decentring regulation: Understanding the role of regulation and self-regulation in a 'post-regulatory world'. *Current Legal Problems, 54*(1), 103.

Braithwaite, J. (1989). *Crime, shame and reintegration*. Cambridge University Press.

Domestic Abuse Bill. (2020a, June 17). Public bill committee proceedings. Retrieved 18 July 2020, from https://publications.parliament.uk/pa/bills/cbill/58-01/0096/amend/domestic_rp_pbc_0617.pdf

Domestic Abuse Bill. (2020b). Public bill committee. *Minutes of the Eighth Sitting*, 284–285, Retrieved 18 July 2020, from https://hansard.parliament.uk/commons/2020-06-11/debates/2b88e3cc-6f84-42a0-a440-136bbc9f-be0b/DomesticAbuseBill(EighthSitting)

Graham, C. (2018). *Norfolk county community safety partnership*. Domestic homicide review report: Review into the death of April in January 2017.

Hansard HL Deb vol 809 col 1640. (2021, January 27). [Electronic version].

Hansard HL Deb vol 810 col 360. (2021, February 10). [Electronic version].

HM Government. (2020a, February). Domestic Abuse Bill 2020 – Impact assessment. Retrieved June 30, 2020, from https://publications.parliament.uk/pa/bills/cbill/58-01/0096/IAFEB2020.pdf

HM Government. (2020b). Domestic Abuse Bill – European convention on Human Rights Memorandum. Retrieved June 30, 2020, from https://publications.parliament.uk/pa/bills/cbill/58-01/0096/ECHR%20memo%20Domestic%20Abuse%20Bill%20Commons%20introduction%20March%202020.pdf

HM Government. (2020c, March). Explanatory notes to the Domestic Abuse Bill. Retrieved June 30, 2020, from https://publications.parliament.uk/pa/bills/cbill/58-01/0096/en/20096en.pdf

House of Commons. (2020a). *April 28 Debate* (vol 675, col 293). [Electronic version].

House of Commons. (2020b). *June 11 debate* (col 281–283). https://hansard.parliament.uk/commons/2020-06-11/debates/2b88e3cc-6f84-42a0-a440-136bbc9fbe0b/DomesticAbuseBill(EighthSitting)

House of Commons. (2020c). *June 11 debate* (col 284–285). https://hansard.parliament.uk/commons/2020-06-11/debates/2b88e3cc-6f84-42a0-a440-136bbc9fbe0b/DomesticAbuseBill(EighthSitting)

House of Commons. (2020d). *July 26 Debate* (vol 678, col 715). [Electronic version].

House of Commons. (2021). *April 26 Debate* (vol 693, col 129). [Electronic version].

Joint Committee on the Draft Domestic Abuse Bill. (2019). Draft Domestic Abuse Bill, First Report of Session 2017–19.

Miles, J. (2011). Defining 'domestic violence': Housing law and beyond. *The Cambridge Law Journal, 70*(3), 511.

Neyroud, P., & Beckley, A. (2001). *Policing, ethics and human rights*. Willan.

Oppenheim, M. (2021). Anger as ministers reject register for serial domestic abuser and stalkers. *The Independent*, 15 April. Retrieved May 10, 2021, from https://www.independent.co.uk/news/uk/home-news/domestic-abuse-bill-stalkers-register-b1832164.html

Proctor, K. (2021). Home office admits 112,000 people have had part of their police records deleted. [Online]. *Politics Home*. Retrieved March 31, 2021, from https://www.politicshome.com/news/article/police-records

Safelives. (2021). Safelives' 2020/21 survey of domestic abuse practitioners in England and Wales.

Thomson, C. (2020). Police finding domestic abusers' new partners and warning them off. [Online]. *Romford Recorder*. Retrieved March 30, 2021, from https://www.romfordrecorder.co.uk/news/crime/domestic-abuse-charity-faces-christmas-and-covid-spike-6865094

Topping, A. (2021). Anger as Tory MPs vote against register for stalkers and domestic abusers. *The Guardian*. Retrieved May 10, 2021, from https://www.theguardian.com/society/2021/apr/16/anger-tory-mps-vote-against-register-stalkers-domestic-abusers

Walker, C. (2018). Counter-terrorism and counter-extremism: The UK policy spirals. *Public Law, 725*.

Women's Aid. (2019). *Funding specialist support for domestic abuse survivors*. Women's Aid.

Index

J. Grace, *Domestic Abuse Disclosure Schemes*,
https://doi.org/10.1007/978-3-030-89039-1

The manufacturer's authorised representative in the EU is Springer Nature Customer Service Centre GmbH, Europaplatz 3, 69115 Heidelberg, Germany. If you have any concerns regarding our products, please contact ProductSafety@springernature.com

Printed and bound by CPI Group (UK) Ltd, Croydon, CR0 4YY
22/09/2026
02221067-0007